World Yearbook of Education 2014

This latest volume in the *World Yearbook of Education Series* focuses on a major and highly significant development in the governing of education across the globe: the use of knowledge-based technologies as key policy sources. A combination of factors has produced this shift: first, the massive expansion of technological capacity signalled by the arrival of 'big data' that allows for the collection, circulation and processing of extensive system knowledge. The rise of data has been observed and discussed extensively, but its role in governing and the rise of comparison as a basis for action is now a determining practice in the field of education. Comparison provides the justification for 'modernising' policy in education, both in the developed and developing world, as national policy-makers (selectively) seek templates of success from the high performers and demand solutions to apparent underperformance through the adoption of the policies favoured by the likes of Singapore, Finland and Korea.

In parallel, the growth of particular forms of expertise: the rise and rise of educational consultancy, the growth of private (for profit) involvement in provision of educational goods and services and the increasing consolidation of networks of influence in the promotion of 'best practice', is affecting policy decisions. Through these developments, the nature of knowledge is altered, along with the relationship between knowledge and politics. Knowledge in this context is co-constructed: it is not disciplinary knowledge, but knowledge that emerges in the sharing of experience.

This book provides a global snapshot of a changing educational world by giving detailed examples of a fundamental shift in the governing and practice of education learning by:

- assessing approaches to the changing nature of comparative knowledge and information;
- tracking the translation and mobilisation of these knowledges in the governing of education/learning;
- identification of the key experts and knowledge producers/circulators/translators and analysis of how best to understand their influence;
- mapping of the global production of these knowledges in terms of their range and reach;
- mapping the interrelationships of actors and their effects in different national settings.

Drawing on material from around the world, the book brings together scholars from different backgrounds who provide a tapestry of examples of the global production and national reception and mediation of these knowledges, and who show how change enters different national spaces and consider the effects in these settings.

Tara Fenwick is Professor of Professional Education at Stirling University, UK.

Eric Mangez is Professor in Sociology, University of Louvain, Belgium.

Jenny Ozga is Professor of the Sociology of Education at the University of Oxford, UK.

World Yearbook of Education Series
Series editors: Terri Seddon, Jenny Ozga and Gita Steiner-Khamsi

World Yearbook of Education 2014

Governing Knowledge: Comparison, Knowledge-Based Technologies and Expertise in the Regulation of Education

Edited by
Tara Fenwick, Eric Mangez and
Jenny Ozga

University of
South Wales
Prifysgol
De Cymru

Library Services

Routledge
Taylor & Francis Group

LONDON AND NEW YORK

First published 2014
by Routledge
2 Park Square, Milton Park, Abingdon, Oxon OX14 4RN

and by Routledge
711 Third Avenue, New York, NY 10017

Routledge is an imprint of the Taylor & Francis Group, an informa business

British Library Cataloguing in Publication Data
A catalogue record for this book is available from the British Library

Library of Congress Cataloging in Publication Data
A catalog record for this book has been requested

ISBN: 978-0-415-82873-4 (hbk)
ISBN: 978-1-315-81773-6 (ebk)

Typeset in Minion
by Book Now Ltd, London

MIX
Paper from
responsible sources
FSC
www.fsc.org   FSC® C013604

Printed and bound by CPI Group (UK) Ltd, Croydon, CR0 4YY

Contents

Illustrations

Figures

Tables

Contributors

Sajid Ali is Assistant Professor in the Aga Khan University's Institute for Educational Development, Pakistan. He holds a PhD in Policy Studies from the University of Edinburgh, an MEd in Leadership and Policy from Monash University, and a Masters in Sociology from the University of Karachi. Dr Ali has held an ESRC South Asian Visiting Fellowship at the University of Oxford. He is the current General Secretary of the Pakistan Association for Research in Education (PARE). His research interests include globalisation and education policy, new forms of education governance, policy networks, education reform, privatisation of education and the role of knowledge resources in shaping policy.

Michael Barber is Chief Education Advisor to Pearson, responsible for leading the company's worldwide research and partnership on education policy and learning methods, supporting the development of new products and services and leading Pearson's strategy for education in the poorest sectors of the world. He has worked for over 20 years in education and government reform and improvement, including as head of UK Prime Minister Tony Blair's Delivery Unit (PMDU), where he was responsible for working with government agencies to ensure successful implementation of the Prime Minister's priority programmes, including those in health, education, transport, policing, the criminal justice system, and asylum/immigration.

Luís Miguel Carvalho is Associate Professor of Education Policy and Administration at the Institute of Education, University of Lisbon. His recent research has a focus on the transnational circulation of knowledge and policies, and on the role of knowledge in the fabrication and regulation of education policies.

Philip Wing Keung Chan is an Assistant Lecturer in the Faculty of Education, Monash University. He has worked in course development and training at the Chinese University of Hong Kong, the University of Hong Kong and the Hong Kong Federation of Education Workers. He is leading two publishing projects titled 'Asia as Method in Education Studies' and 'Equity in Education: Fairness and Inclusion' at Monash University. His recent edited book is *Asia Pacific Education: Diversity, Challenges and Changes* (Monash University Publishing, 2012).

Alma Demszky is a Lecturer in Sociology in the Institute of Sociology at the Ludwig Maximilian University of Munich. Her main research areas are the sociology of health and education in international comparison, focussing on the relation of knowledge and policy and the scientific creation of knowledge.

D. Brent Edwards Jr. received his doctorate in international education policy from the University of Maryland, College Park. His work focuses on the political economy of education reform and global education policies, with a focus on developing countries. Previously, he has worked with the University of California, Berkeley; the University of Amsterdam; the Autonomous University of Barcelona; the George Washington University and the World Bank. Currently, he is a post-doctoral researcher at the University of Tokyo. His work has appeared in such journals as *Comparative Education Review, Education Policy Analysis Archives, Research in Comparative and International Education, Current Issues in Comparative Education*, and *The Urban Review*, in addition to numerous book chapters.

Richard Edwards is Professor of Education at the University of Stirling, UK. He has written extensively about lifelong learning and governmentality, and currently focuses on posthumanist theory and digital media in education. He is Director of the Laboratory for Educational Theory (www.stir.ac.uk/education/theorylab). His recent books, both published with Tara Fenwick, include *Actor-Network Theory in Education* (Routledge, 2010) and *Emerging Approaches to Educational Research: Tracing the Sociomaterial* (Routledge, 2011).

Tara Fenwick is Professor at the University of Stirling, UK, with a focus on professional and vocational learning in various work practices. She is Director of ProPEL: international network for research in professional practice, education and learning (www.propel.stir.ac.uk). She is particularly interested in sociomaterial approaches to understanding dynamics of practice and how particular knowledge, identities and relations become performed and regulated in work.

Samuel Isaacs was the founding Executive Officer of the South African Qualifications Authority (SAQA) and led the organisation for fifteen years. He has an honorary doctorate from University of Western Cape where he is an honorary professor.

David Johnson is Reader in Comparative Education and Fellow of St Antony's College, University of Oxford. He is interested in the political economy of education in Africa and has worked closely with education ministers, international donor agencies and policy research units in several developing countries to study the conditions and outcomes of schooling. He is currently working with the World Bank to support the Federal Ministry of Basic Education in Sudan to establish a National Learning Assessment and to use the results for policy dialogue. He is also conducting a large-scale study into student learning and teacher knowledge on behalf of UNICEF, the findings of which will be used to guide policy interventions in the improvement of girls' education in northern Nigeria.

Berit Karseth is Professor at the Department of Education, University of Oslo. Her main research interests are curriculum policy and curriculum traditions within and beyond national boundaries and issues related to professionalism and knowledge. She is currently the Dean at the Faculty of Educational Sciences, University of Oslo.

Steven J. Klees is the R. W. Benjamin Professor of International and Comparative Education at the University of Maryland. He did his PhD at Stanford University and has taught at Cornell University, Stanford University, Florida State University, and the Federal University of Rio Grande do Norte in Brazil. He was a Fulbright Scholar on two occasions at the Federal University of Bahia in Brazil. Prof. Klees' work examines the political economy of education and development with specific research interests in globalization, neoliberalism, and education; the role of aid agencies; education, human rights, and social justice; the education of disadvantaged populations; the role of class, gender, and race in reproducing and challenging educational and social inequality; and alternative approaches to education and development.

Eric Mangez is Professor in Sociology at the University of Louvain (UCL), Belgium, where he teaches sociological theory, research method and political sociology. He is author of *Réformer les contenus d'enseignement* (PUF, Paris, 2008). He is co-editor and co-author of a forthcoming volume on 'Bourdieu's Social Field Theory: Concept and Applications' (Routledge, *Advances in Sociology*).

Tebeje Molla recently received his PhD from Monash University, Australia. Currently he works at the Centre for Research in Education Future and Innovation, Deakin University. His research areas include international educational development aid, transnational education policymaking, and social justice in and through education.

Armin Nassehi is Professor at the University of Munich since 1998. His fields of research and teaching are social theory, theories of modernity and modern society, sociology of culture, political sociology and migration. He has published about 20 books and more than 150 contributions to books and journals. He edits the journal *Kursbuch*.

Monika Nerland is Professor in the Department of Education, University of Oslo. She conducts research on professional knowledge and learning in education and work. She has carried out several comparative projects on these themes, and recently co-edited the book *Professional Learning in the Knowledge Society* (Sense Publishers, 2012).

António Nóvoa is Rector of the University of Lisbon. He holds a doctorate in History from the Sorbonne and a further doctorate in Educational Sciences from the University of Geneva. Throughout his academic career he has held several international visiting professorships (at Geneva, Wisconsin–Madison, Oxford, and Columbia–New York). His work has been published in 15 countries. He is the author and editor of several books, mainly in the fields of History of Education and Comparative Education, discussing issues related to educational policies and the teaching profession.

Jenny Ozga is Professor of the Sociology of Education in the Department of Education, University of Oxford. Her main research area is education policy, and her recent funded research includes investigation of new governing forms and relations in education in Europe, with particular attention to the role of data and inspection. Her most recent book (edited with P. Dahler-Larsen, C. Segerholm and H. Simola) is *Fabricating Quality in Europe: Data and Education Governance* (Routledge, 2011).

Terri Seddon is Professor of Education at Monash University. She investigates globalization and education through studies of boundary politics and knowledge building in adult education spaces affected by global transitions. Terri recently published *Work and Learning and Politics of Working Life* (2010, with Lea Henriksson and Beatrix Niemeyer) and *Educators, Professionalism, and Politics* (2013, with John Levin).

Eneida Oto Shiroma is Associate Professor in the Department of Specialized Studies in Education at the Federal University of Santa Catarina (UFSC) in Brazil. She has a PhD in education from the State University of Campinas and has developed post-doctoral research at the University of Nottingham and the University of Oxford. She is former editor of the journal *Perspectiva*. Her research interests include work, education policies and policy networks. She is co-author of *Politica Educacional* (4th edn). She is a member of the Research Group on Education Policy and Work (GEPETO/UFSC) and researcher of the National Council for Scientific and Technological Development, CNPq-Brazil.

Maarten Simons is Professor at the Laboratory for Education and Society of the KU Leuven, Belgium. His research interests are educational theory and political and social philosophy with special attention to educational policy, Europeanization and government(ality) in education. Specific focus is on the emergence of new forms of power and challenges posed to the public role of (higher) education.

Shirley Walters is Professor of Adult and Continuing Education at University of Western Cape and founding director of the Division for Lifelong Learning. She was chair of the South African Qualifications Authority (SAQA) from 2004 to 2010.

Ben Williamson is a Lecturer in Education at the University of Stirling. His research is mainly in the areas of education policy and technology, focusing particularly on think-tanks and third-sector actors as policy intermediaries and on new technologies as sociotechnical interfaces to education.

Tali Yariv-Mashal, PhD, specializes in comparative education. She is currently a research fellow at the Gilo Citizenship Democracy and Civic Education Center at the Hebrew University of Jerusalem Israel, and head of the Excellence Program at the Beit Berl Teachers College. She has researched various aspects of social and political educational discourse in Israel, as well as aspects of civic education in Israel's multicultural social realities.

Series Editors' Introduction

The study of globalization has experienced several paradigm shifts over the past two decades. Earlier notions of globalization as an 'external force' emphasized the coercive power attributed to global agencies and institutions. Several assumptions of these early conceptualizations have come under attack: globalization is more than simply a spatial or territorial issue, should not be reduced to a matter of agency, and does not by necessity replace local and national agendas. Globalization transforms rather than replaces the local and the national. In addition, as argued in this and previous volumes, it also transforms the way education is conceived, administered, and monitored. In fact, the current debates view globalization as a social category – similar to class, gender, race, nation, etc. – that not only generates new structures and institutions but also new ways of seeing, thinking and governing education.

Unsurprisingly, globalization has been a recurring theme in the Routledge *World Yearbook of Education Series*. Previous volumes investigated, for example, the impact of globalization on the curriculum or analysed the proliferation of 'travelling policies.' This volume, *Governing Knowledge: Comparison, Knowledge-based Technologies and Expertise in the Regulation of Education*, focuses on the governance of education. The authors have examined in great depth how actors, objectives, and mechanisms of educational governance have been transformed in these globalizing times. Arguably, knowledge-based regulation, evidence-based policy planning, or governance by numbers only label and bring to light the tip of the transformation process. The authors of this volume attempt to dig deeper and understand why comparison and knowledge-based regulation have become the preferred tools of governance and how these regulatory mechanisms have been translated in different contexts.

The focus then, in this volume, is not so much on a specific area of policy or practice (e.g., research, or curriculum, or professional practice) but on how governing work is done, what resources are brought into play, how they are deployed, what agencies and actors are involved, what technologies are mobilized, and what knowledge base or evidence is referenced. For the volume examines and explores the idea that in the adoption of new, networked forms of governance, knowledge and knowledge-based regulation tools come into play and acquire new significance. It looks especially closely at the growth of comparison as a governing tool and explores the work that comparison does in ordering and disciplining nation-states. The application of a globalization lens helps to understand the prominence of the Programme for International Student Assessment (PISA), the influence of new networks of expertise through which education consultants come together to produce and circulate so-called best practice, as well as the reasons why private corporations have discovered education as a lucrative business. The new focus on outputs, outcomes, and standards has, for better or worse, diversified the input sources and agencies involved in governing education. Besides state actors, there are now interest groups, professional groups, and business involved in providing and defining education. It has become necessary to critically scrutinize whether the new regulatory instruments and the narrow definition of 'data' has produced, in effect, new knowledge that enables effective interventions to sustain improved opportunities.

The volume does not assume that these developments lead to the automatic delivery of a global agenda for education, rather it seeks to bring together ideas and concepts that often remain isolated from one another. Here, for example, we can begin to see the ways in which changes in knowledge, accompanied by changes in technology, open up simultaneously capacity for development, for democratization, for 'local' design and delivery of education practice, while also promoting private interest, standardizing practices, and global policy transfer. Moreover, these developments are treated within a conceptual framework that delineates and interrogates new forms of governance – notably in the form of networks and partnerships – which in turn enable different capacities and promote new governing relationships.

This volume seeks to capture some of the key developments, to place them in relationship with one another in different contexts, and thus to engender debate about the governing of education.

Gita Steiner-Khamsi, *New York*
Terri Seddon, *Melbourne*
Jenny Ozga, *Oxford*

Introduction

Governing Knowledge

Comparison, Knowledge-Based Technologies and Expertise in the Regulation of Education

Tara Fenwick, Eric Mangez and Jenny Ozga

This book focuses on a major and highly significant development in the governing of education across the globe: the use of knowledge-based technologies to make policy, rather than simply as aids to decision-making. These technologies, we suggest, are themselves becoming the process of governing. A combination of factors has produced this shift. First, the massive expansion of technological capacity signalled by the arrival of 'big data' (McKinsey 2013) allows for the collection, circulation and processing of extensive system knowledge. The second factor is the growth of comparison as a basis for and justification of action. This growth is accompanied, inevitably, by the increasing displacement of contextualised, messy and 'local' understandings and meanings as resources for policy development, along with much of the ideological debate that previously fuelled a politics of education.

Comparison, we suggest, following Nóvoa and Yariv-Mashal (this volume), is now a basis of governing. Indeed it is central to policy-making in the field of education, in the absence, in many contexts but not all, of explicit and identifiable policy agendas beyond the achievement of 'world class' education and improved positioning in relation to the performance of other systems, comparison provides the justification for 'modernising' policy in education, in both the developed and developing worlds. Transnational and national policy-makers (selectively) identify templates of success from the high performers and demand solutions to apparent underperformance through the adoption of the policies favoured by Singapore, Finland and Korea. Comparison as the basis for action is propagated by influential international actors, including the OECD, who in turn support networks of expert-consultants. These then circulate particular kinds of knowledge/evidence/information and extrapolate preferred policy actions or 'best practice', the adoption of which may form part of the assessment of a nation-state's position in league tables of performance.

The rise of data and its uses and abuses has been observed and discussed extensively (Mackenzie 2012; Wind-Cowie and Lekhi 2012), However, the role of data in *governing* education remains underdeveloped as an area of research and publication. Our purpose, in this collection, is to suggest connections between technological developments and practices of governing, to offer ways of conceptualising these interdependencies, and to illuminate their workings in and across different contexts. In doing this we focus on the rise of comparison as a basis for action, on the changes in knowledge produced in the increasing reliance on comparable data, and on the actors who translate and transfer comparative knowledge globally. Our intention is to promote critical engagement with the interaction between these different developments and emergent trends in the governing of the field of education.

This approach reflects, to some extent, our attempt to exploit the opportunities presented by the World Yearbook to do comparison differently. The Yearbook's origins in post-imperial Britain reflected an approach to comparative education that placed the Anglophone world at the centre and provided collections of accounts of 'difference'. In recent years, the Yearbook has consciously engaged with the shifting spaces and relationships of the field of education in globalising times, attempting to find ways of approaching comparison that are neither too deeply embedded in context – in the way of conventional comparative education, which takes key system characteristics and identifies differences and similarities among them – nor too dislocated from context so that everything is explained through reference to an emergent global education policy field or an emergent world education system (Dale 2005; Lingard and Ozga 2007). This attempt to understand and capture global–local interactions follows Sassen's (2010: 10) injunction to think of the global – whether an institution, a process, a discursive practice, an imaginary – as both transcending the exclusive framing of national states and partly emerging and operating within that framing. She goes on to advocate both 'a focus on interdependence and a focus on how the global gets constituted inside the national' in order to theorise and research globalisation.

And yet such approaches are comparatively rare in the field of education. The field's national or imperial framing remains strong, and reflects the historical development of education systems in tandem with nation states. This is especially so in Europe, where most national education and training systems developed in the nineteenth and twentieth centuries as negotiated settlements between nation-building states and education workforces, who advanced agendas driven by enlightenment commitments to individual equality and collective progress. These agendas were framed by nation-building activities and by a modernist scientific rationality that sought evidence about populations and developed a professional workforce of state employees to deal with social problems. Such activities and the people responsible for them were nationally bounded, organised in or by government bureaucracies and negotiated with, or sometimes challenged, the nation state as the regulatory authority.

Globalisation – however we understand it – problematises the nation state. The increasing interconnection of economic and social life produced by technological innovation in advanced capitalism is dissolving global and local distinctions. Thus nation-states simultaneously participate in setting up new frameworks sustaining these global processes while becoming destabilised by the same frameworks (Sassen 2007). The displacement of hierarchical, bordered and boundaried structures of governing has led nation-states to look for ways of managing through coordination rather than a direct regulating role. Hybrid public–private entities emerge in the delivery of education alongside local, national and international networks influencing education policy. These entities and networks offer both threats and solutions to the nation-state, as it seeks new governing forms and processes. In the transformation of *government* to *governance*, hierarchical bureaucratic regimes are displaced by networks of relationships in which cooperation and coordination must be constantly negotiated and managed (Kohler-Koch and Eising 1999), through a mix of particular policy technologies and constant work by policy actors to maintain connections and coherence in re-spatialised governing relations. The work of these actors in maintaining the networks that do governing work is of heightened importance in the context of fluidity and uncertainty about how to govern. There are tensions between centralised and decentralised levels of governance, deregulation and existing or new (re-) regulatory instruments of governance within nation-states and between the pressures for global convergence and embedded national practices and priorities. This work demands new knowledges, skills and roles: it demands skills in translating, mediating and brokering (Clarke 2009; Lendvai and Stubbs 2006; Larner and Craig 2005).

It is against this backdrop that new regulatory instruments emerge and take on significance. They offer capacity to redesign institutions, to organise networks and to monitor individual, institutional, local, national and transnational activity through the flow of comparative knowledge and data. Data and data systems support the activity of networks of governing experts who identify policy problems and frame policy solutions beyond and across the national scale. These problems have a new significance, and their solutions bring with them a re-spatialisation of governing relations. This is because education is now understood throughout the world as a key policy field not only for economic growth and/or recovery but also for offering governing resources to combat societal fragmentation and alienation as inequalities increase and become more evident. There is a discernible, if not universal, shift in governing practices in education globally and within the nation-state, from national and institutionally based governing to governing through networks of new actors. This shift promotes, through simultaneous decentralisation and re-centralisation, the growth of hybrid provision, institutional and individual autonomy, and individual self-governance informed by constant self-evaluation of performance. Such configurations are steered through the benchmarking and competitive performance regimes of transnational and national organisations.

The growth of regulatory technologies makes possible the constant reference to and dependence on comparative knowledge. These include hardware- and software-testing regimes, travelling qualifications systems, performance indicators and benchmarks, standards, league tables and the networks of experts and consultants who construct and promote these instruments globally. There has been a major expansion of educational consultancy, along with the growth of private (including for profit) involvement in provision of educational goods and services. These in turn contribute to the increasing consolidation of networks of influence, with very considerable global reach, promoting standardised and standardising doxa of 'best practice'. Such networks mobilise the reach and therefore the influence of particular international organisations (IOs) and agencies, with very powerful consequences for the shape of education/learning. This is especially evident in the so-called develop-ing world where, for example, adoption of particular forms of hybrid public–private provision is often a key indicator of modernisation.

Data enable this complex education arena to be translated into practices of calcula-tion. Benchmarking and comparison are core governing processes across a 'learning society' shaped by economic reform, citizenship obligations, employability and inter-national comparison and performance testing in education (Grek 2009; Lawn and Grek 2012). Thus a range of sophisticated instruments of standardisation, quality benchmarking and data harmonisation underpin the governance turn and act on and within national systems promoting ways of controlling and shaping national, institu-tional and individual behaviour through the use of comparative information on performance. National systems are opened up to external influence, but this is also a process in which the nation state is able to actively engage. New comparative data enable the nation state to make comparisons between schools, localities and nations, as a resource for steering policy within the state.

Changes in the nature of knowledge that accompany these developments are not coincidental, but reflect the symbiosis between new governing forms, new regulatory instruments and new knowledges. The pursuit of new knowledge is what drives the competitive engine. Growth is dependent on maximising the out-puts of knowledge workers and the productivity of knowledge resources. National systems seek to ensure competitive advantage through the commercial exploita-tion and application of knowledge, which has to be rapidly 'brought to market'. Technologies enable the instantaneous exchange of information, and the exchanges transcend national boundaries, so the constraints of national economies give way to an interdependent global economy. Because of the primacy of information as the new raw material and creator of wealth, world regions prosper or decline 'not so much because of natural resources, but because of the capacity of their managers, engineers, scientists, and workers to harvest knowledge as raw material' (Hughes 2004: 105).

Through these developments, the nature of knowledge is altered, along with the relationship between knowledge and policy. Policy has always governed knowledge production to some degree but with the explosion of knowledge pro-duction in recent years and its capacity to travel, this relationship has become far more intense. Now, in a sense, policy problems do not appear 'out there' but are called into being (Stehr and Meja 2005: 10) through their statistical representa-tion. from which solutions are (apparently) also derived. Knowledge changes in its production and circulation in networks. New knowledge is activated and trans-ferred in situations that are not fully defined through routine processes, where precedent is not referenced and institutional memories are absent. Knowledge is equated with creative problem-solving and optimised through co-production of new knowledge which can be implemented in action. Creative thinking, innova-tion and problem-solving frequently are valued over and above the consolidation of so-called static knowledge stocks. In other words, a new relation between gov-erning and knowledge may be discerned: expertise moves beyond the traditional task of informing policy, and becomes policy forming in a more complex mode of governing (Issakyan and Ozga 2008).

The increased significance of knowledge means that in the developed world, information and expertise are now more widely available and more widely distributed than ever before. At the same time, new governance forms promote the idea of transparency and public accountability as part of their strategic positioning. Knowledge is drawn into supporting the legitimacy and authority of the social and political processes of networked, new governance forms. Discursively, knowledge and policy are produced as a form of cultural political economy (Jessop 2008) which combines semiotic and material elements in changing the nature of knowledge and its role in governing. Policy-makers suggest that social cohesion and effective government now depend on integrating knowledge as well as on integrating, accommodating and managing different interests. This positioning promotes an agenda for the future in which potentially disruptive energies are harnessed to promote a discourse of continuous scientific and technical advance that also ensures social harmony (Mulderrig 2008: 167).

There are, of course, competing perspectives on new knowledge and on the growth of data. Some perspectives stress the transparency that these developments may promote, along with their democratising potential, or emphasise the capacity of large corporate organisations to deliver services where states have failed. It is also important to note that despite our emphasis here on the governing work of comparison and data, there is considerable capacity in this fluid and unstable context for some actors to exploit the opportunities for mediation or translation that new governing forms offer in order to challenge or contain the logic of comparison, and to disrupt its governing work. Such perspectives are represented in this volume. Indeed the volume continues and builds on the engagement of the World Yearbook with the central problematic of globalisation and the transitions that it engenders in systems of education. We exploit the global reach of the World Yearbook to bring together concepts that are often separated in the social science and education literature – comparison, knowledge, technologies and governance – and thus to suggest possible connections and interdependencies that are not generally evident. Our purpose in this volume, as in its predecessors, is to encourage debate about knowledge production, circulations and uses and their governing effects on the regulation of policy, practice and the production of knowledge itself, in globalising times.

The book is divided into two parts. Part I, 'Governing by Comparison', brings together a range of leading scholars from different disciplinary backgrounds who focus on ways of understanding knowledge, comparison and data as governing practices. Chapter 1, 'Comparative Research in Education: A Mode of Governance or a Historical Journey?' by António Nóvoa and Tali Yariv-Mashal, sets the tone of the book: in a wide ranging, original and provocative account of the collaboration between comparativists and new governing forms. The authors identify and discuss some of the key issues that pre-occupy our contributors, and offer a set of theoretical resources for interrogating these developments, that combine historical and Foucauldian scholarship.

Chapter 2 offers a hard-hitting challenge to what Steven Klees and D. Brent Edwards argue is a dominant faith in scientific knowledge as the best determinant of educational governance. Through critical analysis of the World Bank as a knowledge producer and its methods of quantitative research, particularly randomised control trials, they reveal the poverty of this scientistic faith and the problems it creates in education.

In Chapter 3, Tara Fenwick and Richard Edwards show the utility of sociomaterial network analysis, drawing from Bruno Latour, in critical studies of governmentality. Using examples of PISA, standardised achievement testing, and classroom assessment practices, they illustrate how actor-network approaches can trace the micro-processes through which heterogeneous materials (things, texts, technologies, bodies, anxieties, etc.) are assembled and mobilised over time and space to govern educational practices.

In Chapter 4, Luís-Miguel Carvalho addresses the relation of governing and knowledge by focusing on the fabrication, circulation and mobilisation, in the course of public action, of one carrier of international standards that has apparently become a recurrent category in the contemporary lexicon in education – PISA, the OECD Programme for International Student Assessment. PISA is not merely a triennial survey with a subsequent triennial report, but a complex of activities, involving multiple social worlds, sustained by continuous communication and organisation.

Part II, 'Knowledge Technologies in Action', is focused on examples of the global production and national reception and mediation of these knowledges. It maps the field of 'governing knowledge' in terms of the range and reach of such approaches. It identifies and discusses the ways in which comparative data and knowledge-based technologies enter different national spaces and considers their effects in different national settings.

In Chapter 5, Sir Michael Barber, one of the leading and most influential advocates of data use, talks about his experience in UK Prime Minister Tony Blair's delivery unit, and explains the motivations of large corporations – such as Pearson – in engaging in development work in education. Chapter 6 critically examines the World Bank's (WB) support for Ethiopia, specifically for its higher education (HE) system. Tebeje Molla seeks to shed light specifically on instruments and undesirable consequences of non-financial support of the Bank to the Ethiopian HE system. It tries to answer these interrelated questions: What sorts of knowledge-based policy regulatory tools did the WB use to influence higher education reforms in Ethiopia? And with what effects?

In Chapter 7, Eneida Oto Shiroma analyses the growth of networks and the role of expert-consultants in the modernisation of programmes for teacher education in Brazil, outlining the ways in which key ideas are consolidated and circulated by influential expert-consultants, working closely with government.

Chapter 8 looks at the role of scientific knowledge in policy advice, drawing on empirical data from studies of health and education reforms in Germany. Alma Demszky and Armin Nassehi draw on evidence from the Knowledge and Policy project (www.knowandpol.eu) to make an argument for understanding knowledge and policy as governed by diametrically opposed logics.

In Chapter 9, Sajid Ali considers the role of data and the growth of network governance in education policy-making in Pakistan. This chapter looks at the influence of external experts in the Task Force for Education, and at the interplay between 'local' experts and external consultants in influencing policy and circulating key ideas. The chapter highlights some of the practical and political difficulties facing the modernisation agenda in Pakistan. In contrast, Chapter 10, by David Johnson, provides a more positive account of the uses of data in selected Nigerian states, in pursuit of improved quality in the teaching profession there. This chapter makes a strong case for the use of data to develop knowledge as the basis for action, and identifies the significance of particular political conditions in carrying such action to a successful conclusion. Chapter 11, the aim of Maarten Simons is to argue that the evident need for and exchange of comparative information should be regarded as a symptom of a new mode of governing that installs less-evident power relations. The thesis is that the current 'conduct of conduct' takes shape as 'feedback on performance': as far as the actors involved in education come to understand what they are doing as a performance, feedback information is experienced as indispensable.

In Chapter 12, Shirley Walters and Samuel Isaacs examine the profound tensions in developing and implementing National Qualification Frameworks (NQFs), which is becoming a common form of educational governance. Their context of NQF implementation in post-apartheid South Africa offers a particularly challenging terrain where deeply contested knowledges, interests, regions and histories collide. However, they show how NQFs, even in such a difficult space, can be important vehicles for boundary negotiations and cooperation. Chapter 13 turns to contexts of professional education, with a critical focus on the processes of standardisation. Monika Nerland and Berit Karseth draw upon empirical studies of professional associations in nursing, education and accounting to show how various forms of standards act to regulate professional knowledge, and are becoming increasingly powerful in the accelerated concerns for educational quality assurance and accountability internationally.

Chapter 14 discusses the political use of the PISA data in China. Philip Wing Keung Chan and Terri Seddon consider the ways in which the performance of one Chinese city – Shanghai – has been used to represent the national performance in PISA, and offer a re-analysis of the data that takes into account the weaker performance of other cities and regions in China. The chapter discusses the particular form of networked governance emerging in China and illustrates the connections that exist in this context between political change and data use.

Finally, in Chapter 15, Ben Williamson points to powerful forms of governance now emerging in the linkages between new smart software, learning analytics and public policy labs which are acting as new kinds of governing experts in education. His argument is sobering: these new forms of 'knowing learning' and 'transactional pedagogy' work from individuals' digital traces to position learners as governing resources, activated in ways that refashion the future of education.

References

Brown, P. and Lauder, H. (1997) 'Education, globalization and economic development', in A.H. Halsey, H. Lauder, P. Brown and A. Stuart Wells, *Education: Culture economy and Society*, Oxford: Oxford University Press, 172–192.
Clarke, J. (2009) 'Governance puzzles', in L. Budd and L. Harris (eds) *eGovernance: Managing or Governing?* London: Routledge, pp. 29–52.

Dale, R. (2005) 'Globalisation, knowledge economy and comparative education', *Comparative Education*, 41(2): 117–149.

Grek, S. (2009) Governing by numbers: The PISA effect in Europe. *Journal of Education Policy*, 24(1): 23–37.

Hughes, T. (2004) *Human-Built World*. Chicago, IL: University of Chicago Press.

Issakyan, I. and Ozga, J. (2008) 'Chameleon and post-bureaucracy: Changing knowledge about healthcare and education in seven European countries', unpublished paper. Edinburgh: Centre for Educational Sociology.

Jessop, B. (2008) 'A cultural political economy of competitiveness and its implications for higher education', in B. Jessop, N. Fairclough and R. Wodak, (eds) *Education and the Knowledge-Based Economy in Europe*. Rotterdam: Sense Publishers.

Kohler-Koch, B. and Eising, R. (1999) *The Transformation of Governance in the European Union*. London: Routledge/Falmer.

Larner, W. and Craig, D. (2005) 'After neoliberalism? Community activism and local partnerships in Aotearoa New Zealand', *Antipode*, 37(3): 402–424.

Lawn, M. and Grek, S. (2012) *Europeanizing Education: Governing a New Policy Space*. Oxford: Symposium Books.

Lendvai, N. and Stubbs, P. (2006) 'Translation, intermediaries and welfare reforms in South Eastern Europe', paper presented at the 4th ESPANET Conference, Bremen, September.

Lingard, R. and Ozga, J. (eds) (2007) *The Routledge Reader in Education Policy and Politics*. London: Routledge.

Mackenzie, A. (2012) More parts than elements: how databases multiply. *Environment and Planning D: Society and Space* 30: 335–350.

McKinsey and Company (2013) 'Big data: The next frontier for competition', downloadable from: www.mckinsey.com/features/big_data.

Mulderrig, J. (2008) 'Using keyword analysis in CDA: evolving discourses of the knowledge economy in education', in B. Jessop, N. Fairclough and R. Wodak, (eds) *Education and the Knowledge-Based Economy in Europe*. Rotterdam: Sense Publishers.

Sassen, S. (2007) *Deciphering the Global: Its Scales, Spaces and Subjects*. London: Routledge.

Sassen, S. (2010) 'The global inside the national: a research agenda for sociology', *Sociopedia.isa*, online at: www.isa-sociology.org.

Stehr, N. and Meja, V. (2005) 'Introduction: The development of the sociology of knowledge and science', in N. Stehr and V. Meja (eds) *Society and Knowledge: Contemporary Perspectives in the Sociology of Knowledge and Science*. Edison, NJ: Transaction Publishers.

Wind-Cowie, M. and Lekhi, R. (2012) *The Data Dividend*. London: Demos.

Part I

Governing by Comparison

1   Comparative Research in Education

A Mode of Governance or a Historical Journey?

António Nóvoa and Tali Yariv-Mashal

Introduction: Why the Regained Popularity of Comparative Research?

> Disciplines are in their little world rather similar to nation-states, as their tim-
> ing, size, boundaries and character are, of course, historically contingent. Both
> organisations tend to generate their founding and historical myths. Both claim
> contested sovereignty over a certain territory. Both fight wars of boundaries
> and secession. Both have elaborate mechanisms and procedures for the pro-
> duction of organisational identity and loyalty, and both are also undercut or
> transcended by cross-boundary identities and loyalties.
>
> (Therborn 2000, p. 275)

The definitions, boundaries and configurations of the field of comparative education
have changed and reshaped throughout the history of nineteenth and twentieth
centuries, influenced by the way in which educational policy has been conducted,
as well as by distinct conceptions of knowledge. The formulation of educational
knowledge – what is important to know and what should or should not be
reflected in the study and practice of education – has historically been a consequence of social and political as well as academic developments. More than an
epistemological discussion, these developments entail a process that is historically
contingent, vulnerable and reflective of the political mood and intellectual space
that they express.

   In the past decade, it seems that there has been an important process of re-
acceptance of the comparative perspective within various disciplines, among them
within educational research. After being ostracised for several decades, comparative approaches are regaining their popularity, both as a method of inquiry and as
a frame of analysis. It is a situation that has both positive and negative consequences: on the one hand, it can contribute to the reconstitution of a field of
research that has been unable to distinguish itself as a sound intellectual project
over the years; on the other hand, it can be regarded as a vague fashion, and thus
disappear as suddenly as it appeared.

   The renewed interest in comparative education is a consequence of a process of
political reorganisation of the world space, calling into question educational systems
that for centuries have been imagined on a national basis (Crossley 2002). In fact,

developments in comparative education need to be placed within a larger framework of historical and societal transitions. This has been the case in the past and it is the case in the present. In attempting to determine specific times at which this field has gained legitimacy and popularity, a tentative chronology becomes apparent:

- *1880s: Knowing the 'other'.* At the end of the nineteenth century, the transfer and circulation of ideas, in relation to the worldwide diffusion of mass schooling, created a curiosity *to know* other countries and educational processes. International missions, the organisation of universal exhibitions and the production of international encyclopaedias, all led to the emergence of the discipline of comparative education, which was intended to help national reformers in their efforts to build national systems of education.
- *1920s: Understanding the 'other'.* World War I inspired an urgent sense of the necessity for international cooperation and mutual responsibility. Concomitant with this impulse was a desire *to understand* the 'other', both 'other' powers and 'other' countries, bringing with it an interest in different forms of knowledge production, schooling and education. To build a 'new world' meant, first of all, to educate a 'new man' which implied a 'new school'. The need to compare naturally arose, concentrating on educational policies as well as on pedagogical movements.
- *1960s: Constructing the 'other'.* The post-colonial period witnessed a renewal of comparative approaches. The need *to construct* the 'other', namely in terms of building educational systems in the 'new countries', led to the dissemination of development policies, at a time when education was considered a main source of social and economic progress. The work accomplished within international agencies, as well as the presence and influence of a 'scientific approach' that was developed as the basis of comparative studies, created educational solutions that were exported to different countries and regions.
- *2000s: Measuring the 'other'.* In a world defined through a flux of communication and interdependent networks, the growing influence of comparative studies is linked to a global climate of intense economic competition and a growing belief in the key role of education in the endowment of marginal advantage. The major focus of much of this comparative research is inspired by a need to create international tools and comparative indicators to measure the 'efficiency' and the 'quality' of education.

By recognising these *moments of transition* it is possible to recognise the interrelation between comparative research and societal and political projects. This connection is visible in recent developments, as much as it was in historical processes of change – see, for example, the overview provided by Kazamias (2001) of the episteme of comparative education in the USA and England, providing yet another point of view of the history of the field.

Currently, we are witnessing a growing interest in comparative approaches. On the one hand, politicians are seeking 'international educational indicators', in order to build educational plans that are legitimised by a kind of 'comparative global enterprise'. On the other hand, researchers are adopting 'comparative methods', in order to get additional resources and symbolic advantages (for instance, the case of the European Union where the 'comparative criterion' is a requisite for financing social research). The problem is that the term *comparison* is being mainly used as a flag of convenience, intended to attract international interest and money and to entail the need to assess national policies with reference to world scales and hierarchies. The result is a 'soft comparison' lacking any solid theoretical or methodological grounds.

Studies conducted and published by such organisations as the *International Association for the Evaluation of Educational Achievement* (IEA), the *Programme for International Student Assessment* (PISA/OECD) or the indicators set up to assess the *Quality of School Education* (European Union) illustrate well this construction of knowledge and policy. The significance of these organisations is immense, as their conclusions and recommendations tend to shape policy debates and to set discursive agendas, influencing educational policies around the world (Crossley 2002). Such researches produce a set of conclusions, definitions of 'good' or 'bad' educational systems, and required solutions. Moreover, the mass media are keen to diffuse the results of these studies, in such a manner that reinforces a need for urgent decisions, following lines of action that seem undisputed and uncontested, largely due to the fact that they have been internationally asserted. In fact, as Nelly Stromquist (2000) argues, 'the diffusion of ideas concerning school "efficiency", "accountability", and "quality control" – essentially Anglo-American constructs – are turning schools all over the world into poor copies of a romanticized view of private firms' (p. 262).

The academic critique of these kinds of studies is well established:

> Most recent of all, arguably, has been the advent of the language of performance indicators – the identification of explicit dimensions to represent 'quality', 'efficiency' or 'success' of education systems and of individual institutions within them. The growing internationalisation of this activity in recent years [...] marks perhaps the most powerful and insidious development to date in the process of the world-domination of one particular educational model.
>
> (Broadfoot 2000, p. 360)

Our intention is not to reiterate this intellectual and academic critique, but to insist on the importance of comparative approaches as a way to legitimise national policies on the basis of 'international measures'. What counts is not so much the traditional 'international argument', but instead the circulation of languages that tend to impose as 'evident' and 'natural' specific solutions for educational problems. Curiously enough, education is regarded, simultaneously, through a 'global eye' and a 'national eye', because there is a widely held assumption that education is one of the few remaining institutions over which national governments still have effective powers (Kress 1996). It is important to acknowledge this paradox: the attention to *global* benchmarks and indicators serves to promote *national* policies in a field (education), that is, imagined as a place where national sovereignty can still be exercised.

It is not so much the question of cross-national comparisons, but the creation and ongoing re-creations of 'global signifiers' based on international competition and assessments. This, in turn, fosters specific comparative methodologies and theoretical frameworks that are useful for such analysis. In this never-ending process, questions regarding units of analysis and the influence of 'international categories' arise. What would be the cultural, societal, and even more so, political consequences of these global benchmarks? How can or should the academic research of education, and specifically the field of comparative education, foster such practices? What would all this eventually bring into the practice of educational planning? These questions all arise and become especially significant in the current flow of research and knowledge (Crossley 2002; Grant 2000).

Let us elaborate on the European situation to make this point more visible. In an official document of the European Union (EU Documents 2001a), *The Concrete Future Objectives of Education and Training Systems*, it is stated:

> While we must preserve the differences of structure and system, which reflect the identities of the countries and regions of Europe, we must also recognize that our main objectives, and the results we all seek, are strikingly similar. We should build on those similarities to learn from each other, to share our successes and failures, and to use education together to advance European citizens and European society into the new millennium.
>
> (p. 37)

In practice, since the mid-1980s, but particularly in recent years, the programmes and guidelines that have been implemented at the European level reflect the adoption of a 'common language' of education. New ways of thinking about education have been defined, carrying on governing principles that tended to impose 'one single perspective' and, consequently, tended to de-legitimise all alternative positions. Of course, no country will abdicate a rhetoric affirming its 'national identity'. Yet, all European Union member states end up incorporating identical guidelines and discourses, all of which are presented as the only way to overcome educational and social problems. The strength of these guidelines resides in their acceptance by different countries with a 'sense of inevitability'. In the upcoming years we will witness the deepening of this contradiction: national politicians will proclaim that education is the exclusive responsibility of each member state, even as they adopt common European programmes and policies (Nóvoa 2002).

The recent popularity of comparative education must be explained through this internationalisation of educational policies, leading to the diffusion of global patterns and flows of knowledge that are assumed to be applicable in various places. It is important to underline that these international indicators and benchmarks are not spontaneously generated. On the contrary, they are the result of policy-oriented educational and social research. In saying this, we come to the heart of this chapter. These current trends, as presented, create a unique occasion for comparative educational research that can either lead to the impoverishment of the field, reducing it to a 'mode of governance' or, on the contrary, can contribute to its intellectual renewal, through more sophisticated historical and theoretical references. These two possibilities will be analysed in the following sections.

Comparability as a Mode of Governance

Although the world is witnessing the emergence of new forms of political organisation, and a renewed attention is being paid to questions of how communities are imagined, it is clear that the political and societal form of the nation-state will not disappear in the near future, and the end of the era of nationalism is not remotely in sight (Anderson 1991). World relations tend to be defined through complex communication networks and languages that consolidate new powers and regulations. International criteria and comparative references are used as a reaction to the crisis of political legitimacy that is undermining democratic regimes around the world. The statement 'We are all comparativists now' illustrates a global trend, one that perceives comparison as a method that would find 'evidence' and hence legitimise political action. This perception of the political role of comparative research places the comparative approaches in a position that carries a responsibility, and consequently entails the production of policy decisions and actions by definitions of standards, outcomes and benchmarks.

The enthusiasm towards comparative research has two major consequences that we believe are crucial to the academic field of comparative education: the society of the 'international' spectacle and the politics of mutual accountability.

- *The society of the 'international' spectacle.* In conceptualising the idea of the 'spectacle' one should consider a societal sphere in which the definitions of reality, history, time and space are all transformed into a symbol. Even if there is no single core of control, the society of the spectacle 'functions as if there were such a point of central control' (Hardt and Negri 2000, p. 323). In this societal sphere there is an excess of mirrors, creating the illusion of several images that, indeed, always reflect the same way of thinking. That is why 'surveillance' and 'spectacle' are not divergent positions. Surveillance is exercised through an exposure to public opinion, a spectacular display of indicators, ultimately serving to control individuals and performances. Spectacle is subject to rules of surveillance (surveys, audits, etc.) that define its own characteristics, creating an interpretative framework. According to Hardt and Negri, the spectacle 'destroys any collective form of sociality and at the same time imposes a new mass sociality, a new uniformity of action and thought' (2000, pp. 321-322). Politics is influenced, and in a certain sense constructed, through a systematic exposure to surveys, questionnaires and other means of data collection that would, or are perceived to have the ability to, estimate 'public opinion'. This ongoing collection, production and publication of surveys leads to an 'instant democracy', a regime of urgency that provokes a permanent need for self-justification. Hagenbüchle (2001) rightly points out that 'the mediatisation of political life reduces politics to a public spectacle', impeding any critical discussion (p. 3). We argue that by using comparable measures and benchmarks as policy we are, in fact, creating an international spectacle, one that is deeply influencing the formation of new policies and conceptions of education.

- *The politics of mutual accountability.* The second important consequence relating to the changing roles of comparative research has to do with a politics of mutual accountability. Here, the expert-discourse plays an important role through the production of concepts, methodologies and tools used to compare educational systems. The idea of 'mutual accountability' brings a sense of sharing and participation, inviting each country (and each citizen) to a perpetual comparison to the other. In fact, much more than a horizontality of exchanges, this process brings a kind of verticality, that is, a system of classification of schools according to standards that are accepted without critical discussion. To illustrate this process, a look at the European context is again useful. Within this context the idea of 'Europeanisation' of education has provoked the development of a strong feeling of mutual accountability, based on an evaluation of, or a comparison between, national systems of education, using a series of indicators, outcomes, benchmarks and guidelines. The important point here is that political intervention of the European Union in education is legitimised through this process of comparison. There is no danger of adopting homogeneous or uniform lines of development in each member state, because EU regulations don't allow this possibility. But through 'agreements', 'communication', 'exchange', 'transfer' and 'joint reflection', that is, through a logic of comparison, the European nations will progressively adopt a common understanding of the 'best practices', and hence will implement similar policies in the so-called European educational space. The construction of comparable indicators serves as a 'reference point' that will eventually lead the various national institutions to adopt 'freely' the same kind of actions and perspectives within the educational field.

Our perspective is that both the processes of 'international spectacle' and 'mutual accountability' are achieved by way of comparison, defining a new mode of governance. In using the term governance one is bound to fall into various and often confusing definitions. Ironically, with the ever-enhancing discourses of 'liberalism', 'democracy' and 'freedom' the discussion of governance is increasingly becoming a central topic for any societal analysis, bringing with it different conceptions of hierarchy and power. Curiously enough, governance is often defined through a series of related terms and expressions, such as soft-regulation, open method of coordination, contract culture, flexible frameworks, partnerships, target setting, auditing, open-ended processes, or benchmarking.

In trying to grasp the concept of governance, political scientists end up showing how it works as a kind of 'screen' that, in fact, keeps our sight away from new processes of power formation. The crucial point is that of *legitimacy*. Let us look again at the European Union and the efforts that are being made to overcome its famous 'democratic deficit'. Interestingly enough, the issues that are being raised do not direct our attention to a deepening of democratic decisions, but instead to a reinforcement of 'new means' (governance, benchmarking, exchange of 'good practices', etc.) and 'new powers' (networks, informal groups, mass media, etc.).

Hence, the strong rhetoric of 'transparency' turns into a form of action that enhances the opacity of institutions, groups and networks that lack a visible 'face'.

Therefore, it is not surprising that the European Union in its *White Paper on European Governance* (EU Documents 2001b) defines as its main goal to 'enhance democracy', because 'despite its achievements, many Europeans feel alienated from the Union's work' (p. 7). This 'disenchantment' would only be overcome through the implementation of principles of 'good governance', that is, openness, participation, accountability, effectiveness, and coherence, governmental aspects that gain legitimacy from the practice of comparability resulting in a generalisation of benchmarks, standards, and policy guidelines.

This new approach to European affairs reveals, clearly, a strategy to move the discussion away from matters of *government* (habited by citizens, elections, representation, etc.) and place it in the more diffused level of *governance* (habited by networks, peer review, agreements, etc.). Policy formulation and government action are no longer matters of 'straightforward' decision-making by citizens, representatives and politicians. Policy is constructed, legitimised and finally put into action through 'new means' that are intended to find the most beneficial or efficient solution. A logic of *perpetual comparison* legitimises a policy that is built around a rhetoric of 'identity' and 'diversity', leading nevertheless to similar solutions. This is the current paradox of comparative approaches, and that is why we should carefully analyse their uses in political and educational debates.

Moving away from definitions, one must seek current strategies that are used as modes of governance, as in the case of 'benchmarking practices'. Initially used in management, these practices are nowadays one of the most successful tools for implementing governance policies. Sisson and Marginson (2001) claim that benchmarking offers a way to achieve co-ordination without 'apparent' (*sic*) threat to national sovereignty. They quote the President of the European Commission in a speech to the European Round Table of Industrialists:

> Increasingly, rather than legal regulation and collective bargaining being the main engines of Europeanization, it is developments involving benchmarking that are to the fore. Indeed, it is no exaggeration to suggest that, in terms of EU policy making, benchmarking is acquiring quasi-regulatory status, raising major questions for theory and practice.
>
> (Sisson and Marginson 2001, p. 2)

This statement clearly defines the practice of benchmarking not only as a technique or a method of inquiry, but as a political stance. Benchmarking – and, for that matter, *comparability* – is constructed as a political solution that will become *the* policy. By articulating a regulatory status to standards of achievement and production, national politicians will have no choice but to relate to them and hence provide a practice that will achieve the benchmarks signalled at an international level. This is, in fact, a new form of organisation that ultimately creates a process of regulation and governing that is to be relocated into every political context, as is obvious in the analysis of the *European Report on Quality of School Education* (European Commission 2002) which addresses the 'challenge of data and comparability' (p. 9). This document identifies 'the need to set quantifiable targets, indicators and benchmarks as a means of comparing best practice and as instruments for monitoring and reviewing the progress achieved' (p. 6), in order to provide a basis for 'educational policy making'. The question is not if it is reasonable to organise a league table for schools or for nations, but if it is reasonable to create an educational discourse, one that includes indicators, outcomes, data and knowledge, ultimately becoming a regulating rule, obliging everyone to refer back to it.

This kind of comparative mood is far from the traditional logic that has for many years dominated the field of comparative education, and that resides on ideas of borrowing or lending of 'successful' reforms and practices. It is also distanced from the idea of the 'international argument' which claims that the reference to foreign experiences is one of the main legitimising strategies for educational reforms at the national level. Rather, the current *comparability* is not only promoted as a way of knowing or legitimising, but mainly as a way of governing. Comparative research is important regardless of its conclusions or even its recommendations. It is important as a *mode of governance*, one of the most powerful being administered not only in Europe but also worldwide.

Against this background, we will argue, in the next section, that it is necessary to historicise comparative approaches, in order to contextualise concepts and to avoid a circulation of ideas that lack social roots or structural locations. We are aware of the obvious criticism that may arise here: does not the motive for comparative analysis reside in its 'displacement', allowing for an interpretation that goes beyond the historicity of each individual case? This would be a valid criticism only if we limit the discussion to traditional conceptions of 'comparison' and 'history'. To be able to overcome these traditional conceptions, we are calling for a re-conceptualisation of the relations between space and time in historical and comparative research, building the bridge for reconciliation between comparison and history.

In fact, it would be possible to elaborate on the idea that global forces are changing the role of the state in education, and demand attention to factors that go beyond the local level, and hence we should call for a methodology that highlights these supranational trends (Dale 1999). But it would also be possible to sustain that 'the effects of globalisation differ from place to place', drawing our attention back 'to the nature and implication of such differential effects even at the national level' (Crossley 2002). It is not our intention to argue in one or another direction. Our question is placed at a very different level. What we want to understand are the different uses of comparative approaches. For this purpose we distinguish a use that builds up comparison as a mode of governance from a perspective that looks at comparison as a historical journey.

Comparability as a Historical Journey

In the past decade, the word *turn* has invaded epistemological debates in several disciplines: the *linguistic turn*, the *pictorial turn*, and so on. Recently, some scholars have been referring to the *comparativist turn*, as a way of overcoming the fragilities and the weaknesses of the comparative field (Chryssochoou 2001). In fact, looking at different disciplines dealing with comparative approaches, such as anthropology, literature, political science or education, it is easy to identify a feeling of fragmentation and incompleteness. For some scholars, this fragmentation is not an impediment, but rather implies a sense of 'methodological opportunism': 'If game theory works, I use it. If what is called for is a historical account, I do that. If deconstruction is needed, I will even try deconstruction. I have no principles' (Prezeworski 1996, p. 10). There is no doubt that the plasticity of the field is, at the same time, one of the main reasons for its popularity as well as for its ambiguity. This plasticity is also the reason that scholars, like ourselves, are calling for a clarification of the concept of *comparability*, in order to understand the limitations and the potentialities of comparative research. By doing so, we are not introducing a new discussion to the field, but exploring ways in which we can enhance and re-introduce what Cowen (2000) calls 'the core question of the field'.

Building a case in favour of a deeper historical perspective of comparative studies, we will argue that this is one of the ways – not the only way, of course – of clarifying comparison, avoiding the 'vaporous thinking' that infiltrates research approaches, namely in education. In fact, many of the current works in the field of comparative education are part of an inquiry that perceives change as part of a 'global change', one that is not located in specific contexts or histories, but that is a consequence of 'global winds'. These winds of change seem 'vapour' in the sense that they are not rooted in a concrete reality, that is, in a well-identified *space-time*. Not only is it impossible to analyse any educational problem without a clear understanding of its historical location, but this way of thinking – and here the metaphor of the *gas* is useful – occupies the totality of the space available, therefore eliminating the possibility of alternative methods and approaches.

Before moving forward, we must explain the notion of 'history' that we are referring to. This is the notion of history as portrayed by Michel Foucault – a history of problems located in the present:

> The question I start off with is: what are we and what are we today? What is this instant that is ours? Therefore, if you like, it is a history that starts off from this present day actuality. [...] I will say that it's the history of problematizations, that is, the history of the way in which things become a problem. [...] So, it is not, in fact, the history of theories or the history of ideologies or even the history of mentalities that interests me, but the history of problems, moreover, if you like, it is the genealogy of problems that concerns me.
>
> (Lotringer 1996, pp. 411–414)

'The genealogy of problems', as Foucault presents it, is a history that understands *facts* to be objects of knowledge brought into view and highlighted in a conceptual system in which specific processes are seen as *problems*. We argue that strengthening a 'comparison in time' is the best position through which we may be able to divert comparative studies from being directly organised as 'policy' instead of 'research'. We are aware of the fact that analyses of educational reforms, even when they adopt a 'chronological reference', are often characterised by their lack of historical thickness. That is why we call for a reconceptualisation of space–time relations, in order to build a historical understanding that allows a reconciliation of history with a comparative perspective.

Re-conceptualising Space–Time Relations

One of the main topics of the current historiographic debate is the re-conceptualisation of space and time, the 'space–time of historical reflection'. The heart of the argument in this debate resides in acceptance of the idea that a purely physical definition of space and a chronological definition of time are no longer sufficient. In a post-modern era, it has become clear that we cannot continue to think of space and time as autonomous entities, ignoring the fact that space and time tend to merge into the same reality. We have become so used to thinking in a fixed (bordered) space and concentrating on time as a variable of change that it is difficult to break away from this framework. The metaphors of an 'arrow of time' or of history as a 'river that flows' are clear illustrations of this basic understanding.

For the past decade, globalisation theories have come to authorise a way of thinking that has had fundamental influence upon academic research and episte-mological orientations. Among these, there is the notion that events happening in one place and time may have important impact upon other places. Anthony Giddens (1990), for instance, refers to the idea that in the pre-modern world, time and space were inseparable, congealed in the local, that is, in a specific 'place'. In the transition to modernisation, space separates itself from place, and time becomes the abstract time on the calendar or the clock. Nowadays, time and space should be conceived as virtual entities, with space being defined through global interconnections and flux of communication, and time separating itself from the clock. Hence, the concept of globalisation creates a non-linear dependency between peoples, places, organisations and technological systems worldwide. In such multi-systems, there is always a 'disorder within order', in which these inter-dependencies problematise the notion of global relations (Urry 2002).

The re-conceptualisation of space–time relations is problematic, because it implies a rupture with the sensorial conception of space and time, as 'things' that can be physically touched. The process of re-conceptualising space and time entails a need to adopt a perspective of an immaterial space (a space of flows and communications, of meanings and interpretations), and, simultaneously, to understand the different 'times' that co-exist in a given 'time period'. This discussion has been present in the scientific debates for over a century, but the social sciences have been unable to incorporate it into their own ways of conceiving research:

> The mechanistic world-view indeed officially ended at the beginning of this century. Einstein's relativity theory broke up Newton's universe of absolute space and time into a multitude of space-time frames each tied to a particular observer, who therefore, not only has a different clock, but also a different map. Stranger still, quantum theories demanded that we stop seeing things

as separate solid objects with definite (simple) locations in space and time. Instead, they are de-localized, indefinite, mutually entangled entities.
(Ho 1997, p. 44)

In this statement Ho is directly addressing the need to move away from a fixed conception of space and time. In fact, the production of new knowledge is related to the possibility of distancing ourselves from a 'sensorial perspective', adopting displacements and ways of looking that create new 'illuminations', in the sense portrayed by Walter Benjamin (1968). Somewhat similarly, Stephen Greenblatt's (1998) concept of 'new historicism' shifts the centre of the comparative-historical literary research to a space of time rather than a thread of time. Greenblatt conceptualises time as a 'contested space' in which periods and 'linear' time overlap each other, highlighting the different objects and subjects of power preserved, modified or intensified over time. Or, to use the words of Ho: 'the here and now contains in its essence a myriad of there and thens' (1997, p. 44).

Another important example of efforts to rethink notions of time and space was introduced in a recent book, which compares the perspectives of space and time in the work of Einstein and Picasso. In this book, Arthur Miller shows the early twentieth century fascination with a 'fourth dimension', with all its implications for principles of movement and history: 'The main lesson of Einstein's 1905 relativity theory is that in thinking about these subjects, we cannot trust our senses. Picasso and Einstein believed that art and science are means for exploring worlds beyond perceptions, beyond appearances' (Miller 2001, p. 4).

It is interesting to note that similar processes of re-conceptualising space–time in comparative studies has been evident in various comparative disciplines. In ethnography, Michael Burawoy (2000) challenges notions of a global, one-dimensional place and time, explaining the need 'to understand the incessant movement of our subjects, the mosaic of their proliferating imaginations' (pp. 4–5). Within the discipline of comparative literature, works by diverse scholars such as Hayden White, Stephen Greenblatt, Richard Terdiman, Stephen Kern, Lyndia Liu and many others, try to provide the tools for re-envisioning literary history and re-conceptualising it within modern conceptions of cultural studies. Historical documents (and literature) become more than objective records or transcription of experience. They must be assessed as to their participation in a cultural exchange or struggle for meaning and power. Literature, in this framework, works as a text among many cultural texts, all of which can illuminate the contest for meaning and power in history. These methodological approaches attempt to define concepts of space and time in a non-linear way, enabling comparative research to free itself from traditional notions of place (those that usually have to do with the nation-state) and time (a concept that usually would refer to linear time chronology placed in the western modern history).

In these various interpretations of space and time, as well as the role of these concepts in different disciplines and research, we are confronting a new idea that invites us to look at the *width* and *thickness* of time. Width enables historical fluidity, conceiving the present not as a 'period' but as a process of transformation of the past into the future (and vice-versa). It is unfeasible to conceive historical thinking without inscribing 'memories' and 'imaginations' into our inquiry. The invention of history was not possible in 'cold societies', that is, societies without an idea of future. To analyse the French Revolution, for example, is not only to recon-struct past events in an attempt to describe what 'really happened', rather, it is to understand how the French Revolution became a 'problem' that is present in our current discussions and debates. It is also to understand how histories of the French Revolution have been constructed and reconstructed throughout different periods, legitimising ideologies and political stances, as well as giving rise to inter-pretations and projects that define our ways of thinking about this event, and about its importance and influence on current events. It is only by 'widening' the concept of time, creating a historical conception that is multidimensional and capable of capturing more than the one-dimensional linear time continuum, that history can be understood in all its fluidity.

It is, however, at the same time crucial in comparative research to be aware of the thickness of time. This thickness makes us live, simultaneously, different temporalities overlapping in such a manner that time is no longer a single 'thread' (the thread of time) but is represented with a string in which many threads are intertwined. Let us think, for example, of colonial and post-colonial studies, where this dimension is quite evident. Traditionally, when discussing colonial and post-colonial regimes, the argumentation is based on distinct cul-tures and identities with different relations to time and space, and with diverse conceptions of history. A useful metaphor to illustrate this idea is a 'geological formation', where we find several layers of time that cannot be understood with-out taking into account their specificities, as well as the commonalities that connect and influence each and every layer. More than introducing a device into these different strata, the historian needs to provoke an earthquake in order to understand how these layers work, how they are connected and disconnected, producing contested explanations for the same 'event'. It is only in such form of analysis that we can conceptualise post-colonial realities, that is, by looking at various layers of power, culture, imagination and identity. Then, we will be able to understand how different discourses, languages, histories and times are connected, where they are disconnected, and how they ultimately create 'new' communities and societies.

Reconciling History and Comparison

To overcome the current state of comparative studies we must reconcile history and comparison. Both may inform one another, but we resist the notion that comparative education 'has the capacity to do in space what educational history does in time' (Grant 2000, p. 316). Accounting for space and time is a necessity for both disciplines. Our argument is that we need to consider the manner in which a historical study deals with *space*, and a comparative study deals with *time* (and vice-versa).

In the post-modern era the world is within easy reach to those with the power to determine meaning. It is in this context in which we witness an increasingly instantaneous moment in time, a compression of space and time: 'The present being dramatized as much as the past seems a cause without effect and the future an effect without cause' (Santos 1998). This presumed lack of ability to differentiate between places, times, causes and effects, the immediateness of events, is why one of the main tasks of comparative scholars, and also of historians, is to make an effort to *multiply space* (spaces) and to *unfold time* (times) opening up visions towards new understandings. This is the theoretical basis that would allow reconciliation between history and comparison.

In order to accommodate such developments in comparative and historical research, the 'come-back' of comparative research needs to be accompanied by two related movements: on the one hand, the adoption of methodological perspectives that do not consecrate models of analysis exclusively centred on national geographies, and that are able to understand the multiplicity of levels of affiliation and belonging that characterise communities around the world (Cowen 2000; Crossley 2002); on the other hand, the reinforcement of a thinking that lies in the logic of comparison in time, moving away from a floatation of concepts, lacking roots or locations. It is basically a question of overcoming the gulf between experience and expectation, conceiving comparative-historical research as a constant production of meanings; or, in other words, as an immense playing field defined by the necessity to produce sound and rigorous statements, and at the same time, being open to an infinity of interpretations. Let us further elaborate on these two movements.

Multiplying Spaces

Despite its evolution, comparative education has remained deeply attached to the *materiality* of the nation-state as the main unit of observation and analysis. This is, of course, not a phenomenon unique to comparative education. The study of comparative literature, for example, has a similar tradition of basing comparisons on the premises of nation-focused concepts. Some leading literary figures, such as Pierre Brunel, Claude Pichois, and Andrea-Michele Rousseau, ironically claimed that the comparative literary study should have been called 'comparative national literatures' (Hokenson 2000). Also, if we consider the field of political science, we recognise that the tradition of seeing politics as taking place either within or among independent states is still predominant (Stepan 2001). The re-examination of this one-dimensional bordered space is a precondition for the renewal of comparative studies.

Appadurai (1996) presents a clearly articulated description of the way in which space should be depicted in current research in his book *Modernity at Large*. Appadurai suggests that in order to conceptualise the new role that 'space' and 'nation' have in the global era, one must adopt the concept of *scapes* (ethnoscape, ideoscape, mediascape, etc.), advocating an alternative spatial rendering of the present, one that is not 'fixed' as a typical landscape may be: 'Imagination is now central to all forms of agency, is itself a social fact, and is a key component of the new global order' (p. 32). This concept is one that is detached from any geographical scape, but is located in imaginary and virtual 'flows' through which communities are created.

These ideas invite us to look to a space that is not limited to its physical margins. In truth, as Thomas Popkewitz (1999) shows, temporal concepts are displaced by spatial ones through 'the making of maps', 'the development of discursive fields', 'regionality', 'localities', 'terrain', 'imagined communities' and 'institutional geographies', 'ideological space' and 'topographies of the person':

> The use of spatial concepts entails rethinking the ideas of history, progress, and agency that have been inscribed from nineteenth century social theory. The concept of space in post-modern theories has both representational and physical qualities. [...] The focus of post-modern literature is how social spaces are constructed not as geographical concepts alone but as discourses that produce identities.
>
> (pp. 27–28)

We are arguing in favour of a conceptualisation of space that can capture virtual, imaginary and geographical spaces at once, moving away from a sensorial perspective, that is, a space that can be fixed, bordered and touched. This does not mean that we should ignore the role still played by nation-states, as stated by Burawoy (2000):

> The dense ties that once connected civil society to the state are being detached and redirected across national boundaries to form a thickening global public sphere. Yet these connections and flows are not autonomous, are not arbitrary patterns crossing in the sky, but are shaped by the strong magnetic fields of nation states.
>
> (p. 34)

Yet we need to take into account a redefinition of space and time, in order to recognise the importance of an *immaterial space*, built around memories and imaginations, identities and affiliations, networks and communication.

Unfolding Times

Koselleck (1990), in his work *Futures Past*, hypothesises that, in determining the difference between past and future (or between experience and expectation), we create conditions to apprehend the time of history: 'We saw throughout the centuries a time construction of history, that led to this singular form of acceleration that is characteristic of the current world' (pp. 20–21). Koselleck portrays history as though there is past in the present, not only as a 'before' and as an 'after', but as a 'during' that resides in a present of several modes. It does not reside as a 'physical action', but as a complexity of memories and projects building senses of identity. Similarly, in comparative literature, the concept of 'imaginative space' is the basis of an argument that transfers the centre of literary studies from the writer to the reader, that is, creating a space in which the reader's imagination compensates and creates new realities (Iser 2000).

Adopting a different approach, Laïdi (1998) talks about a collective renegotiation of our relation to space and to time: 'a space that is extended and a time that is accelerated' (p. 10). Comparative scholars, as well as historians, are asked to take into consideration not only 'geographical' spaces, but more importantly 'spaces of meaning' (Laïdi 1998). These spaces of meaning are placed in a social and conceptual environment where the 'instant' (immediateness) is linked with a deeper understanding of the very long duration of origins and universes. In this sense, historical time is also compressed and extended, underlining the limits of our interpretations.

In this, we are facing an important role for historical research within the comparative discipline, one that would enable comparative work to trace the conceptualisation of ideas and the formation of knowledge over time and space. One could picture such a theoretical framework for comparative studies as a multidimensional process in which research is grounded in 'local histories', but is based and embedded in different forces, connections, times and places. The reception of each of these histories in different 'presents' will produce an individual, historically contingent social, cultural and educational discourse.

> Historicism contents itself with establishing a causal connection between various moments in history. But no fact that is a cause is for that very reason historical. It became historical posthumously, as it were, through events that may be separated from it by thousands of years. A historian who takes this as his point of departure stops telling the sequence of events like the beads of a rosary. Instead, he grasps the constellation which his own era has formed with a definite earlier one. Thus he establishes conception of the present at the *time of the now* which is shot through with chips of Messianic time.
>
> (Benjamin 1968, p. 263)

Educational systems have been defined as a consequence of events in which they play a role in determining, and of which they are themselves a result. There is in addition a clear connection between comparative research and social and political processes of historical change. Benjamin's notion of 'Messianic time' refers to the idea that human history is a nearly undetectable fraction of the totality of historical time, coinciding with the fact that the historical present is merely an abridgement of the entire history of humankind. Benjamin thus opens up another possibility for a comparative-historical approach.

We call for a re-conceptualisation of space–time relations, so as to build a historical understanding which allows for a reconciliation between history and comparison. Stille (2002) refers to the idea that the 'loss of historical memory' is hardly unique to our age (p. xiii), but we believe it requires an added dimension in the contemporary context, calling for the construction of an interpretative space which is historically grounded. The definition of new zones of looking is, probably, the most important challenge for comparative research in the twenty-first century. This implies a sophistication of our theories, binding together historical and comparative approaches so as to gather a new understanding of problems in the educational field.

Final Comments

By presenting the current condition of comparative educational research and the research trends that have resulted in its renewed popularity, our intention was to present the extremes. On the one hand, the definitions of comparative education as a *mode of governance* and on the other hand, its importance as a *historical journey*. Between these two extremes there is room to imagine different positions and dispositions for comparative education. In a certain sense, one can argue that the interest of the field resides precisely in the presence of several and distinct traditions. But these various traditions need to be analytically separated. Otherwise, we are bound to be entangled in an amalgamation of principles and concepts, a mixture that is the main reason for the depreciation of comparative education and for its transformation into an 'academic folklore'.

This is why, counter-current to mainstream comparative thinking, we are advocating the need for a deeper historical perspective. We are not referring, obviously, to a 'narrow history', enclosed within a linear vision of time and a geographical notion of space. Such a linear understanding of history is useless for comparative purposes. Rather, we are referring to a history that enables us to understand the problems of the present through an analysis of the way they have been and are constituted throughout the past and present, enabling a constitution of the future:

> History, with its rigid paradigms of order, comes to shore up the insecure ramparts of a failing memory. Untangling the strands of the past – or submitting to their confusing but exhilarating intricacy – cannot simply be an act of recognition, of fitting events into fixed patterns, of just seeing the light. It must begin, rather, by apprehending the sources of light and the present objects they shed or illuminate, and follow with an active, incessant engagement in the process of naming and renaming, covering and uncovering, consuming and producing new relations, investigating hierarchies of power and effect: distilling light into sun, moon and fire. Just as maps interpret and redefine terrain in the image of their makers, history can yield both past and prospective orders.
>
> (Alcalay 1993, p. 2)

Here, we are referring to an analysis of the present as part of historical practices that produce ways of thinking, acting, and feeling. In this sense, as Popkewitz *et al.* (2001) claim, history is not the movement toward some form of reliable representation, it is rather a part of the present: 'A cultural history as a history of the present considers reason as a field of cultural practices that orders the ways that problems are defined, and possibilities and innovations sought' (p. 4).

The project of raising an understanding of the historical specificity of educational phenomena and simultaneously acknowledging the radical presence of the other(s) defines a new agenda for comparative research. As argued by Ringer, 'there is simply no other means of arriving at explanations, and not just descriptions, of change in education than the comparative approach' (cf. Schriewer and Nóvoa 2001, p. 4222).

The focus of comparative education should not be on the 'facts' or the 'realities', but on *problems*. By definition, the facts (events, countries, systems, etc.) are incomparable. It is possible to highlight differences and similarities, but it is hard to go further. Only problems can constitute the basis for complex comparisons: problems that are anchored in the present, but that possess a history and anticipate different possible futures; problems that are located and relocated in places and times, through processes of transfer, circulation and appropriation; problems that can only be elucidated through the adoption of new zones of looking that are inscribed in a space delimited by frontiers of meaning, and not only by physical boundaries.

References

Alcalay, A. (1993) *After Jews and Arabs*. Minneapolis: University of Minnesota Press.

Anderson, B. (1991) *Imagined Communities: Reflections on the Origin and Spread of Nationalism*. London and New York: Verso.

Appadurai, A. (1996) *Modernity at Large: Cultural Dimensions of Globalization*. Minneapolis: University of Minnesota Press.

Benjamin, W. (1968) *Illuminations*. New York: Harcourt, Brace & Jovanovich.

Broadfoot, P. (2000) 'Comparative education for the 21st century', *Comparative Education*, 36(3): 357–371.

Burawoy, M. (ed.) (2000) *Global Ethnography: Forces, Connections and Imaginations in a Postmodern World*. Berkeley: University of California Press.

Chryssochoou, D. (2001) *Theorizing European Integration*. London: Sage.

Cowen, R. (2000) 'Comparing futures or comparing pasts?', *Comparative Education*, 36(3): 333–342.

Crossley, M. (2002) 'Comparative and international education: contemporary challenges, reconceptualization and new directions for the field', *Current Issues in Comparative Education* (online journal), 4(2), www.tc.columbia.edu/cice.

Dale, R. (1999) 'Specifying globalization effects on national policy: a focus on the mechanisms', *Journal of Educational Policy*, 14(1): 1–17.

EU Documents (2001a) *The Concrete Future Objectives of Education and Training Systems*. Report from the Education Council to the European Council. Brussels: Council of the European Union.

EU Documents (2001b) *White Paper on European Governance*. Brussels: Commission of the European Communities.

European Commission (2002) *European Report on Quality of School Education*. Brussels: Directorate-General for Education and Culture.

Giddens, A. (1990) *The Consequences of Modernity*. Stanford, CA: Stanford University Press.

Grant, N. (2000) 'Tasks for comparative education in the new millennium', *Comparative Education*, 36(3): 309–317.

Greenblatt, S. (1998)' 'Culture', in D. Keesey (ed.) *Contexts for Criticism* (3rd edn). Mountain View, CA: Mayfield.

Hagenbüchle, R. (2001) 'Living together as an intercultural task', *Comparative Literature and Culture* (online journal), 3(2), http://clcwebjournal.lib.purdue.edu.

Hardt, M. and Negri, A. (2000) *Empire*. Cambridge, MA: Harvard University Press.

Ho, M. (1997) 'The new age of the organism', *Architectural Design*, 67(9–10): 44–51.

Hokenson, J.W. (2000) 'Comparative literature and the culture of context', *Comparative Literature and Culture* (online journal), 2(4), http://clcwebjournal.lib.purdue.edu.

Iser, W. (2000) *The Range of Interpretation*. New York: Columbia University Press.

Kazamias, A. (2001) 'Re-inventing the historical in comparative education: reflections on a protean episteme by a contemporary player', *Comparative Education*, 37(4): 439–449.

Koselleck, R. (1990) *Le futur passé: contribution à la sémantique des temps historiques* [Futures Past – on the semantics of historical time]. Paris: Éditions de l'École des Hautes Études en Sciences Sociales.

Kress, G. (1996) 'Internationalisation and globalisation: rethinking a curriculum of communication', *Comparative Education*, 32(2): 185–196.

Laïdi, Z. (1998) *A World Without Meaning: The Crisis of Meaning in International Politics*. New York and London: Routledge.

Lotringer, S. (ed.) (1996) *Foucault Live – Collected Interviews 1961–1984*. New York: Semiotexte.

Miller, A. (2001) *Einstein, Picasso: Space, Time, and the Beauty that Causes Havoc*. New York: Basic Books.

Nóvoa, A. (2002) 'Ways of thinking about education in Europe', in A. Nóvoa and M. Lawn (eds) *Fabricating Europe – The Formation of an Education Space*. Dordrecht: Kluwer Academic Publishers.

Popkewitz, T. (1999) 'A social epistemology of educational research', in T. Popekiwtz and L. Fendler (eds) *Critical Theories in Education: Changing Terrains of Knowledge and Politics*. New York and London: Routledge.

Popkewitz, T., Franklin, B. and Pereyra, M. (eds) (2001) *Cultural History and Education*. New York: Routledge-Falmer.

Prezeworski, A. (1996) 'The role of theory in comparative politics: a symposium', *World Politics*, 48(1): 1–49.

Santos, B.S. (1998) 'No Verao com exposcopio', *Visao*, 13 August.

Schriewer, J. and Nóvoa, A. (2001) 'History of education', in *International Encyclopedia of Social and Behavioral Sciences*, Vol. 6. Oxford: Elsevier, pp. 4217–4233.

Sisson, K. and Marginson, P. (2001) *Benchmarking and the 'Europeanisation' of Social and Employment Policy*. Sussex, ESRC 'One Europe or Several' Programme – Briefing note 3/01.

Stepan, A. (2001) *Arguing Comparative Politics*. Oxford: Oxford University Press.

Stille, A. (2002) *The Future of the Past*. New York: Farrar, Strauss and Giroux.

Stromquist, N. (2000) 'Editorial', *Compare*, 30(3): 261–264.

Therborn, G. (2000) 'Time, space and their knowledge', *Journal of World System Research*, 2: 275–292.

Urry, J. (2002) *Global Complexity*. Cambridge: Polity.

2 Knowledge Production and Technologies of Governance in Education

Steven J. Klees and D. Brent Edwards Jr.

We live in a society obsessed with knowledge – there is endless talk of the knowledge economy, the knowledge society, the knowledge revolution, knowledge management, etc. (Garnham 2000). Knowledge has long been seen as a major contributor to better governance. As one example, the policy sciences, developed in the years following World War II, held the promise to take some of the politics out of politics by using science and expertise to discover facts (Deleon and Martell 2006; Fuguitt and Wilcox 1999). Most particularly, these were causal facts that measured the impact of potential policies. Politics could still argue over the value of and values in policies, but science could and would determine best practice, at least in so far as the impact of policies. Thus, the governance and regulation of education and other endeavors would be determined, in large part, by technical knowledge (Mingat and Tan 1988). Today, this trend continues unabated (Walters *et al.* 2009; Meyer and Benavot 2013).

Unfortunately, this simplistic connection between knowledge and governance is false. The policy sciences have been criticized since their inception (Lindblom and Cohen 1979; Rein and White 1979; Sapru 2011; Wittrock and Deleon 1986). The field, for the most part, has dropped the science label and explicitly recognizes the limits of so-called rational models, even sometimes paying attention to the need for more democratic and participative approaches to policy analysis and choice (Deleon and Martell 2006; Hoppe 1999). Another important field at the intersection of knowledge and governance – program evaluation – has also been subject to considerable contestation. It began, at least in education, as very much oriented towards scientific testing and measurement and wound up opening to an array of qualitative, participatory, and empowerment approaches (Stufflebeam *et al.* 2000). More generally, the objectivity and supremacy of knowledge has been challenged by the postmodern turn and the variety of poststructural, postcolonial, and other post-perspectives (Hoppe 1999).

However, despite contestation and challenge, the predominant view is still fairly simple and linear – that objective knowledge can be discovered and that this knowledge in turn can be used to direct governance (Mosteller and Boruch 2002; Slavin 2002). This chapter tries to dispel this myth by focusing on two issues. First, we look at the problems of the predominant view in relation to the World Bank (known as the Bank), perhaps the preeminent global governance institution in education. Second, we look at the failure of the primary technology of knowledge generation used by the World Bank and most other researchers and research institutions around the world – namely, quantitative research methods.

The World Bank as a Knowledge Bank and Knowledge Producer

World Bank as Knowledge Bank

While the World Bank downplays the importance of resources in the governance of education (Verger and Bonal 2012), the same is not true for knowledge (King 2002). Beginning with President Wolfensohn, the World Bank

> embarked on a 'new' vision in 1996 – to become the Knowledge Bank that spurs the knowledge revolution in developing countries and acts as a global catalyst for creating, sharing and applying the cutting-edge knowledge necessary for poverty reduction and economic development.
>
> (World Bank 2001:1, as cited in Klees 2002:459)

This "new vision" yielded re-organization within the Bank, "knowledge managers," a World Development Report (1998/99) devoted to "Knowledge for Development," and a new rhetoric that permeates everything the Bank does (World Bank 1999a), including its education work.

To that end, the Bank's 1999 education strategy paper emphasized the importance of the Education Knowledge Management System (EKMS), which, according to the Bank's intentions at the time, "creates, captures, distills, and disseminates relevant development knowledge on education" (World Bank 1999b: 42). More recently, in its *Education Strategy 2020* (WBES2020), the World Bank declared not only the need to build "a global knowledge base powerful enough to guide" educational reform (World Bank 2011: 1) but also its "aspirations to be both a generator of new knowledge and a synthesizer of existing knowledge" (53).

WBES2020 also highlights the World Bank's latest initiative in this area, SABER, or System Approach for Better Education Results. According to the SABER overview document, this "initiative is helping the World Bank and its development partners to collect and analyze information on policies and identify actionable priorities for strengthening education systems" (World Bank 2013: 4), with the goal being to "make it possible for stakeholders to obtain simple, objective, up-to-date snapshots of how their system is functioning, how well it is performing, and what concretely the system can do to achieve measurably better results" (World Bank 2011: 61). By collecting information on numerous aspects of education systems around the world, the World Bank will create a "global knowledge base on education policies and institutions" in order to provide evidence-based guidance to countries on education reform (World Bank 2013: 4).

World Bank as Knowledge Producer

The World Bank has not only focused on benchmarking country performance and storing knowledge. As "the largest development research institution in the world" (Gilbert and Vines 2006: 49), it also produces hundreds of knowledge products each year, including reports, academic articles and books, impact evaluations, working papers, seminar proceedings, and policy briefs. Indeed, between 1998 and 2005 alone, the Bank "undertook 705 research projects and published 3,635 research publications in English" (Dethier 2007: 471). The Bank's research on education is no exception to this extraordinary observation.

In WBES2020, the World Bank devotes some space to lauding its own contribution to the "global knowledge base" on education (World Bank 2011:52). It talks of producing some 500 journal articles and another 500 books, book chapters, and working papers. It compares its publication record in the economics of education favorably with top universities – "only Harvard University comes close" (53). Moreover, between 2001 and 2010 the education sector at the World Bank spent $49 million dollars on research and produced "about 280 pieces of research and other analytical work" (52). On average, then, a single piece of research costs approximately $175,000! This indicates the incredible amount of resources that this institution dedicates to such purposes.

Issues in World Bank Knowledge Production and Governance

Although the World Bank's production of research is impressive by its sheer volume, and though its stated desire to be a clearing-house for "best practice knowledge" from everywhere – its own and that of all its partners (World Bank 1999a: 42) – is alluring, there are ample reasons to suggest that we should be highly critical of these efforts. That is to say, we should approach with skepticism activities by the Bank to produce, collect, and disseminate objective knowledge in the service of governance because they belie the well-known neoliberal economics bias that is inherent to this institution (Lauglo 1996; Rao and Woolcock 2007).[1] This bias manifests in a number of ways.

Most egregious and widely recognized is that Bank research is almost exclusively self-referential: it cites research done by Bank staff or its consultants, all of whom share a neoliberal ethos (Steiner-Khamsi 2012).[2] When research by Bank staff does not accord with the neoliberal framework and policy prescriptions of this institution, that research is suppressed (Broad 2006, 2007; Klees 2012). On the other hand, for those particular policy reforms which do resonate with the Bank's biases, as well as with the staff who champion them, they have been promoted vigorously around the world – at times without even the pretense of any evidentiary base (Broad 2006; Klees 2012; Nielsen 2007).[3] The development of public–private partnerships in education is a recent example of a policy that has been supported by Bank staff despite a research base which, even by the standards of the methods we problematize here, shows a lack of positive results (Patrinos *et al.* 2009; Verger 2012).[4] Moreover, the Bank's bias is apparent in the conduct of analysis itself: scholars found that the Bank has manipulated data and/or repeatedly offered overly sanguine interpretations of the available evidence (Broad 2006; Edwards 2012, 2013; Samoff 1993; Steiner-Khamsi 2012). As a final example, consider that the consultations in the process of producing the WBES2020 revealed the inability of the Bank to document and seriously consider commentary and suggestions which did not mesh with its neoliberal approach to understanding and reforming education – and this after intentionally seeking the perspectives of progressive educators from outside the Bank (Arnove 2012).[5] The Bank's biases make a mockery of the policy sciences idea that objective knowledge can direct governance in the public interest.

Even at its best, the idea of a central repository of "best practice" is problematic. As a case in point, although the World Bank suggests that it can pool knowledge through SABER about "what works," there is no free marketplace of ideas in the real world, where best ideas win out. To the contrary, in the real world, knowledge is contested and power, influence, and political considerations govern the outcome of that contestation (Broad 2006; Samoff and Stromquist 2001).[6] Furthermore, given the commonly held belief within the Bank that quantitative studies produce more credible, reliable, and valid findings, consider the implications for studies based on qualitative and other alternative forms of research. Such studies would likely not be included in any database developed by the Bank (Samoff and Stromquist 2001) – and would thus have no chance of influencing governance. The Bank approaches education and development policy not only from its own economic perspective but also on the basis of a narrow and flawed set of research methods. It is to the latter issue that we now turn.

Quantitative Methods as a Technology of Governance

The dominant approach by Bank researchers and most others – across many fields – for determining the supposedly objective knowledge needed for policy choice is based on quantitative research methods. In this section we focus on regression analysis, the primary statistical technique for uncovering the causal impact of one variable on another. While some might see this as technical and esoteric, regression analysis is the dominant methodology for studying the impact of educational and social policy and practice. Regression analysis is the principal technology for knowledge generation and it is important that all researchers and practitioners recognize its fundamental flaws.

Regression analysis and its offshoots (path analysis, hierarchical linear modeling, structural equation modeling, etc.) try to determine the effect of one or more independent variables on a dependent variable of interest. Regression analysis begins with three key assumptions. These assumptions are that the model being estimated includes all relevant variables, that those variables are measured correctly, and that their functional interrelationships are accurately specified. If the assumptions hold true, then regression coefficients, which are supposed to measure the impact of each independent variable, are accurate estimators of causal impact. However, in the real world these assumptions never hold true; there are always multiple failures of the assumptions. Regression analysis theory does talk about the failure of one assumption at a time, but offers no guidance as to how inaccurate the resulting regression coefficients are under real-world misspecification conditions, that is, deviation from the three key assumptions. Thus, in practice, regression analysis is always misspecified. With so many alternative specifications from which to choose, regression analysts can almost always find their favorite variable to be significant, and thus the empirical literature becomes a debate over who has the best specification. To illustrate these fundamental flaws, below we briefly discuss the use of regression analysis to explain student achievement.

Education Production Function Studies

Perhaps the most common use of regression analysis in education is to estimate what are called educational production – or input–output – functions. The dependent variable usually studied is the student score on an achievement test. As always, the three conditions for proper specification are impossible to fulfill. First, the array of potential independent variables is huge, including, for example: socioeconomic status, gender, race, ethnicity, age, homework effort, computer use in the home, previous learning, ability, motivation, aspiration, peer characteristics, teacher degree level, teacher practices, teacher ability, teacher experience, class size, school climate, principal characteristics, and curriculum policies, to name a few. Second, there is no agreement on how to measure most, if not all, of these variables. Third, the possible functional interrelationships are innumerable. Contrary to the linear formulation usually run, multiple equation formulations with an array of interaction terms among the independent variables have been posited as preferable, though they are little used.

Literally hundreds of these educational production function studies have been done. With such an infinite array of specification choices, almost every study is unique and idiosyncratic. Eric Hanushek (2004, 1979) has, over the long term, studied and summarized the results of such studies. Not surprisingly, he and others have found inconsistent results. However, he and the vast majority of quantitative researchers cling to the hope that improvements in models and data can eventually show some clear results. To the contrary, we see the indeterminacy of this form of research as a result of the very assumptions on which it is based.

The result of this state of affairs is endless misspecification – by necessity. As we said, researchers have an almost infinite array of choices in how they specify the function they estimate and, as such, each regression study is never a replication. Studies are always different from others, often in many respects. The upshot for researchers is that each regression study is idiosyncratic. Since it is relatively easy to get significant coefficients, especially with large data sets, each researcher finds their particular variable of interest to be significant. As a result, when there is controversy, each side of the debate can find empirical evidence to support their perspective.

An Example: The Effects of Textbooks

When a particular finding that could be useful to policy is reported across several studies, it turns out that the consistency is more in the eye of the beholder than in the data. One of the few examples of a finding from educational production functions that has been consistently touted over the years is the positive effect of textbooks on student achievement. In the late 1980s and early 1990s, three studies based on regression analysis were singled out in major literature reviews (Lockheed and Verspoor 1991; Fuller 1987) as offering convincing research on this point. Upon examination, however, fundamental flaws were uncovered in each of these studies.

For example, Lockheed *et al.* (1986), looking at textbook use in Thailand, used a very difficult-to-interpret textbook variable, controlled for hardly any teacher or school variables, and actually found that textbooks did not matter in some of their regressions. Stephen Heyneman and colleagues (1984), who looked at textbook use in the Philippines, had no pretest measure, did not include school or teacher variables, and relied on a variable for textbook usage that was very unclear. The third study reported the results of an experiment that looked at textbook usage in Nicaragua (Jamison *et al.* 1981). While, in theory, experiments might not need regression analysis controls, in practice they mostly do because experimental controls in field settings are always inadequate (see discussion below). To that end, Dean Jamison and colleagues controlled for a few variables that might have affected the coefficients of interest, but again left out almost all home and school variables. Moreover, the textbook variable was not statistically significant in their individual (i.e., student-level) data (though it was in their group averages) and only showed an effect for first – but not fourth – grade.

We go back to this old research because the effectiveness of textbooks is one of the few consistent findings from this input–output research, yet we see that the research is fundamentally problematic and subject to inconsistent specification and contestable interpretations. These regressions provide no credible evidence of the impact of textbooks. That said, we want to point out that these are well-known, competent researchers. It is not our contention that they did an especially poor job as much as that good regression analysis practice is simply not possible.[7]

Consequences of Methodological Limitations

In theory, when using regression analysis, you are supposed to start with a complete model specification (informed by the relevant literature), and then take your data and estimate it, a one-shot deal. Given the indeterminacy of model specification, this is uncommon in practice. In his now classic article, "Let's Take the Con Out of Econometrics," Leamer (1983: 36) describes regression analysis in the real world and its consequences:

> The econometric art as it is practiced at the computer … involves fitting many, perhaps thousands, of statistical models … . This searching for a model is often well-intentioned, but there can be no doubt that such a specification search invalidates the traditional theories of inference. The concepts of unbiasedness, consistency, efficiency, maximum likelihood estimation, in fact, all the concepts of traditional theory utterly lose their meaning by the time an applied researcher pulls from the bramble of computer output the one thorn of a model he likes best, the one he chooses to portray as a rose.

The practical question then becomes, have we learned anything from all this research? Most quantitative researchers would say they have, but we believe that such learning, if examined, would likely turn out to be from a subset of studies done from a perspective with which the researcher agreed. As Leamer (1983: 37) put it: "Hardly anyone takes data analyses seriously. Or, perhaps more accurately, hardly anyone takes anyone else's data analyses seriously."

We believe that this type of quantitative methodology is a dead end – not just in education but in all fields – no better than alchemy and phrenology, and someday people will look back in wonder at how so many intelligent people could convince themselves otherwise. This is not a situation that better modeling and data can fix. But we should say that we do not see the essence of the problem as quantification. Quantifying social phenomena clearly has its limits and, at best, yields approximations (Samoff 1991). But cross-tabulations and correlations are useful to suggest interrelationships. As is well known, however, any associations found may be spurious and can have a number of alternative explanations. The problem is that the causal relations underlying such associations are complex and that the mechanical process of regression analysis is incapable of unpacking them. If we are interested in looking at quantitative data, we are afraid we are stuck with arguing from cross-tabulations and correlations. This is an unwelcome prospect for most quantitative researchers who have spent years becoming virtuosos at data analysis.

Randomized Control Trials

In partial recognition of the limits of the type of statistical modeling offered by regression analysis, there has been considerable recent interest in knowledge and evidence from experiments, or randomized controlled trials (RCTs), as they are commonly known. Frequently, RCTs have been portrayed as a magic bullet offering unambiguous estimates of policy impact (Matthews 2012). Advocates market them as Science and Truth, the "gold standard" for research. Yet, they are no more reliable than other research methods. Just as with regression studies, the underlying issue is what causes what.

RCTs supposedly get around the issues faced by regression analysis through the use of careful physical, experimental controls instead of statistical ones. The idea is that doing so will let one look at the effect of an individual factor, such as whether the student attended a reading program. In order to do this, one randomly assigns students to an experimental group and control group, which, in theory, will allow for firm attribution of cause and effect. Having done this, one hopes that the difference in achievement between the groups is a result of being in the reading program. Unfortunately, it may or may not be. You still have the problem that the social and pedagogical processes are so complex, with so many aspects for which to account, that, along some relevant dimensions, the control and experimental group will not be similar. That is, control groups always turn out systematically different from the experimental group, and the result is we no longer have the ability to make clear inferences. Instead, we must use some form of statistical analysis to control for differences between the two groups. However, the application of statistical controls becomes an ad hoc exercise, even worse than the causal modeling regression approach. In the latter, at least there is a pretense of developing a complete model of potentially intervening variables whereas with the former a few covariates are selected rather arbitrarily as controls. In the end, one does not know whether to attribute achievement differences to the reading program or to other factors.

Conclusions

The policy sciences were, for some, a clarion call of hope that more and better knowledge could improve governance. Although the policy sciences themselves have been critiqued and more modestly conceptualized, the original conception still dominates today, perhaps stronger than ever. There is a widespread belief that institutions like the World Bank, Ministries of Education, school districts or foundations can uncover Truth, what works, best practice, and the like through reliance on rigorous quantitative research methods. In our view, this is simply ideology and power talking. As one example, the self-referential Knowledge Bank has a track record of finding theoretical and empirical support for neoliberal policies, such as: emphasizing primary school over higher education; introducing or expanding fees for schooling; and supporting private and charter schools, vouchers programs, and decentralized community control of schools, etc.

While regression analysis or RCT evidence to support these policies are amassed, there is almost always contrary evidence. Claims that RCTs and regression analyses uncover regularities can be made when there are only one or two studies in a particular area or country, but when there are dozens of studies done on a topic, those studies always disagree. The ubiquitous call for "evidence-based policy" always means "my evidence." There is not one area of public policy, including education, where we have results that we can agree tell us the Truth.[8]

Research is necessarily partisan. There is no objective knowledge. Who is doing the research and who is funding the research affects the findings. This fact is enshrined in our institutions. In the United States, Democrats and Republicans intentionally draw on different researchers who will support their positions. Institutions like the Heritage Foundation, the Cato Institute, the Brookings Institution, UNESCO or the World Bank, all have their own biases. But these biases are not individual or idiosyncratic. Neoliberalism predominates throughout much of the world, and while many institutions have a neoliberal bias, perhaps none is so globally influential as the World Bank. The Bank is not some source of objective knowledge about what is in the public interest, it is a right-wing think tank, similar in perspective to Cato and Heritage. Even Bank staff complain of the "thought police" within the Bank that enforce ideological conformity (Broad 2006), Hegemonic neoliberal ideology should simply be unacceptable. Whereas Heritage and Cato are private institutions, the World Bank is funded publicly through its member countries and, as such, should be offering a more balanced reflection of the debates about different views of what is in the public interests.[9] This argument is not a call for despair. It is a call for realism and alternatives. To that end, we have two points to offer in conclusion.

First, alternative research methodologies abound. Under the label qualitative or interpretive there are a variety of methods, including: case study, ethnography, grounded theory, phenomenology, narrative, and oral history, to name a few. Additional alternatives are offered by critical/transformative methodological approaches. These perspectives criticize the fundamental lack of objectivity of positivist/quantitative research and qualitative/interpretive research, arguing that there is no neutral research, and that too often such studies are done in support of dominant interests. Critical/transformative research takes an explicit position to work in the interests of marginalized people. Research in this vein falls under the labels of participatory, action, feminist, indigenous, critical, critical ethnography, and critical race (Denzin *et al.* 2007; Klees 2008; Mertens 2004; Pawson 2006). While none of these methods can uncover some unattainable notion of Truth, they can contribute different perspectives on the governance choices we face.

Second, if evidence, based on any research methodology, is always debated, it means we must take exceptional care with the nature and structure of those debates. This means we greatly need to circumscribe the role of expertise and focus, above all, on how to democratize decision-making processes. Beneficiaries and other stakeholders, especially those without a current voice in the policy arena, must have a major say in the design, management, and evaluation of education and other policy areas.

None of this is easy or straightforward. Neoliberalism is hegemonic. What kind of research and whose research gets funded depends on ideology and power. Similarly, the ability for all relevant stakeholders to significantly participate in the policy arena is circumscribed. Nonetheless, hegemonic does not mean monolithic and neoliberalism is constantly challenged in myriad ways around the world (Griffiths and Millei 2013; Muhr 2013). Challenging the supposedly scientific approach taken to knowledge and the methods used to generate it is an important part of the struggle for transformation.

Notes

1 Neoliberal policies call for great reliance on the market, minimizing government, privatizing, de-regulating business, and attacking labor unions (Colclough 1996).
2 Some years back, in 1999, when it felt especially stung by this self-referential critique, the World Bank actually hired the U.S. Comparative and International Education Society to add 400 references to the World Bank's database so it would look like they had a broader vision (Samoff and Stromquist 2001).
3 For example, Dean Nielsen, former Senior Evaluation Officer of the World Bank's own Independent Evaluation Group, has pointed out that the education sector of the Bank included community-level decentralization of education management in its 1999 Education Sector Strategy without offering "any evidence that decentralization made a difference in valued education outcomes," though there was "clearly a determination [by the Education Sector] to support countries in their movements towards more local decision-making" (Nielsen 2007: 84). Though we critique in this chapter the foundations of the evidentiary base usually offered by the World Bank, the point here is that, according to Nielsen (2007), no evidence was provided in the Sector Strategy which promoted this policy, not even one based on the methods critiqued in this chapter.
4 For comprehensive reviews of the effects of public–private partnerships in education, see Jeynes (2012), Lubienski (2006), McEwan (2004), and Rouse and Barrow (2009).
5 When not ignoring progressive ideas, the Bank has a track record of co-opting them (Bonal, 2002). One example is how the Bank co-opted notions of participation and empowerment in development (Edwards and Klees 2012; Leal 2007).
6 To that end, simply the proposition is amazing. This could never be done in the North. Imagine if an institution in the United States said it was or wanted to be the central

clearinghouse for distilling all ideas about educational or economic best practice. They would be laughed at. Given the diversity of views, for example, in think tanks and universities, no one would even consider having some such central knowledge manager or broker.

7   We should also point out that, of course, textbooks can contribute to student achievement (depending on what is in them, how they are used, etc.), but our point is that this kind of research cannot capture whether, in a particular case, textbooks affect achievement, let alone the more important policy question: To what extent?

8   Our argument applies to all social policy. The recent controversy over the economic policy recommended in Harvard economist Kenneth Rogoff's regressions is a case in point. One particular misspecification became a focal point in that an alternative specification would have yielded a major change in government policies (Pollin and Ash 2013). What is not discussed is that this was only one misspecification out of an almost infinite array of reasonable alternative specifications that could yield quite different policies.

9   In our world of conflicting interests, there really is no singular public interest.

References

Arnove, R. (2012) 'The World Bank's Education Strategy 2020: a personal account', in C. Collins and A. Wiseman (eds), *Education Strategy in the Developing World: Revising the World Bank's Education Policy*, Bingley, UK: Emerald.

Bonal, X. (2002) 'Plus ca change … the World Bank global education policy and the post-Washington consensus', *International Studies in Sociology of Education*, 12: 3–22.

Broad, R. (2006) 'Research, knowledge, and the art of 'paradigm maintenance': The World Bank's development economics Vice-Presidency (DEC)', *Review of International Political Economy*, 13: 387–419.

Broad, R. (2007) '"Knowledge management": a case study of the World Bank's research department', *Development in Practice*, 17: 700–708.

Colclough, C. (1996) 'Education and the market: which parts of the neoliberal solution are correct?', *World Development*, 24: 589–610.

Deleon, P., and Martell, C. (2006) 'The policy sciences: past, present, and future', in B. Peters and J. Pierre (eds), *Handbook of Public Policy*, Thousand Oaks, CA: Sage.

Denzin, N., Lincoln, Y., and Smith, L. (2007) *Handbook of Critical and Indigenous Methodologies*, Thousand Oaks, CA: Sage.

Dethier, J. J. (2007) 'Producing knowledge for development: research at the World Bank', *Global Governance*, 13: 469–478.

Edwards Jr., D. B. (2012) 'The approach of the World Bank to participation in development and education governance: trajectories, frameworks, results', in C. Collins and A. Wiseman (eds), *Education Strategy in the Developing World: Understanding the World Bank's Education Policy Revision*, Bingley, UK: Emerald.

Edwards Jr., D. B. (2013) 'The development of global education policy: a case study of the origins and evolution of El Salvador's EDUCO program', unpublished dissertation, University of Maryland, College Park.

Edwards Jr. D. B. and Klees. S. (2012) 'Participation in international development and education governance', in A. Verger, M. Novelli, and H. Kosar-Altinyelken (eds), *Global Education Policy and International Development: New Agendas, Issues and Programmes*, New York: Continuum.

Fuguitt, D. and Wilcox, S. (1999) *Cost-Benefit Analysis for Public Decision Makers*, Westport, CT: Quorum.

Fuller, B. (1987) 'What factors raise achievement in the Third World?', *Review of Educational Research*, 57: 255–92.

Garnham, N. (2000) '"Information society" as theory or ideology: a critical perspective in technology, education and employment in the information age', *Information, Communication and Society*, 3: 139–152.

Gilbert, C. L., and Vines, D. (2006) *The World Bank: Structure and Policies*, Cambridge: Cambridge University Press.

Griffiths, T., and Millei, Z. (eds) (2013) *Logics of Socialist Education: Engaging with Crisis, insecurity, and Uncertainty*, New York: Springer.

Hanushek, R. (1979) 'Conceptual and empirical issues in the estimation of educational production functions', *Journal of Human Resources*, 14: 351–388.

Hanushek, R. (2004) 'What if there are no "best practices"?', *Scottish Journal of Political Economy*, 51: 156–172.

Heyneman, S., Jamison, D., and Montenegro, X. (1984) 'Textbooks in the Philippines: evaluation of the pedagogical impact of a nationwide investment', *Educational Evaluation and Policy Analysis*, 6: 139–150.

Hoppe, R. (1999) 'Policy analysis, science and politics: from 'speaking truth to power' to 'making sense together', *Science and Public Policy*, 26: 201–210.

Jamison, D., Searle, B., Galda, K., and Heyneman, S. (1981) 'Improving elementary mathematics education in Nicaragua: an experimental study of the impact of textbooks and radio on achievement', *Journal of Educational Psychology*, 73: 556–567.

Jeynes, W. (2012) 'A meta-analysis on the effects and contributions of public, public charter, and religious schools on student outcomes', *Peabody Journal of Education*, 87: 305–335.

King, K. (2002) 'Banking on knowledge: the new knowledge projects of the World Bank', *Compare: A Journal of Comparative Education*, 32: 311–326.

Klees, S. (2002) 'World Bank education policy: new rhetoric, old ideology', *International Journal of Educational Development*, 22: 451–474.

Klees, S. (2008) 'Reflections on theory, method, and practice in comparative and international education', *Comparative Education Review*, 52: 301–328.

Klees, S. (2012) 'World Bank and education: ideological premises and ideological conclusions', in S. J. Klees, J. Samoff, and N. Stromquist (eds), *The World Bank and education: critiques and Alternatives*, Boston: Sense.

Lauglo, J. (1996) 'Banking on education and the uses of research. A critique of: World Bank priorities and strategies for education', *International Journal of Educational Research*, 16: 221–233.

Leal, P. A. (2007) 'Participation: the ascendancy of a buzzword in the neo-liberal era,' *Development and Practice,* 17: 539–548.

Leamer, E. (1983) 'Let's take the con out of econometrics', *American Economic Review*, 73: 31–43.

Lindblom, C., and Cohen, D. (1979) *Usable Knowledge*, New Haven, CT: Yale University Press.

Lockheed, M., and Verspoor, A. (1991) *Improving Primary Education in Developing Countries*, Washington, DC: Oxford University Press.

Lockheed, M., Vail, S., and Fuller, B. (1986) 'How textbooks affect achievement in developing countries: evidence from Thailand', *Educational Evaluation and Policy Analysis*, 8: 379–392.

Lubienski, C. (2006) 'School diversification in second-best education markets: international evidence and conflicting theories of change', *Educational Policy*, 20: 323–344.

Matthews, D. (2012) 'Taking the guesswork out of policy', *The Washington Post*, December 7.

McEwan, P. (2004) 'The potential impact of vouchers', *Peabody Journal of Education*, 79: 57–80.

Mertens, D. (2004) *Research Methods in Education and Psychology: Integrating Diversity with Quantitative and Qualitative Methods,* 2nd edn, Thousand Oaks, CA: Sage

Meyer, H., and Benavot, A. (eds) (2013) *PISA, Power, and Policy: The Emergence of Global Educational Governance,* Oxford: Symposium.

Mingat, A., and Tan, J. P. (1988) *Analytical Tools for Sector Work in Education,* Baltimore: Johns Hopkins.

Mosteller, F., and Boruch, R. (eds) (2002) *Evidence Matters: Randomized Trials in Education Research,* Washington, DC: Brookings.

Muhr, T. (2013) *Counter-Globalization and Socialism in the 21st Century: the Bolivarian Alliance for the Peoples of our America,* New York, Routledge.

Nielsen, H. D. (2007) 'Empowering communities for improved educational outcomes: some evaluation findings from the World Bank', *Prospects,* 37: 81–93.

Patrinos, H., Barrera-Osorio, F., and Guáqueta, J. (2009) *The Role and Impact of Public-Private Partnerships in Education,* Washington, DC: World Bank.

Pawson, R. (2006) *Evidence-Based Policy: A Realist Perspective.* London: Sage.

Pollin, R., and Ash, M. (2013) 'Debt and growth: a response to Reinhart and Rogoff', *New York Times,* April 29. Available at: http://www.nytimes.com/2013/04/30/opinion/debt-and-growth-a-response-to-reinhart-and-rogoff.html?_r=0

Rao, V., and Woolcock, M. (2007) 'The disciplinary monopoly in development research at the World Bank', *Global Governance,* 13: 479–484.

Rein, M., and White, S. H. (1979) 'Can policy research help policy?', *The Public Interest,* 49: 119–136.

Rouse, C., and Barrow, L. (2009) 'School vouchers and student achievement: Recent evidence and remaining questions', *Annual Review of Economics,* 1: 17–42.

Samoff, J. (1991) 'The façade of precision in education data and statistics: A troubling example from Tanzania', *Journal of Modern African Studies,* 29: 669–689.

Samoff, J. (1993) 'The reconstruction of schooling in Africa', *Comparative Education Review,* 37: 181–222.

Samoff, J., and Stromquist, N. (2001) 'Managing knowledge and storing wisdom? New forms of foreign aid?', *Development and Change,* 32: 631–656.

Sapru, R. (2011) *Public Policy: Art and Craft of Policy Analysis,* 2nd edn, New Delhi: Raj Press.

Slavin, R. (2002) 'Evidence-based education policies: transforming educational practice and research', *Educational Researcher,* 31: 15–21.

Steiner-Khamsi, G. (2012) 'For all by all? The World Bank's global framework for education', in S. Klees, J. Samoff, and N. Stromquist (eds), *The World Bank and Education: Critiques and Alternatives,* Boston: Sense.

Stufflebeam, D., Madaus, G., and Kellaghan, T. (eds) (2000) *Evaluation Models: Viewpoints on Educational and Human Services Evaluation,* 2nd edn, Boston: Kluwer.

Verger, A. (2012) 'Framing and selling global education policy: the promotion of public-private partnerships for education in low-income contexts', *Journal of Education Policy,* 27: 109–130.

Verger, A., and Bonal, X. (2012) '"All things being equal?": policy options, shortfalls, and absences in the World Bank Education Strategy 2020,' in S. Klees, J. Samoff, and N. Stromquist (eds), *The World Bank and Education: Critiques and Alternatives,* Rotterdam: Sense.

Walters, P., Lareau, A., and Ranis, S. (eds) (2009) *Education Research on Trial: Policy Reform and the Call for Scientific Rigor.* New York: Routledge.

Wittrock, B., and Deleon, P. (1986) 'Policy as a moving target: a call for conceptual realism', *Policy Studies Review,* 6: 44–60.

World Bank (1999a) *Education Sector Strategy.* Washington, DC: World Bank.

World Bank (1999b) *World Development Report 1998/99: Knowledge for Development*. New York: Oxford University Press.

World Bank (2011) *Education Strategy 2020: Learning for All: Investing in People's Knowledge and Skills to Promote Development*, Washington, DC: World Bank Group. Available at: www.worldbank.org/educationstrategy2020

World Bank (2013) *SABER Overview: The What, Why, and How of the Systems Approach for Better Education Results (SABER)*, World Bank. Available at: http://siteresources.worldbank. org/EDUCATION/Resources/278200-1290520949227/7575842-1365797649219/SABER_ Overview_Paper_4_17.pdf

3 Network Alliances

Precarious Governance Through Data, Standards and Code

Tara Fenwick and Richard Edwards

Introduction

We share the general concerns of this book about the ways in which education, alongside most other social services from health care to air travel and banking, is being managed through comparative technologies. These effectively translate complex knowledge processes and human relationships into data. Such translations render processes calculable, and enrol them into massive digital networks that track, sequence, assess, procure and direct most social activity in advanced societies. To better understand how these processes mobilize particular educational practices, we argue for the utility of network analysis following Bruno Latour (2005). While controversial, versions of actor-network theory are increasingly brought to bear in educational studies of governmentality and knowledge. These approaches tend to avoid the limitations inherent in explanations that rely upon dominant 'paradigms' and political ideologies. They also deliberately decentre human actors, their meanings and politics. Instead, we argue for analysis that traces myriad negotiations among material devices, embodiments, and technologies with social desires and discourses. Through these sociomaterial vitalities, particular forms of knowledge become performed and stabilized.

In an actor-network analysis, it is the 'translation' of complex processes into comparable, calculable items such as numeric items of data that can exercise control in knowledge and education. Calculation works through material practices that depend upon things like written benchmarks, inspection forms, achievement tests, databases, league tables, and so forth. Callon and Law (2005: 718) offer the term 'qualculation' to capture the ways that arithmetic and qualitative accounts are melded in acts of calculation. Things have to be valued in particular ways, they must *qualify* for calculation, which involves qualitative processes. And, acts of qualculation involve all sorts of ways to manipulate things within a single spatio-temporal frame, only some of which are arithmetic. Similarly, standards of practice attempt to create comparability by controlling conduct across space and time. In both cases of governance through data manipulation or through standards implementation, regulation is accomplished through traces and representations that can fix an idea and move it around – through specifying texts, required tools, or mandated protocols. These traces become enacted and represented through codes and algorithms that naturalize and quantify, but tend to obscure the politics of their own performances.

In this chapter we outline how actor-network approaches can trace the micro-processes through which associations of heterogeneous materials of things, technologies, bodies, etc. are accomplished, and how these become translated into networks and mobilized over time and space to govern educational practices. We use the term actor-network theory (ANT) lightly: like any analytical orientation, it has developed a wide range of distinct sensibilities, preoccupations and methods that are highly diffused and internally contested, and that we have discussed in detail elsewhere (Fenwick and Edwards 2010; Fenwick and Edwards 2013). While we do not wish to flatten these into one enactment, we also do not wish to become caught up here in debates about what ANT or 'after-ANT' is, was, or should be. Our approach is to signal what appear to be particularly salient conceptual resources and approaches for studying educational governance, and we tend here to draw from the writings of Bruno Latour (2005). We also feature examples of studies claiming to work with Latour's concepts to analyse various processes of educational governance through practices of comparison. These include standardized achievement testing, PISA, an implementation of educational policy, the negotiation of standards in professional healthcare practices, and the increasing proliferation of code in processes of learning and knowledge production. All of these point to the materiality and the politics of negotiation in the network dynamics through which governance is realized. As Latour (2005: 261) has argued, the value of such analyses is 'to highlight the stabilizing mechanisms so that the premature transformation of matters of concern into matters of fact can be counteracted'.

A Network Analysis of Governance

Let us begin with an example. This one is a commonplace and particularly powerful form of governance: standardized tests of student achievement, which are increasingly mandated across states and provinces in North America. An actor-network analysis of this phenomenon has been produced by Jan Nespor (2002), showing how such tests themselves embed a history of network constructions, struggles and mediations which have settled into one fixed representation. The fixed items of such tests work to 'translate' complex learning practices into limited categories. The calculation of these translates year-long and vastly different educational processes around the state into numeric scores. Teachers become bypassed as mediators of pedagogy and knowledge, and students become directly enrolled into subject matter that has been translated into the test's limited forms of knowledge. Because the stakes are high in the calculative process (schools scoring less than a certain percentage lose their accreditation), Nespor shows that the test mobilizes a whole series of events and people to align with its forms: administrators force curricula to conform to the test's demands, teachers drill classes in test preparation, remedial classes are arranged to improve students' test achievement, and fear is mobilized among all. The result is a funnelling, hierarchical network in which the state becomes a centre of accumulation collecting standardized representations of all the students in its political borders. The state can then summarize and compare students as a class, and more importantly speak for and act upon them.

(Nespor 2002: 375)

In these extended networks of evaluation, as Nespor (2002) points out, particular materials and people are assembled and translated to become aligned with the standardized form, while others such as the testers, supervisors and the state are not. But these actors also are effects of network processes. They are combined with other forms, representations and artefacts. They are 'hooked up' with other networks already on the move: 'historically and geographically stretched out in materially heterogeneous networks that overlap and interact with one another' (Nespor 2002: 376). As Latour (2005) points out, a war room can command and control anything only as long as it maintains connection with distributed sites of action through continuous transport of information. Evaluation and accountability 'is made only of movements, which are woven by the constant circulation of documents, stories, accounts, goods and passions' (Latour 2005: 179). The test effectively circulates across time and space: an intermediary that mobilizes particular pedagogies and knowledge, and inscribes them within new texts and data bases. The circulating test and the networks that are created around and through it become linked with massive assemblages in other domains, such as the networked activities that generate mandated curricula, supra-national policies, media reports about educational crises, etc. Latour (2005) argues that when we trace the specific micro-processes and political negotiations through which heterogeneous elements become allied to form these different networks, and the specific ongoing linking labour through which they and their associated networks sustain and expand the network's movements, we can better understand how centres of power come into being and exercise influence in local sites of activity.

In sum, then, this analysis traces the micro-interactions through which diverse elements are performed into being: how they come together – and manage to *hold* together – in assemblings that can act. As we see in the example of standardized achievement tests, these complex, interwoven 'networks' can spread across space and time, and produce policies, knowledge and practices. Pushing the network logic even further, this analysis understands that all elements are enacted as they become assembled into particular collectives of activity. A student memorizing study notes late into the night or a teacher designing test preparation classes does not exist outside the test network, any more than the test materials or data base calculations. In Michel Callon's (1991) terms, the nature of all agents and what they do depends on the morphology of relations in which they are interwoven.

Network sensibilities are particularly useful for following these relational strategies. The empirical approach notices how things become invited or excluded, how some linkages work and others don't, and how connections become more stable and durable by linking to other assemblages. Analysis can focus on minute negotiations that go on at potential points of connection, and trace the kinds of connection or partial or dis-connection that materialize. The connections are never settled, but constantly being renegotiated, shifting the alignments and forms of the entities that have come together.

At the heart of actor-network analysis is attention to 'translation', a term used by Latour to signify the ways in which elements shape or change one another in these connections, and how they become reconfigured and redirected as they become enrolled into new networks of activity. Nespor (2002) for example shows how test items translate complex knowledge and learning processes into limited categories and numeric scores that can be easily compared and calculated. Latour's particular contribution is to highlight, in particular, the powerful role played by moving materials in such governance processes – the objects, bodies, texts and technologies that become entangled in enactments of teaching and learning.

Another emphasis for actor-network analysis in questions of governance is upon 'matters-of-concern', which Latour (2005: 19) has continued to argue are often mistaken for 'matters-of-fact'.

> What we are trying to register here … is a huge sea change in our concep-
> tions of science, our grasps of facts, our understanding of objectivity. For
> too long, objects have been wrongly portrayed as matters-of-fact. This is
> unfair to science, unfair to objectivity, unfair to experience. They are much
> more interesting, variegated, uncertain, complicated, far reaching, hetero-
> geneous, risky, historical, local, material and networky than the pathetic
> version offered for too long by philosophers.

In Latour's reading, our everyday lives are infused with things regarded as matters-of-fact. The laptops and software we use, the cars and road systems we drive, the routines and social rules of our work, the science that informs our perception, etc. – these tend to be treated as settled, evident and mostly stable. But of course, all of these embed many live networks and controversies that once were matters-of-concern. For Latour (2005), the political project is to highlight the controversies and uncertainties of matters-of-concern, and to prevent their premature closure into matters-of-fact. Take accounts of governance. A network analysis can trace how they circulate and how certain accounts become accepted and used as though they are matters-of-fact. The notion of hegemony, for example, can be followed to examine how consent to ideology is actually achieved and how hegemonic projects become anchored through particular networked activities and objects of everyday life.

However, what is also important to foreground is that networks do not simply fix and circulate entities in ways that control processes, identities, knowledge and so forth. The process is of continual becoming, as social and material elements become entangled and mutually constitutive. These processes are highly political, bringing certain things into presence, concentrating value, and creating differential distributions of capacity. There also are many forms of network assemblages, some more open and provisional, others more tightly prescriptive, or highly diffuse. There are usually always counter networks and supplemental networks at work – and these assemblages co-exist in a complex multiplicity in any given occasion of practice. Network analysis is not only about tracing how things become entangled into particular assemblages, but also can point to the weak points and the creative openings. Where are the gaps where elements are not joined up sufficiently to mobilize particular practices? What networks supposedly are cooperative but do not link coherently? Actor-network analysis can help to illustrate what are sometimes very ambiguous lines of control and competing webs of elements in play, as we see in examples below.

Governance Through Mediating Data

Turning to another example, Radhika Gorur (2012) draws from Latour in her study investigating how PISA both translates complex educational processes into static data, and becomes powerful in itself as a form of scientific knowledge. What Gorur shows is that practices associated with PISA stabilize and extend knowledge through everyday material practices. These assemble and then align wide-ranging objects, ideas and behaviours, including a vast array of information from diverse locations and contexts:

> [PISA] has mapped the world, ordered knowledge and disciplined people into taking up their assigned positions at regular intervals. It has coded, classified and marked people and concepts, and produced new and interesting associations. When PISA becomes a matter of chains of translation, [then acts of] intervening at points along that chain, requesting verification or reference or challenging a translation become practical matters.

PISA is a prominent example of the larger policy shift in education whereby data production and calculation have become critical mediators in new governance processes (Ozga 2009). Output measures to monitor accountability, such as test scores of pupil achievement and school inspection scores, have become increasingly powerful in the rise of deregulated and decentralized service. This in turn has led to rapid growth in data production by various actors, further demands for data, and changing modes of gathering and translating information in a relentless process of 'breeding' and integrating data (Ozga 2009: 154). In her analyses of these processes, Jenny Ozga shows how actors such as local authorities become clearing houses in mediating data. Their local contextual knowledge is flattened or lost in large-scale national data systems, and their roles reduced to servicing the data production systems as calculating devices. Although Ozga (2009:158) doesn't draw explicitly from an ANT analysis, she very much focuses on the importance of non-human elements in this 'network of agencies that are held together in webs of data' to form new governing relations. For Ozga, data itself plays the pivotal role in these disaggregated, distributed forms of governance. These items of data, as Nespor showed through his actor-network analysis of data produced through achievement testing, each embed and freeze a history of complex processes and network relations that have been reduced to a comparable, calculable material form.

Thus it is important to recognize the translation processes that produce this data, and the wider effects of these translations. Jill Koyama (2009) shows how very local activities become translated and integrated vertically into massive alliances of private and public sectors in her study of the implementation of the USA policy 'No Child Left Behind' (NCLB) in the New York City District. She examined in detail how for-profit 'supplemental educational services' (SES) providers became legitimated and integrated into the school system through the alliances and circulation of material and social bodies. These included hot lunches, enrolment packages, district officials, school administrators, parent coordinators, databases, test scores, timetables, and profit. A particular device that became pivotal in creating the required assemblage as it circulated was the enrolment packet given to students to enable them to receive the remedial instruction provided to the school system by the for-profit SES tutoring agency. Only students who received free hot lunch were eligible. The enrolment form not only selected and excluded students for the SES service, but also accounted for billable service by the for-profit SES tutorial agency, and guaranteed sufficient overall student enrolment numbers to transfer funds from the school district to the SES provider. At one point, however, schools began reporting serious shortages of SES enrolment packets, or packets in languages unsuited to their students. Additional packets were refused by district officials, citing previous wastages caused by insufficient monitoring of student eligibility. School administrators began restricting the number of enrolment forms made available to parent coordinators of the tutoring programs, suspecting improper distribution of the forms. But a problem in the system was that SES enrolment occurred during weeks in the year before determinations were made about which children were eligible for free lunch. Superintendents suspected parent coordinators of 'hijacking' the forms to help children receive enrolment packets in time to join the SES program. One explained,

> I can't just be sending more and more forms out there. I don't mean to sound paranoid, but each form represents 2000 dollars for a provider and we have been told that [SES] providers are out there buying enrolment forms.

Some parent coordinators, ever resourceful to meet angry parent demands, began to simply photocopy more forms. Schools in turn refused to accept these 'counterfeit' forms even for students that legitimately qualified for the services, prompting further parental outcry.

As we have explained elsewhere (Fenwick and Edwards 2011), the enrolment form links the SES agency directly with free lunch in ways that bypass a child. It can be exchanged directly for cash, or calculated in billing practices that transfer funds from a school to a for-profit company. It also helps mobilize unexpected responses that reconfigure the relations among parents, the dynamics of parental relations with the school, and the school's relations with the district. The enrolment form ultimately is a powerful device that determines students' access to remedial instruction, enabling assemblages that acted to prevent qualified students from accessing the very programmes to address inequity that the programme was set up to provide.

Thus we see the micro-conduits of material linkages through which a school system becomes accountable to data production rather than to student learning. Koyama shows us how the for-profit SES provisions became translated into specific and stable practices among various entities – tests, reports, databases, school principals, tutoring enrolment packages, district officials, private tutoring companies – which all enacted practices of calculation that ultimately produced inequities. The NCLB's SES mandates were closely dependent on calculations that compared, categorized, valued then linked data with consequences such as provision of privatized remedial tutoring for disadvantaged students. Teachers, administrators, parents and the for-profit tutoring company all become focused upon the numbers rather than children's specific learning requirements. Test processes appeared to be measuring student learning, but were actually intended to fulfil the company's contractual stipulation with the school district to track and record progress. In all of this, however, numbers can be messy and unreliable mediators in the network. In one example, a supervisor from the tutoring company fabricated low test scores so that the numbers following his intervention would reflect enough improvement that the firm's contract would be renewed. The suspicious test scores, despite questions, finally became accepted by all as a consequence of a defective database. The network's durability held, despite counter-factual evidence, because the matters-of-concern enrolling most participants in the SES network involved reporting high numbers subsequent to low numbers.

In Koyama's study we can see how the global is assembled in policy, aligning complex dynamics into a single frame where they can be flattened, calculated and compared against other powerful networks. Gorur's ANT analysis also shows how data-driven alignments such as PISA, as an assemblage of knowledge and governance, are also precarious. They are held together through ongoing work that sustains their connections and enactments. What appears to be entrenched authority and universality of powerful PISA actor-networks actually depend upon fragile, provisional linkages that can be interrupted, weakened or refused. Even when a policy and its associated enactments have become black boxed, therefore, it can be rendered vulnerable when assailed by persistent questions: what do these figures and explanations actually represent? PISA, like the SES network, is a fragile assemblage performing itself as solid and immutable. However, the assemblage is never stable. It constantly moves as values are renegotiated. Such networks are matters-of-concern through which to challenge the matters-of-fact that represent comparisons of student achievement across the globe.

Standards and Standardisation

PISA is one example of how the standardizing of data enables calculation processes that govern a range of educational practices and forms of knowledge. For standardization to actually work, as Bowker and Starr (2000: 232–233) suggest, there must emerge a difficult balance of comparability across sites alongside 'margins of control', opening spaces of 'intimacy' for actors in practice. Excessively high levels of control can threaten the local intimacy at each site that brings standardization to life in myriad networks of action. Actor-network accounts of standardization in education make this abundantly clear. But we need to be careful. Some have misinterpreted network analysis to focus upon an 'immutable mobile', such as a powerful text, travelling around different regions and insinuating itself into different messy negotiations among actors in ways that translate all into an extended network. However, this representation is inadequate to describe educational practice, or arguably any practice. Different assemblages are possible in the network of standardization, assemblages that emerge among the nodes and folds of extended networks, but not as stable entities. These assemblages themselves emerge and shift and dissolve into new forms as their constituting entities encounter interruptions and discover new approaches. Local network negotiations will always be influenced by humans' creative tinkering, objects' limitations, and other networks functioning in the same space that reinforce different meanings of quality and priorities. These ongoing disturbances jostle alongside a standard's attempt to control and demand compliance. While the resulting assemblages often bear sufficient comparability to sustain certain necessary dimensions of consistency, they also demonstrate Law's (2004) admonition that there are no orders, only orderings, and these are always precarious.

A nuanced example of this is available in Mulcahy's (1999) study of vocational cooking instructors working with students in kitchens. She shows how different forms of competency standards are present and held in tension in a series of embodied relations. National industry standards in hospitality are important, of course. They circulate in various forms: as representations on a piece of paper, but also in teachers' unique interpretations of these standards in their demonstrations and directions to students. Alongside these, however, Mulcahy detects instructors' very personal, embodied standards of practice that are too 'materially complex' for formal representation as competency – such as predicting the effect of a flavour on a particular dish. And there are other local standards at work. Certain networks of practice that had become stabilized and treated as standards in this site arose historically from instructors' accommodation over time to the materiality of their particular context (such as unavailability of certain ingredients and local abundance of others). Further, instructors drew from accumulated experience of watching and assessing students' growing capacity, knowing when students came to embody acceptable performance in some aspects of a skill while not quite mastering others. Instructors' work with students, then, unfolded through embodied negotiation of these different forms of standards. No one formal standard or term of competency is privileged over another, in everyday practice. Mulcahy concludes that, at least in teaching–learning and vocational encounters, standards are accomplished face to face, through interactional work. They

> are not so much read off the written specifications and then applied, as recreated on the job, using the written specifications as a resource or guide.

Achieving competence is a matter of using embodied skills, face-to-face communication, and collective negotiation by which the outcomes of the work can be taken into account.

(Mulcahy 1999: 94)

In health-care research, Stefan Timmermans and Marc Berg (2003) argue for more attention to the multiple outcomes produced through these local enactments of standards. Their work is developing a sociology of standards that radically challenges notions of control and uniformity. One of their earlier studies drew from actor-network approaches to examine professional practice of the standard protocol for cardio-pulmonary resuscitation (CPR). In the 80 different cases of CPR they observed, Timmermans and Berg (1997: 288) found that in most, professionals adapted the standard: 'seen from their perspectives, it is the protocol's trajectory which is secondary and which is aligned to their own goals and trajectories ... it is dealt with in terms of their local specificities'. Nurses acted beyond their scope by dropping hints to inexperienced physicians, which may prompt more aggressive treatment by the physician, new drugs not specified by the protocol were introduced, and strict directives of the protocol were altered in situations of 'the very hopeless patient'. Tight control is unreasonable for non-human elements in medical situations where machines break down, X-rays can show unexpected images, and blood cells can behave oddly. The protocol's explicit demands always need tinkering.

Local universality, then, implies a context of practice, of multiple crystallizing and dispersed trajectories, of reappropriation, repairing, combining, and even circumventing the protocols and standards, of leaving margins of freedom, of reminding, of long processes of negotiation, of diverse interests, and so forth.

(Timmermans and Berg 1997: 298)

A standard functions not as one professional's strict performance of a universal standard but as the outcome of negotiation processes among various actors. Furthermore, the protocol itself is what Timmermans and Berg describe as a techno-scientific script that crystallizes multiple trajectories.

The protocol designers, funding agencies, the different groups of involved physicians, patients' hopes and desires, organizational facilities, laboratory capabilities, drug companies, the patients' organs' own resilience, and so forth, all come into play in the negotiation processes leading up to the 'final' protocol. What kind of drugs are used, how they are to be dosed, who should receive them: all these 'decisions' are not so much a product of consciously developed *plans* as a result of these continuous, dispersed and often contingent *interactions*. The actual shape of the tool, in other words, resembles no one 'blueprint' but is accomplished 'in-course'.

(Timmermans and Berg 1997: 283, emphasis added)

Protocol as a standard interferes in these different trajectories, changing them in the moment when they are brought together. This moment not only gathers and transforms, but also creates visibility of all the trajectories and roles and purposes of those involved. This is why Timmermans and Berg call it a 'crystalliza-tion' of multiple trajectories. As a network moment, a moment of translation in Latour's terms, this transaction is contingent and temporary. Whatever is per-formed in that moment is not guaranteed to have any prescriptive power for subsequent action.

This conception illuminates what goes on in the translation of standards. In the moment of translation, the protocol is one actor with a historical trajectory, in a commotion of actors each with their own trajectories. These are drawn together to perform that protocol with some reasonable outcome aligned with their own desires. Timmermans and Berg (2003) are working with these concepts of local universality and immanent crystallization of multiple trajectories to help interrupt assumptions that standards function as an exercise of domination. They focus instead upon the interplay that is performed anew in each setting while maintain-ing sufficient consistency, opening new possibilities for health care practice.

These various representations of standards incorporating bodies in motion, equipment, blood, ingredients, dishes produced, politics, talk and texts are not static and separate. They flow constantly in movement and relations in sites of everyday practice. Mulcahy (1999: 97) suggests that practitioners knowingly engage in a 'strategic juggling of representational ambiguity' among these varied standards. This juggling translates the formal competency standard into diverse representational forms of competency that settle the 'problem' of difference at the local level. The question then becomes not only, 'where *are* standards?' but also what political negotiations enable certain performances of standards and constrain others. A network analysis can trace the material specificities of these performances, showing how bodies, dispositions, pedagogical encounters and understanding are produced at the point of situated performance in specific environments.

Code and Algorithms

Fundamental in these actor-networks that order and govern education, among other social processes and entities, are data, calculation and comparison across space and time. It is not surprising that Foucault's (1991) concept of governmen-tality has become so important to those studying policy processes, or that network analysis is influentially drawn upon to frame the actions at a distance through which power is exercised. However, while the centrality of calculation and com-parison is often asserted, what have been less explored are the forms of computer coding and algorithms through which this work is actually performed. Critical to enabling networks to work and extend across space and time are technologies. These technologies have taken various forms across historical time, e.g. railways, printed books, the telephone, standardized coding. However, it is arguable that there is a qualitative leap taking place in the potentialities for networked govern-ance through the growth, extension and mobilities of computing.

Computing has also become a key means of performing these networks through common processes of tagging, classification, calculation and circulation. These require codes and algorithms. It is the work of codes that is being opened up by the emerging area of critical software studies (Kitchin and Dodge 2011). Thrift (2005: 240) observes that:

> software has grown from a small thicket of mechanical writing to a forest of code covering much of the globe ... code runs all manner of everyday devices, from electric toothbrushes to microwave ovens, from traffic lights to cars, from mobile phones to the most sophisticated computers.

To do this requires enacting data infrastructures. Integral to this are the development, adoption and application of the standards that enable data to be organized, net-worked and moved. It is not simply data mobilized through such practices. Thus,

> It is not just bits and bytes that get hustled into standard form in order for the technical infrastructure to work. People's discursive and work practices get hustled into standard form as well. Working infrastructures standardize both people and machines.
>
> (Bowker, 2005: 111–112)

And, as Kitchin and Dodge (2011: 4) suggest, 'although code in general is hidden inside the machine, it produces visible and tangible effects in the world'. They identify coded objects, coded infrastructures, coded processes and coded assem-blages as participating in shaping sociospatial organization.

Yet, if ever there is an area that is black boxed, it is the nature, production and performance of computer software. Effectively, computing is presented as a form of prosthesis, rather than as part of more complex networked assemblages within which the software is one element, and which necessarily involve their users in a wide range of socio-material relationships. Computers order, preserve, and allow access to resources, but they also promote and preclude certain kinds of social and spatial relationships. How the codes they draw upon come to do those things is not usually examined and, for us, this is potentially part of what Thrift (2004) has termed a 'technological unconscious' of contemporary life.

This requires standardized ways of describing content and the development of ontologies and typologies (Lampland and Star, 2009). In order to be encoded, to be read as data therefore, content is required to be reduced. However, by insisting that things are described and knowledge represented in particular ways, much is hidden, including the very means of concealment. Qualifications are taken as proxies of learning and equivalences enacted between different qualifications and contexts in order to generate national tables of achievement. The picture here is one of multiple hidden translations, some effected by human and some by non-human actants, that are incorporated into technology applications through codes, ontologies and metadata (Miller and Bowker, 2009).

In actor-networks that govern education, it is the coding and the linking of data, the applications of technical standards, and the decision-making and reasoning processes articulated through computer code that mobilize objects and information flows to perform very particular practices through coded infrastructures: e.g. student and school records, e-learning systems, libraries and information access services, assessment of students, teachers and indeed all educational dynamics. What hidden codes do is to make it more difficult to determine how and when they are acting, and on what basis. While, as Bowker (2005, p. 140) argues, 'you can't store data without a classification system', our argument is that how this occurs and with what effects, is largely left unexamined and unquestioned in analysis of networked governing in education. With the passing of time and the incorporation of such data into new assemblages and applications, the pre-history of data capture, calculation processes, emergence of standards, and general application of rules disappears from view and becomes part of the taken for granted 'evidence', for instance on levels of achievement, upon which to develop educational policies and practices.

Conclusion

As education becomes networked into global configurations authorizing particular knowledge, standardized audit procedures and league tables, a network analysis helps to reveal how these alignments are formed and held together through much more than ideologies and discourses. It is to the mundane materials and their infusions with human desires and fears that we need to look. Nespor (2002: 376) suggests important questions about 'how and in what forms people, representations and artefacts move, how they are combined, where they get accumulated, and what happens when they are hooked up with other networks already in motion'. For understanding processes of knowledge regulation, this approach breaks through the 'gap' between policy as prescription and as local enactment, and traces how all performances are produced as effects of unfolding material networks.

What is the specific contribution of this approach? As we have argued in this chapter, a network analysis offers methodologies and questions to trace assemblages that enact governing moments. The analytic focus shifts from the social and discursive to the socio-material, and from structures to contingent negotiations and translations. Through these negotiations of connection, standards of knowledge become developed and mobilized, performed in different ways and sometimes resisted. But different negotiations and connections increasingly act to translate these performances into data, calculate and compare them numerically, and extend the growing data assemblages across large populations or regions. By following the linkages forging these actor-networks together, as well as the dynamics playing out around them in the penumbra of marginalized and counter-networks, educational analysis can better appreciate the directions and forces that perform some practices and beliefs, dissolve others, and create contradictions.

What is revealed in such analysis is not just a simple story of powerful networks and infrastructures. As the examples in this chapter indicate, network analysis shows the interplay among myriad, often contested or incoherent, network trajectories in everyday practice that carry force in governing knowledge and activity. This raises new questions for considering governance of knowledge in specific settings. What is the nature of the different network assemblages at play? Which network trajectories become crystallized in moments of enacted practice? What practices of knowledge and identity become produced in these networks? What negotiations occur as elements take up, resist, or compete with attempts to enrol them into particular patterns of action and knowledge? How do actors juggle competing networks of standardization? What and who becomes included and excluded?

When governing assemblages are exposed as a series of precarious connections exercising variable force, educators might find it easier to see how their own everyday work becomes inscribed into these powerful networks. They might also more easily identify the most productive entry points and strategies to interrupt entrenched practices or to propel new emergences.

Acknowledgements

This chapter draws on material previously published and subsequently modified from Fenwick and Edwards (2011, 2013) and Fenwick (2010).

References

Bowker, G. (2005) *Memory Practices in the Sciences*, Cambridge, MA: MIT Press.
Bowker, G. and Star, L. (2000) *Sorting Things Out: Classification and Its Consequences*, Cambridge, MA: MIT Press.
Callon, M. (1991) 'Techno-economic network and irreversibility', in J. Law (ed.) *A Sociology of Monsters: Essays on Power, Technology and Domination* (pp.132–165), London: Routledge.
Callon, M. and Law, J. (2005) 'On qualculation, agency, and otherness', *Environment and Planning D: Society and Space,* 25(5): 717–733.
Fenwick, T. (2010) '(un)Doing standards in education with actor-network theory', *Journal of Education Policy,* 25(2): 117–133.
Fenwick, T. and Edwards, R. (2010) *Actor-Network Theory in Education*, London: Routledge.
Fenwick, T. and Edwards, R. (2011) 'Considering materiality in educational policy: messy objects and multiple reals', *Educational Theory,* 61(6): 709–726.
Fenwick, T. and Edwards, R. (2013) 'Networks of knowledge, matters of learning, and criticality in higher education', *Higher Education*, online first, DOI: 10.1007/s10734-013-9639-3
Foucault, M. (1991) 'Governmentality', trans. Rosi Braidotti, in G. Burchell, C. Gordon and P. Miller (eds) *The Foucault Effect: Studies in Governmentality* (pp. 87–104), Chicago, IL: University of Chicago Press.
Gorur, R. (2012) 'ANT on the PISA trail: following the statistical pursuit of certainty', *Educational Philosophy and Theory,* 43(1): 76–93.
Kitchin, R. and Dodge, M. (2011) *Code/Space: Software and Everyday Life*, Cambridge, MA: MIT Press.
Koyama, J.P. (2009) 'Localizing No Child Left Behind: Supplemental Educational Services (SES) in New York City', in F. Vavrus and L. Bartlett (eds) *Critical Approaches to Comparative Education: Vertical Case Studies from Africa, Europe, the Middle East, and the Americas*, New York: Palgrave Macmillan.
Lampland, M. and Star, S. (eds) (2009) *Standards and Their Stories: How Quantifying, Classifying, and Formalizing Practices Shape Everyday Life*, Ithaca, NY: Cornell University Press.

Latour, B. (2005) *Reassembling the Social: An Introduction to Actor-Network Theory*, Oxford: Oxford University Press.

Law, J. (2004) *After Method: Mess in Social Science Research*, London: Routledge.

Miller, F. and Bowker, G. (2009) 'Metadata standards: trajectories and enactment in the life of an ontology', in M. Lampland and S. Star (eds) *Standards and Their Stories: How Quantifying, Classifying, and Formalizing Practices Shape Everyday Life*, Ithaca, NY: Cornell University Press.

Mulcahy, D. (1999) '(actor-net) Working bodies and representations: Tales from a training field', *Science Technology Human Values*, 24(1): 80–104.

Nespor, J. (2002) 'Networks and contexts of reform', *Journal of Educational Change*, 3: 365–382.

Ozga, J. (2009) 'Governing education through data in England: from regulation to self-evaluation', *Journal of Education Policy*, 24(2): 149–162.

Thrift, N. (2004) 'Remembering the technological unconscious by foregrounding knowledges of position', *Environment and Planning D: Society and Space*, 22: 175–190.

Thrift, N. (2005) 'Beyond mediation: three new material registers and their consequences', in D. Miller (ed.) *Materiality*, Durham, NC: Duke University Press.

Timmermans, S. and Berg, M. (1997) 'Standardization in action: Achieving local universality through medical protocols', *Social Studies of Science*, 27(2): 273–305.

Timmermans, S. and Berg, M. (2003) *The Gold Standard: The Challenge of Evidence-Based Medicine and Standardization in Health Care*, Philadelphia: Temple University Press.

4 The Attraction of Mutual Surveillance of Performances

PISA as a Knowledge-Policy Instrument

Luís Miguel Carvalho

Introduction

Nowadays policy-makers advocating policy transfers tend more to refer to international standards rather than to a specific educational system (Steiner-Khamsi 2012: 9). This chapter addresses the relation of governing and knowledge by focusing on the fabrication, circulation and mobilization, in the course of public action, of one carrier of international standards that has apparently become a recurrent category in the contemporary lexicon in education – PISA, the OECD Programme for International Student Assessment.

Throughout the last decade products generated under the PISA label (reports, methods, tables) have been differently used in diverse social spaces (research agencies, state and supranational bureaucracies, media) and scales (local, national, regional). Thus, the acronym seems to pervade multiple knowledge and policy contexts: one may see PISA results (or analysis, or implications) mobilized in order to galvanize disputes or to legitimize policies, but one may also note the presence of PISA in the making of secondary research or in the making of assessment tools (based on their rationale and method). In parallel, PISA has expanded, since the first assessment (2000), in various ways: broadening the geographical–political scope, with a growing number of countries involved (specially non-OECD countries); increasing the number and focus of the surveys and target populations; connecting with other OECD programmes; extending the number of experts and public and private organizations associated with the development of PISA-related activities of inquiry, exchange and publication.

Not forgetting the cultural specificities of the contexts through which PISA travels and the already acknowledged variability of form, content, amplitude and intensity of its impact in national policies (Bieber and Martens 2011; Dobbins and Martens 2012; Ertl 2006; Greger 2012; Grek 2009; Gür *et al.* 2012; Pons 2012; Rautalin and Alasuutari 2009; Rinne *et al.* 2004; Steiner-Khamsi 2003; Takayama 2008), PISA may nonetheless be analysed as an object around which (and based on which) there has been a recurring creation of perceptions about today's educational problems and appropriate ways of dealing with them. Informed by the hypothesis that new forms of governing are connected with new ways of knowing (Nóvoa and Yariv-Mashal 2003; Ozga 2008), the analysis developed in this chapter focuses on the processes that sustain the expansion of this exemplar of comparative governing knowledge and the ways it achieves the status of an indispensable resource for thinking-acting in policy, for the imagination and/or the scrutiny of educational problems and policies.

The OECD's self-portrayed quality monitoring tool is here analysed as a 'public policy instrument' (Lascoumes and Le Galès 2007). Further, drawing on contributions from the sociology of science and technology, the fabrication, circulation and mobilization PISA are here analysed as processes related with the creation of the ecology of the instrument.[1] We clarify these two central features of our approach in the first part of the chapter. Considering that each policy instrument develops a 'particular representation' and a 'specific problematization' of the issue that it is created to handle (Lascoumes and Le Galès 2007: 9–10), in the second part of the chapter we consider the cognitive and normative features of PISA, and we analyse them as examples of OECD's agenda and modes of governance. In the third part of the chapter, we examine the practices that support the fabrication of the policy instrument. We give a closer look to the processes related with the gathering and coordination of the diverse social worlds involved in the making of the instrument, as well as to the making and diffusion of regulatory knowledge. Finally, in the last part of the chapter, we consider the circulation of PISA through national contexts, where different social groups are interested by PISA and using it differently in their own policy contexts and practices, though frequently attached to PISA's *dicta* on knowledge-based regulatory processes. We conclude by arguing that more than a national policy convergence this exemplar of comparative governing knowledge achieves power through the creation of convergence *towards* mutual surveillance as an appropriate way of knowing-governing – thus allowing PISA to become, following the term coined by Callon (1986), an 'obligatory passage point' for the imagination and/or the scrutiny of educational problems and policies.

Points of Departure

Advocating the idea that 'public policy is a sociopolitical space constructed as much through techniques and instruments as through aims or contents', Lascoumes and Le Galès (2007: 4-6) use the notion of public policy instrument to refer to the devices used to organize social relations between administrative and administered subjects according to specific interpretations of the social world they address and based on a specific concept about the ways it should be oriented, coordinated and controlled. From their perspective, instruments are a combination of technical components (e.g., calculating techniques, a type of law, a specification of procedures) and social components (as they sustain and are sustained by values, interpretations, concepts about the social realities they envisage). Accordingly, we approach PISA as a policy instrument that combines comparative assessment techniques with a set of representations about education and a philosophy of (transnational and national) regulation of education policies and practices. Moreover, PISA is here envisaged as a 'knowledge-based' and 'knowledge-oriented regulation instrument' (van Zanten 2011: 33; see also Pons and van Zanten 2007): it draws on knowledge 'but also produce[s] and diffuse[s] knowledge in order to shape the behavior of actors in a given policy domain'. Therefore, PISA exemplifies the presence, in the contemporary policy processes, of forms of regulation that favour information and persuasion (and acting through the actors' reflexivity) instead of command and control (Lascoumes and Le Galès 2007).

The fabrication, circulation and mobilization of PISA (as a knowledge-based and knowledge-oriented instrument) is here analysed as a 'complex of interdependent practices' (see Latour, 1989): from constructing a subject of inquiry (the competences of literacy) to establishing a 'monopoly of competence' around the issue; from convincing politicians, bureaucrats, experts, researchers, in order to guarantee informational, financial, and human resources, to building 'public confidence'. From this perspective the accomplishment of PISA depends on interesting, bringing together and encouraging co-operation among diverse actors (experts, OECD professionals, politicians, high-level civil servants, researchers) around a complex flow of activities that guarantee the making, circulation and legitimacy of a knowledge-policy instrument that, consequently, is accepted as appropriate to the understanding and to governing of education systems. These processes go hand in hand with the making of definitions of and expectations about the conduct of young people, and scripts for policy-making. In sum, to analyse the making and the trajectory of PISA one needs to consider the processes that connect diverse social worlds in the production and use of cognitive and normative frames about education and the ways it should be governed and that guarantee (concurrently) the indispensability of OECD as an 'ideational authority' (Marcussen 2004).

Our analysis draws also on the idea that when PISA products (rationale, results, methods, etc.) circulate they may be put to different political uses and, most of all, acquire new meanings. PISA travels and drives people, but it also shifts while travelling across different social worlds and discursive spaces. This multidirectional analytical orientation (Carvalho 2012) invites scrutiny of knowledge-policy instruments as potentially changeable and multi-usable products of such intertwining of ideas and agencies. This perspective is compatible with the socio-political approach to policy instruments: if, as institutions, instruments 'structure public policy according to their own logic of policy' (and, therefore, have 'their own force of action'), it is also evident that they have trajectories and are submitted to controversies and modifications (Lascoumes and Le Galès 2007: 10, 17).

The Emergence and Cognitive Features of PISA

> But it is the OECD's Programme for International Student Assessment (PISA) survey, which tests young people's acquisition of knowledge and skills for life, that is the most powerful and extensive tool for considering educational outcomes and transforming public policy.
>
> (OECD 2011: 17)

This self-laudatory judgement shows the importance assigned to PISA by OECD as one of its major means of action in the education sector, created with an overt policy orientation. PISA's aim is to provide 'a stable point of reference against which to monitor the evolution of education systems' (OECD 2007: 17). And it is developed from an explicit perspective about the relation between policy and knowledge and about the making of knowledge, 'a collaborative effort, bringing together scientific expertise from the participating countries, steered jointly by their governments on the basis of shared, policy-driven interests' (op. cit.: 10).

PISA did not emerge from nowhere. It has a social-historical foundation linked with phenomena external and internal to the OECD, as has been documented and analysed (see Bottani 2006; Lundgren 2011; Mons 2007; Morgan 2007). For the analysis developed here, it is important to keep in mind that PISA is part of a long-term movement towards the institutionalization of a form of comparative knowledge and a script for knowledge-policy relationships. Put briefly, this comparative perspective states that: regular and systematic assessments are truthful practices for the improvement of national education systems, and that such improvement has to be analysed by taking into account the pace of change of other countries; international comparison of performances are responsible for changing the concept of quality applied to education systems, reaching to the core issue – student achievement – and are also recognized as being able to consider educational complexity (by collecting relevant data on learning structures, on students social-economic backgrounds, on school structures and policy choices). In sum, PISA may be seen as part of a comparative project that Nóvoa (1998) has characterized as steered by pragmatic reasoning, committed to the building of indicators for decision-making.

However, OECD's PISA also reshapes this knowledge tradition. PISA has a set of characteristics that make it different from other similar instruments and that may be related to its success in the field of international comparative assessments (Bottani 2006: 82–88). These are: the frequency of tests (triennial) and its 'diachronic coherence'; the focus on a narrow set of expertise; the 'flexibility' of the programme owing to its modular structure; the 'stability of the population' (15-year-old pupils); the focus on competencies instead of the official school curriculum and the 'politicization of the programme', ensuring that the funding governments have a say in controlling the priorities of the programme and its application. Further singularities of PISA (and the emergence of the programme) evidence the scope of OECD's political work – in brief, an intervention through soft modes of governance, with the focus on 'surveillance of performances' and 'assessment of policies', impacting on national policies as a 'creator, purveyor and legitimator of ideas' (Mahon and McBride 2008: 7–15; see also Martens and Jakobi 2010) and an agenda that, since the 1990s, is marked by the idea of monitoring quality and in which educational problems are equated with the requirements of a knowledge-based economy (Rinne *et al.* 2004: 459–62; see also Henry *et al.* 2001; Rubenson 2008).

In this context, PISA became an important instrument because with it, as Henry *et al.* (2001) noted, the agency no longer depends on statistical data created by national systems and may produce its own data, and OECD's capacities to participate in transnational governance in education increased when the agency made a turn towards comparative studies (Martens 2007). The point here is: with PISA OECD does not only generate its own data – but also may claim to be the provider of an expert-based independent framework for the monitoring and steering of school systems. We should now ask, what are the main cognitive and normative features of PISA regarding education and regarding policy processes in education?

School systems have to adapt to changes in the economy and society, from industrial to post-industrial knowledge economies and societies – this is a recurrent topic in PISA documents. The Programme incorporates and disseminates ways of thinking-doing that are supposed to enable policy-makers to naturally take part in the exercises of monitoring and mutual surveillance (practices seen as appropriate for – and thus defining – their identities and roles). The arguments developed in OECD texts or by OECD's executives and/or collaborators (Hugonnier 2008; Schleicher 2007; Turner 2007; Weinberg 2008) assert that PISA supplies policy-makers with rigorous comparative data that allows them to: conduct themselves rationally; learn about the place of each educational system in the worldwide competitive space; identify their country's relative positioning *vis-à-vis* the 'knowledge society' and/or 'knowledge economy'; and, consequently, to make their education systems move to the (physical and symbolic) time of 'tomorrow's world'.

If PISA sustains particular cultural *dicta* about policy-making in contemporary times, it also enacts representations and problematizations regarding the educational model of contemporary societies: it operates through redefining students as life-long learners; redefining teaching–learning relationships and settings; redefining school knowledge.[2] The frames, questions and indicators used in the assessment of 'literacy performances' define young people's characteristics and expected modes of action or repertoires of 'competent' attitudes and behaviors.[3] What is more, such a common expected background of performance and engagement in social life is, also, an imagination of a common educational model for an imagined knowledge society.

A good example of this relates to the innovative focus that PISA claims to bring to assessments – 'rather than examine mastery of specific school curricula, PISA looks at students' ability to apply knowledge and skills in key subject areas and to analyse, reason and communicate effectively as they examine, interpret and solve problems' (PISA website).[4] This definition allows OECD to introduce a double shift: first, a move away from the conventional self-reflection of national school systems based on their own categories and outputs (with assessments relying on tests and examinations based on national curriculum goals and content) and towards the territory of outcomes, thus directly connecting the contexts, practices and results of teaching/learning with the so-called demands of the school system environment and enabling a move away from the rationale of previous comparative studies of student performances and their dependency on national *curricula*. The second element of this double shift is a redefinition of what constitutes appropriate school knowledge. The notion of competence enacts a utilitarian perspective on knowledge as it takes practical usefulness in solving everyday problems as the main criterion for the assessment of school knowledge (Mangez 2008). Therefore it promotes a restructuring of curriculum as trans-disciplinary or cross-disciplinary. Furthermore, these shifts go hand in hand with calls for change in teaching–learning structures (e.g., from hierarchical to organic models) and in the formal education model in order to move towards the so-called knowledge economy and society.

Fabricating PISA

The emergence of PISA and the legitimacy that it seems to have in current debates on educational issues cannot be separated from a cultural and political environment that disseminates the conceptions of global economic competitiveness and the knowledge economy (Broadfoot 2000), and from the emerging age of accountability (Hopmann 2007). It surely cannot be separated from the status achieved by OECD as an 'expert organization' (Noaksson and Jacobsson 2003) – the recognition of OECD precedes and fosters the recognition of PISA. For instance, the justifications made by national authorities regarding their adhesion to and participation in PISA are strongly inhabited by symbolic elements related to OECD status: that from looking for a position among the advanced nations of the world and its major forums (of policy and expertise) to the recognition of the agency as an instance specialized in the production of knowledge relevant to policy-making (Carvalho *et al.* 2009).

Thus, one might simply see PISA as an OECD capitalization on such conditions. Our point though is that to understand the indispensability searched for and apparently achieved by PISA, one needs also to keep under scrutiny the collection of practices that keep the instrument alive and confronting successfully other agencies that also produce monitoring instruments, either at international, regional or national scales. OECD's intervention occurs also in a multilateral space where international, national and local agencies compete and cooperate in educational lending–borrowing practices (see Steiner-Kahmsi 2004).

From this perspective, in order to achieve the status of an indispensable instrument, OECD's PISA depends of the creation of a favourable ecology. Such a quest for legitimation partly determines the very characteristics of the instrument as well as how it develops. We retrieve here the idea that PISA is a complex instrument made to attract and to attach to social actors, public debates and public policies. We will develop this idea focusing on two related issues: the organizational aspects of PISA and the rules and social processes that support the production and dissemination of PISA's knowledge.

Connecting Worlds

PISA is not merely a triennial survey with a subsequent triennial report, but a complex of activities, involving multiple social worlds, sustained by communication and organization. When we refer to diverse social worlds we have in mind those who are involved in PISA's formal structures (public and private research centres, experts, OECD professionals, policy-makers, high-level civil servants and technicians from multiple countries), as well as those indirectly involved: media and national politicians who selectively discuss the results; national and/or regional governing and/or administrative structures that use PISA knowledge for creating their own assessment devices; even researchers from various fields who use PISA data in order to build secondary analysis. Thus, the accomplishment of PISA depends on bringing together those actors through an organized flow of activities and produces inquiry-related activities (for example the preparation of the framework of the surveys, preparation of the questionnaires and other tools, 'pilot testing' of related activities, conduct of the 'main assessment', analysis of data). These activities also include the production of the 'field trial' (including the definition and selection of items, the translation and face-to-face activities (in meetings, workshops, etc.), and numerous publications (main reports, technical reports, thematic reports, national reports, manuals, databases, etc.). In sum the success of PISA depends on the establishment of effective associations with (and between) multiple social actors in the activities of inquiry, publication and exchange that support the production, dissemination and use of its own knowledge-related materials.

When we explore who is who in the making of PISA frameworks and main technical tools, we might say that the monopoly of expertise created around PISA rests on a somewhat narrow social basis that includes a nucleus of between ten and twenty actors (from private and public organizations, experts from different areas, and OECD members) that also participate in the coordination of PISA's multiple activities

(Carvalho with Costa 2009). OECD's PISA Secretariat (the structure formally responsible for the 'management of everyday activities of PISA') is just one of the actors, but it is a central player that takes seriously the international agency's scripts, playing the (self-described) role of catalyst – acting on the mobilization, enlargement and selection of collective (and sometimes individual) actors to be involved in/by PISA and operating as a purveyor of data and visions. In fact, in order to be a facilitator or an accelerator of interactions between research and policy, the OECD has generated through its own initiative the production of a specific (and singular) framework – the competencies of literacy. With such a frame it became possible to interest others in new ways of thinking and doing knowledge and policy.

But the achievement of PISA does not depend only on bringing actors and ideas into relation; it depends also on 'keeping them in' and acting with specific scripts and, simultaneously, on fulfilling their informational needs. Having the formal role of manager of everyday activities of PISA, the Secretariat is able to regulate the timings, the resources and the flow of the activities and relationships between the actors. Throughout the several sequences of tasks that make PISA – preparing frameworks, testing instruments, implementing the survey, treating and discussing data, preparing publications – the 'manager' ensures that certain procedural protocols but is as much concerned to ensure that interactions follow the common values and rules expected in a social space created by a putative expert organization: consensus building, high-trust in expertise, responsiveness to external changes and criticisms, even co-optation of criticisms and/or competitors. PISA meetings and internal documents are two examples of the coordination forms and rules we are referring to here.

An examination of the narratives from national representatives about the dynamics of the PISA Governing Body meetings (Carvalho with Costa 2009) reveals three themes: the OECD Secretariat has a leading role in the meetings; the meetings are political spaces where conflicts between visions of education take place, and where compromises are established between participants with unequal resources (e.g. the nearness to / distance from the specific technical knowledge of PISA, the mastery of the English language, the unequal status of each country in the political-economic hierarchy of the OECD). There are also unequal capacities to exercise those resources: the technical argument has a central role for the achievement of political consensus, as for many the (political) building of consensus seems to be secondary to the technical expertise. Regarding documents, the use of (written) consultation practices emerges as an effective strategy for reaching consensual decisions. The practice of producing an enormous number of documents – mobilizing people to work on successive draft versions – throughout the flow of PISA activities, constitutes a complex system of normative and functional coordination. These 'open' processes of writing generate perceptions of membership and belonging and of (at least) partial authorship and they effectively contribute to the production of consensual decisions (for example regarding the framework, or regarding the structure and writing style of the reports) and to the adoption of standardized procedures that steer the participants (for example the technical norms that guide the implementation of PISA enquiries).

Assemblage, Plasticity and Multiplication of Knowledge

All these practices are related to the production of a specific kind ok knowledge. This is knowledge for policy, generated in order to assist policy-making and/or to provide policy-makers with steering tools (Desjardins and Rubenson 2009; Nassehi 2008; Ozga 2008), and is created by specific practices and referencing specific criteria. In the making and flow of this type of knowledge, it is not only the quality of scientific or technical credibility that counts; the criterion of 'contextuality' – that is, following Lindquist (1990: 31-35) the quality or condition of being relevant and able to be handled by an audience – also counts. The making of PISA ecology rests on the capacity to engage social actors in practices that uphold mutual surveillance as an appropriate way of knowing–governing. Such ability relates to three qualities we address here regarding the making and the diffusion of knowledge: the assemblage, plasticity and multiplication of knowledge for policy.

Knowledge used and generated by PISA surveys and reports is disciplined by the so-called literacy framework and by assumptions, concepts and methods from the psychometric world. But it also entails contributions generated by experts related to teaching and learning (specifically of science, reading and mathematics). In fact, the development of the surveys and the reports in each PISA domain – the core domains of mathematics, reading and science, but also problem-solving, ICT or financial literacy (included in the 2012 survey) – is diverse and depends on the degree of consensus between experts, their permeability to political and cultural factors or pressures, and their alignment with OECD discourse. Furthermore, other sources of knowledge and actors have influence, such as those who work on the relationships between the performances and the so-called contextual variables – streams of knowledge coming from policy evaluation and analysis, and from the school effectiveness tradition. Thus, knowledge produced and disseminated within the PISA programme rests on consensus, among OECD staff, research consortiums, experts, national representatives, about what counts as usable knowledge. This assemblage – in which the allocation and the relocation of epistemic and methodological authority occurs – is played out under the 'transgressive', 'collective' and 'self-organized and self-authorizing' dispositions and practices highlighted in studies of the contemporary making of expert knowledge (see Nowotny *et al.* 2001). From the point of view of those who steer PISA – these practices prove the advantages of the existence of the forum of supranational deliberation that accommodates experts and countries, independent of national parochialisms and interests.

What we label here as plasticity of knowledge is perceptible in PISA documents and relates strongly to the need for contextuality. Two examples quickly suggest themselves when one reads several PISA main reports: the editing work which creates a para-text that step by step summarizes and selectively highlights the information from the body of the report; or the attention given by the editors to the creation of a readable document, for instance by means of the relatively frequent introduction of texts that inform the reader how data may or may not be interpreted. Perhaps less evident, but more interesting are the metamorphoses of data/information/knowledge throughout the PISA main reports: there is a shift from moments of revelation (for instance of the core results of the survey – the performance of the students and the profiles of literacy competence) to moments of explanation (the interpretation of the results through relationships between variables, like socio-economic status or factors associated with national and/or school policies); and, finally, to spaces of condensation, where selected findings meet selected policy questions – school autonomy, accountability, privatization, involvement of stakeholders in the management and financing, school choice and school improvement – most of them related to the move towards new modes of governing the school system.

A multiplier effect is evident when one considers the variety of publications produced under the PISA label (Carvalho with Costa 2009: 67-69). In each PISA cycle there are several reports displaying results and analyses: the general report (prepared by the OECD secretariat, with the support of several experts); the thematic report (on selected topics, produced by external researchers) and the extensive reports (which result from partnerships between the OECD and other international agencies). Together with the national reports (elaborated by national teams) these documents express an amplification of PISA data through varied analysis. Other types of reports deal with the methodology implemented in PISA. These are oriented towards audiences with diverse interests and skills: the technical reports display specific information about tests, scales, samples and quality control mechanisms, while the databases and the reports on the databases supply information that enables secondary analyses to be carried out in line with the methodologies used for data collection and processing. Finally, some documents disseminate the basic assessments and are written for teachers, parents and pupils. There we may find examples of test tasks (and how they are graded); a (limited) number of questions used in the surveys (and their respective answers) and others used in the development and experimentation phases of the survey.

In sum, among these materials publicly disseminated it is possible to detect different kinds of documents. Importantly, this variety of publications (and other informational products) has explicit target populations and opens up a multiplicity of possible uses, whether in order to reproduce and/or re-contextualize the data/information or in order to produce (new) knowledge from it. In its capacity to attach to and to attract people (and their informational needs), the instrument is able to extend its reach. The 'plasticity' of the tool is a crucial quality in explaining why and how PISA is used differently by so many diverse actors – national researchers, media, policy players, bureaucrats and even by teachers (though they do not necessarily know that they are using it). The ecology of PISA rests on this feature too.

But what happens when these products circulate in diverse social and knowledge contexts?

From the Circulation and the Multiple Uses to the Attraction of PISA

For more than ten years supplementary visions have been added to PISA and new knowledge, policies and politics have been assembled within it. Comparative analyses of the effects of PISA on national policies, though scarce, have identified different kinds of responses to PISA. Steiner-Khamsi (2003), based on existing research, identifies contrasting responses in Germany and the UK regarding PISA 2000: 'scandalisation' and 'glorification'. Grek (2009) examines three different kinds of effects: 'surprise' (Finland), 'shock' (Germany) and 'promotion' (UK), further pointing out different paths and uses of the PISA data by English and Scottish political actors. Bieber and Martens (2011) conclude their comparison of the impact of PISA, as a marker of OECD soft governance, on national policies in Switzerland and the USA – respectively, a 'well scoring' and a 'underperforming' country – and point out the contrasting reception of the instrument: 'from comprehensively reforming the education system' to 'no echo'. Analysing the impact in two countries with similar results – Germany and the Czech Republic – Greger (2012) contrasts the numerous policy measures being adopted in the former with the absence of reaction from policy-makers in the latter. Pons (2012), analysing the effects of PISA in six European countries (Portugal, Romania, France, francophone Belgium, Scotland and Hungary) moves away from the idea of a PISA shock in order to emphasize the diverse ways in which their results are analysed, translated and reinvested, and points out that the main effects of PISA may well be to confirm national predetermined opinions on various topics.

In fact the studies conducted on the circulation and use of PISA in those European spaces show conspicuous diversity in the use of PISA in national/regional contexts (see Carvalho *et al.* 2009): for example, its mobilization for the making of analysis and argumentation, based upon data/knowledge about specific educational policy issues; its use as a resource for the development of studies on national educational realities and its use for purposes of making or improving domestic knowledge-based and knowledge-oriented instruments, particularly in environments where accountability and/or quality assurance issues are already central. With respect to the representations and rules that the instrument carries, it is also clear that these may be filtered, corrected, modified, sometimes even strongly contested when moving through different socio-cultural contexts. In fact policies that invoke the knowledge generated by PISA vary from country to country and even within each country (over time). They may differ regarding the solutions advocated and the goals to be achieved, their targets (students, teachers, families) or even their declared values. There is, once more, a selective mobilization of knowledge, so that recurring public policy issues remain, return or gain greater visibility as education problems in political agendas.

Such selection is not independent of the knowledge and/or political orientation of the contenders. Clearly, the differences stated above are not separable from factors related to political and cultural factors, for example, knowledge traditions within the field of assessment and the degree of their philosophical, theoretical or methodological proximity–distance regarding the PISA international comparative assessment framework; the strength of the previous national involvement in international studies/ organizations; the agenda of on-going reforms (PISA is seemingly more present in public debates when issues of accountability, monitoring, or changing conceptions of curriculum, are at stake) and the agency of policy-brokers or entrepreneurs.[5] Therefore, PISA objects/texts are reinterpreted, made acceptable and efficient for specific socio-cognitive contexts, and each context may exhibit different abilities and knowledge resources and circumstances in which to do so.

However – and alongside such a multiplicity of uses – a few commonalities in the reception of PISA are also manifest. We emphasize three common trends in public action scenes. First, there is a kind of a resizing of the knowledge deliverable in PISA reports – quantitative data related to the results by country, in the form of league tables, tends to be overstated. Second, the debate takes one of two epicentres – it is either directed towards the issue of equity in education systems (with an emphasis on the effects of socio-economic variables on the variability of student results or on inter-mediate factors like school curricula, school social composition, school resources, and an appeal for State policies against inequality in education) or dominated by the issue of the efficiency and efficacy of the system (namely focusing on the relationship between public spending on education and student performance, and frequently advocating the redefinition of the State's role in school provision and administration). Thus, the debates tend to provide continuity to established debates but and this is significant – they are now based on other indicators generated by another knowledge provider that is taken as truthful. Finally – and this is the third trend – despite the existence of critical voices, PISA is usually perceived by political actors as capable of raising public awareness about education systems, as capable of helping to identify problems and provide good examples, and as accurately portraying the performance of education systems, their weaknesses and strengths.

Towards a Conclusion

To sum up, it seems reasonable to state that PISA is currently perceived in the public space as almost an obvious provider of information based on evidence and also that it may be used to support the debating of established problems and/or the imagination of new futures for education in contemporary societies. At the same time, one needs to recognize that if the products generated by PISA provide a framework of possibilities for policies, one cannot say that there is an automatic or an inevitable convergence of policies as an effect of PISA. Thus, the perception of the existence of conspicuous differences in the mobilization of PISA by diverse knowledge communities in different political contexts (be they national, regional, local or transnational) coexists with the recognition of their attractiveness.

This is not necessarily a contradiction if we think that the success of PISA does not depend on effectively generating convergence in terms of policy options or solutions, but rather in creating a functional and/or a symbolic dependence in the various social worlds that it reaches. On the one hand, the instrument is an organizational and discursive platform for making durable connections with and between the worlds of politics and knowledge, by taking into account the differences between these and by creating products able to feed their different interests and dispositions regarding the use of PISA. From this point of view, the success of PISA resides in the ability to maintain its attraction for diverse social worlds and their attachment to the activities of inquiry, exchange and publication under the PISA label. That is its strength and form of power: to operate from the participation (from the uncondi-tional to the critical) of various social worlds in production, dissemination, use and consumption. On the other hand, the acceptance of PISA as an obvious resource for policy, even if only rhetorical or in order to justify already adopted courses of action, even if triennially (following each PISA cycle), is also a signal of the strength achieved by a set of rules for the governing of education: the primacy of an evidence-based model for the coordination and control of activities in the education sector, contrasting and disqualifying forms of coordination based on opinions and/or philosophies; the free acquiescence of politicians to mutual surveillance as a proper and efficient practice for the administration of the social and the endorsement of systematic comparative assessment of 'literacy competences and domains of competence' as a useful and reliable tool for the steering educational systems. This is another aspect of the strength of the instrument: that controversies, disputes over data or analyses of solutions to the problems of education, and/or the scrutiny of educational policies and practices are engaged in with some kind of commitment to the tool.

The attraction of national policy actors around this device of mutual surveillance of competences may well be understood as an indicator of the strengthening of their dependence regarding the expert organization that provides it. However, such a relation should not be seen only as one of dependence in relation to a trusted resource for the administration of each national educational realm. This dependence operates also at the cognitive level. For instance, one might talk of a PISA effect in the revision of reference societies in national education debates: there is a move towards the observation of those countries associated with the best results or with the making of progress between PISA surveys, but also – and this is perhaps more important – towards those countries that are imagined to be equivalents because they share certain educational problems that are depicted by PISA categories and analysis.

To conclude, the effect of the attraction occurs in a wider cognitive level: when the surveillance of performances is made through the measurement of the outcomes of every school system, each one of these is connected to the so-called demands of an imagined global environment (the 'knowledge society' and the worldwide competitive 'knowledge economy') and each one is assessed through categories other than those nationally generated. Thus, the attractiveness of PISA may well be related, as others as have pointed out (Mangez and Hilgers 2012: 199) to the changing relations of power between transnational and national policy fields and to the decrease of the latter's abilities to delineate their own understanding of education and to drive their choices regarding the 'legitimate means of making sense' of their own activity.

Acknowledgements

This chapter has been published thanks to the support of the European Union's Sixth Framework Programme for Research and Technological Development on the theme of socio-economic sciences and the humanities – the KNOWandPOL (Knowledge and Policy in Education and Health Sectors) project, Contract Number 028848-2. The information and views set out in this chapter are those of the author only and do not necessarily reflect the official opinion of the European Union. The analysis made in this text draws on information from two reports on the fabrication, circulation and use of OECD's PISA (Carvalho with Costa 2009, Carvalho *et al.* 2009) produced in the context of the aforementioned project. I would like to thank Estela Costa and Natércio Afonso for their significant collaboration in the making of those studies and reports. I want also to thank João Barroso for his valuable comments on a previous version of this text. Of course, any problems that remain unresolved in the text are entirely my responsibility.

Notes

1   Following Everett Hughes' notion of 'ecology of institutions', as quoted by Star and Griesemer (1989 [1999]: 506), by ecology we mean the existing contextual factors of PISA but also OECD/PISA's choices about its sources (materials, information and human) as well as the agency skills to establishing continued and lasting exchanges with selected actors.
2   For an extended discussion, see Carvalho (2011).
3   On the strong normative function of PISA regarding the identity of youngsters in contemporary societies, see Popkewitz (2011). On the OECD cognitive and normative orientations regarding lifelong learners, see Rizvi and Lingard (2006)
4   See www.oecd.org/pisa/pisafaq/. Accessed 13 November 2012.
5   On the diversity of PISA reception in those six countries, see the thematic issue of *Sísifo – Educational Sciences Journal*, 10 (2009), 'PISA and educational public policies: studies in six European countries'. Online, available at: http://sisifo.fpce.ul.pt/?r=26

References

Bieber, T. and Martens, K. (2011) 'The OECD PISA study as a soft power in education? Lessons from Switzerland and the US', *European Journal of Education*, 46(1): 101–116.
Bottani, N. (2006) 'La más bella del reino: el mundo de la educación en alerta con la llegada de un príncipe encantador' [The most beautiful girl in the kingdom: the excitement in the education field with the arrival of a very charming prince], *Revista de Educación*, extraordinario: 75–90.
Broadfoot, P. (2000) 'Comparative education for the 21st Century: retrospect and prospect', *Comparative Education*, 36(3): 357–371.
Callon, M. (1986) 'Some elements of sociology of translation', in J. Law (ed.) *Power, Action, and Belief*, London: Routledge and Kegan Paul.
Carvalho, L.M. (2011) 'Look at the mirror! On the cognitive and normative features of a knowledge-policy tool', in J. Kush (ed.) *Knowledge, Differences, and Harmonies in the Time of Globalization*, Cambridge: Cambridge Scholars Publishing.
Carvalho, L.M. (2012) 'The fabrications and travels of a knowledge-policy instrument', *European Educational Research Journal*, 11(2): 172–188.
Carvalho, L.M. with Costa, E. (2009) *Production of OECD's PISA: Final Report*, Project KNOWandPOL, WP 11. Online. Available at: www.knowandpol.eu/
Carvalho, L.M., Costa, E. and Afonso, N. (2009) *PISA – Fabrication, Circulation and Use in 6 European Countries: Integrative report*, Project KNOWandPOL, WP 17. Online. Available at: www.knowandpol.eu/
Desjardins, R. and Rubenson, K. (2009). 'The tension between research of policy and research for policy in an era of transnational education policy-making: an introduction', in R. Desjardins and K. Rubenson (eds) *Research of versus Research for Education Policy*, Saarbrücken: Verlag Dr. Müller.
Dobbins, M. and Martens, K. (2012) 'Towards an education approach à la *finlandaise*? French education policy after PISA', *Journal of Education Policy*, 27(1): 23–43.
Ertl, H. (2006) 'Educational standards and the changing discourse on education: the reception and consequences of the PISA study in Germany', *Oxford Review of Education*, 32(5): 619-634.
Greger, D. (2012) 'When PISA does not matter? The case of the Czech Republic and Germany', *Human Affairs*, 22(1): 31–42.
Grek, S. (2009) 'Governing by numbers: the PISA effect', *Journal of Education Policy*, 24(1): 23–37.
Gür, B.S., Çelik, Z. and Özoğlu, M. (2012) 'Policy options for Turkey: a critique of the interpretation and utilization of PISA results in Turkey', *Journal of Education Policy*, 27(1): 1–21.
Henry, M., Lingard, B., Rizvi, F. and Taylor, S. (2001) *The OECD, Globalisation and Education Policy*, Oxford: Pergamon Press.

Hopmann, S. (2007) 'Epilogue: No child, no school, no state left behind', in S.T. Hopmann, G. Brinek and M. Retzl (eds), *PISA According to PISA: Does PISA Keep What It Promises?* Wien/Berlin: Lit Verlag.

Hugonnier, B. (2008) 'Les acquis des adolescents' [The learning achievement of adolescents], *Futuribles,* 344: 47–61.

Lascoumes, P. and Le Galès, P. (2007) 'Introduction: understanding public policy through its instruments – from the nature of instruments to the sociology of public policy instrumentation', *Governance,* 20(1): 1–21.

Latour, B. (1989) 'Joliot : l'histoire et la physique mêlées' [Joliot: history and physics merged], in M. Sèrres (dir.) *Eléments d'Histoire des Sciences,* Paris: Bordas.

Lindquist, E.A. (1990) 'The third community, policy inquiry, and social scientists', in S. Brooks and A.-G. Gagnon (eds) *Social Scientists, Policy, and the State,* New York: Praeger.

Lundgren, U.P. (2011) 'PISA as a political instrument: one history behind the formulation of the PISA programme', in M. Pereyra, H.-G. Kotthoff and R. Cowen (eds) *PISA Under Examination: Changing Knowledge, Changing Texts, and Changing Schools,* Rotterdam: Sense Publishers.

Mahon, R. and McBride, S. (2008) 'Introduction', in R. Mahon and S. McBride (eds) *The OECD and Transnational Governance,* Vancouver: UBC Press.

Mangez, E. (2008) 'Knowledge economy, knowledge policy and knowledge regimes' in B. Delvaux and E. Mangez, *Towards a Sociology of the Knowledge-Policy Relation,* KNOWandPOL Literature Review – Integrative Report. Online. Available at: www.knowandpol.eu/

Mangez, E. and Hilgers, M. (2012) 'The field of knowledge and the policy field in education: PISA and the production of knowledge for policy', *European Educational Research Journal,* 11(2): 189–205.

Marcussen, M. (2004) 'The Organization for Economic Cooperation and Development as ideational artist and arbitrator', in B. Reinalda and B. Verbeek (eds) *Decision Making Within International Organisations,* London: Routledge.

Martens, K. (2007) 'How to become an influential actor: the comparative turn in OECD education policy', in K. Martens, A. Rusconi and K. Leuze (eds) *New Arenas of Education Governance,* New York: Palgrave Macmillan.

Martens, K. and Jakobi, A. (2010) 'Introduction: The OECD as an actor in international politics', in K. Martens and A. Jakobi (eds) *Mechanisms of OECD Governance: International Incentives for National Policy-Making?,* Oxford: Oxford University Press.

Morgan, C. (2007) 'The OECD Programme for International Student Assessment: Unraveling a knowledge network', unpublished thesis, Carleton University.

Mons, N. (2007) 'L'évaluation des politiques éducatives: apports, limites et nécessaire renouvellement des enquêtes internationales sur les acquis des élèves' [The evaluation of educational policies: contributions, limitations and needed renewal of international surveys of student achievement], *Revue Internationale de Politique Comparée,* 14(3): 409–423.

Nassehi, A. (2008) 'Making knowledge observable. Short considerations about the practice of "doing knowledge"', KNOWandPOL unpublished working paper, Munich: Institut für Soziologie.

Noaksson, N. and Jacobsson, K. (2003) *The Production of Ideas and Expert Knowledge in OECD,* Stockholm: SCORE (Score Rapportserie).

Nóvoa, A. (1998) *Histoire & Comparaison (Essays sur l'Éducation)* [History and Comparison (Essays on Education)], Lisboa: Educa.

Nóvoa, A. and Yariv-Mashal, T. (2003) 'Comparative research in education: a mode of governance or a historical journey', *Comparative Education,* 39(4): 423–438.

Nowotny, H., Scott, P. and Gibbons, R. (2001) *Re-Thinking Science,* Cambridge: Polity Press.

OECD (2007) *PISA – The OECD Programme for International Student Assessment.* Online. Available at: www.pisa.oecd.org/dataoecd/51/27/37474503.pdf

OECD (2011) *Education at a Glance 2011: OECD Indicators*. OECD Publishing. Online. Available at: http://dx.doi.org/10.1787/eag-2011-en

Ozga, J. (2008) 'Governing knowledge: research steering and research quality', *European Educational Research Journal*, 7(3): 261–272.

Ozga, J. (2012) 'Assessing PISA', *European Educational Research Journal*, 11(2): 166–171.

Pons, X. (2012) 'Going beyond the "PISA shock" discourse: an analysis of the cognitive reception of PISA in six European countries, 2001-2008', *European Educational Research Journal*, 11(2): 206–226.

Pons, X. and van Zanten, A. (2007) 'Knowledge circulation, regulation and governance', in B. Delvaux and E. Mangez (coords), *KNOWandPOl Literature Review*. Online. Available at: www.knowandpol.eu/IMG/pdf/lr.tr.pons_vanzanten.eng.pdf

Popkewitz, T.S. (2011) 'PISA: numbers, standardizing conducts, and the alchemy of school subjects', in M. Pereyra, H.-G. Kotthoff and R. Cowen (eds), *PISA Under Examination: Changing Knowledge, Changing Texts, and Changing Schools*, Rotterdam: Sense Publishers.

Rautalin, M. and Alasuutari, P. (2009) 'The uses of the national PISA results by Finnish officials in central government', *Journal of Education Policy*, 24(5): 539–556.

Rinne, R., Kallo, J. and Hokka, S. (2004) 'Too eager to comply? OECD education policies and the Finnish response', *European Educational Research Journal*, 3(2): 454–486.

Rizvi, F. (2004) 'Theorizing the global convergence of educational restructuring', in S. Lindblad and T.S. Popkewitz (eds), *Educational Restructuring*, Charlotte, NC: Information Age Publishing.

Rizvi, F. and Lingard, B. (2006) 'Globalisation and the changing nature of the OECD's educational work', in H. Lauder, P. Brown, J.-A. Dillabough and A. Halsey (eds), *Education, Globalisation and Social Change*, Oxford: Oxford University Press.

Rubenson, K. (2008) 'OECD education policy and world hegemony', in R. Mahon and S. McBride (eds), *The OECD and Transnational Governance*, Vancouver: UBC Press.

Schleicher, A. (2007) 'Can competencies assessed by PISA be considered the fundamental school knowledge 15-year-olds should possess?', *Journal of Educational Change*, 8(4): 349–357.

Star, S.L. and Griesemer, J.R. (1989) 'Institutional ecology, translation and boundary objects: amateurs and professionals in Berkeley's Museum of Vertebrate Zoology, 1907-39', *Social Studies of Sciences*, 19: 387–420; reprinted in M. Biagioli (ed.) (1999) *The Science Studies Reader*, New York: Routledge.

Steiner-Khamsi, G. (2003) 'The politics of league tables', *Journal of Social Science Education*, 1. Available at: www.sowi-onlinejournal.de/2003-1/tables_khamsi.htm

Steiner-Khamsi, G. (2004) *The Global Politics of Educational Borrowing and Lending*, New York: Teachers College Press.

Steiner-Khamsi, G. (2012) 'Understanding policy borrowing and lending: building comparative policy studies', in G. Steiner-Khamsi and F. Waldow (eds), *World Yearbook of Education 2012: Policy Borrowing and Lending in Education*, London: Routledge.

Takayama, K. (2008) 'The politics of international league tables: PISA in Japan's achievement crisis debate', *Comparative Education*, 44(4): 387–407.

Turner, R. (2007) 'PISA – The Programme for International Student Assessment: an overview', *Journal of Applied Measurement*, 8(3): 237–248.

van Zanten, A. (2011) 'Knowledge-oriented instruments and the regulation of educational systems: a comparison of six European countries', in H. Ramsdal and A. van Zanten, *Knowledge Based Regulation Tools in Education and Health*, KNOWandPOL Orientation 3 – National instruments: Integrative report. Online. Available at: www.knowandpol.eu

Weinberg, M. (2008) 'Entrevista: Andreas Schleicher – Medir para avançar rápido', *Veja*, Agosto 17: 20–21. Online. Available at: http://veja.abril.com.br/060808/

Part II
Knowledge Technologies in Action

5   Data Work

Michael Barber in Conversation with Jenny Ozga

This chapter takes the form of a conversation between Sir Michael Barber and Professor Jenny Ozga that took place in the spring of 2013. Michael Barber's heavy commitments meant that it was impossible for him to produce a chapter for this World Yearbook, but the editors were anxious to get a perspective on the use of data from someone who was instrumental in its development in government in the UK, and who has continued to promote and develop the global potential of data – and the interrogation of data – to support education improvement. Sir Michael Barber has worked for over 20 years in education and government reform and improvement. Following a degree in history from Oxford University he trained as a teacher and taught in schools in England and Zimbabwe, before joining the education department of the National Union of Teachers. As a member of the Labour Party, he was elected to the council of the London Borough of Hackney, becoming chair of the education committee. He became Chief Adviser in School Standards to the Secretary of State for Education during Tony Blair's first term as British Prime Minister and Chief Advisor on Delivery to Tony Blair during Blair's second term, from 2001 to 2005. As head of the Prime Minister's Delivery Unit (PMDU), he was responsible for working with government agencies to ensure successful implementation of the Prime Minister's priority programmes, including those in health, education, transport, policing, the criminal justice system, and asylum/immigration. Michael Barber then became a partner and head of McKinsey's Global Education Practice. He is currently Chief Education Advisor to Pearson, responsible for leading the company's worldwide research and partnership on education policy and learning methods, advising on and supporting the innovation and development of new products and services, and leading Pearson's strategy for education in the poorest sectors of the world, particularly in fast-growing developing economies. In November 2012, Michael Barber launched The Learning Curve, the first open and searchable global education data bank (http://thelearningcurve.pearson.com) – drawing on what are described as the world's best existing datasets including the PISA, TIMSS and PIRLS studies.

In the discussion that follows, Michael Barber reflects on the development and work of the Delivery Unit in the UK Government Cabinet Office; on the importance of analytical capacity in interrogating and synthesising data; on the need for the integrity of data to be respected, and on the roles of public and private institutions in taking up the opportunities that the availability and accessibility of data present.

JO: Would you like to start with a reflection on your own work in terms of how the knowledge base has changed in terms of evidence-informed policy-making in recent years?

MB: The way I like to think about my work – obviously you have to factor in bias – is that, in the four years when I was in the department, 1997 to 2001, and then especially 2001 to 2005 when I was in the Delivery Unit and we were looking at 20 big domestic policy priorities in four or five areas, we did more for evidence-informed policy-making than anybody else has done, in Britain anyway. Because we put getting good data at the heart of decision-making in a very, very disciplined way. At a trivial level, I'm sure I've shown more graphs in the Cabinet room than anybody else in history. But at a profound level, what we did by building those routines around delivery on health and education, crime and transport is, that when Blair debated the progress with health policy with Alan Milburn[1] or later John Reid,[2] they did it with the evidence in front of them on a PowerPoint screen. And they were briefed in advance. And I had to make sure obviously that the Department of Health agreed with our interpretation of the data and there was no argument about whether the data was broadly reliable, or if there were questions about the data everybody shared the same questions. So the data was common.

   And then there was a discussion about what to do. Were we on track? Were we not on track? If we weren't on track, what we were going to do about it? To me, that was pretty radical because until then, Prime Ministers and Cabinet Ministers have been meeting obviously for centuries, but they very rarely actually looked at the hard data in close to real time when they were making those decisions. I looked for precedents earlier on. There's some evidence that Macmillan did that with house building in the fifties, and definitely some evidence that Churchill did it with the production of fighter aircraft in 1940 and '41. But there's not a lot of it. And so it was actually very, very important. I think that a lot of my personal work in government was about bringing data to the point of decision. And good data. Data is rarely perfect. But good data, close to real time, well based. And always, wherever possible, using alternative datasets to confirm what we were seeing in our own dataset so we didn't over-depend on one dataset.

JO: Did that work depend on technical advances in the capacity of data? And what about the capacity, the analytical capacity of people to translate data?

MB: Obviously the recent developments in technology and in Big Data enable the collection of massive datasets that make things possible. A lot of what we did in 2001 to 2005 was actually very, very basic. Just to give one example, just making sure that there was a standardised way of collecting crime data in 43 police forces that was then reported monthly. That wasn't a technological advance, it was just a data collection standardisation process. And computers were helpful but they weren't vital to that at the time. But you could see the development coming. So in dealing with road congestion, we kept asking them [the Department of Transport] questions about why they use this completely inadequate process. And we said why don't you use the Global Positioning System. And eventually they got

minute-by-minute data on every motorway. And you could see the benefits of that if you drive around the motorways now. It says Junction 16, 12
minutes or whatever. So all of those were driven by minute-to-minute
collection of data. And it changed the way they thought about policy.
Instead of reacting afterwards, they could use the data to drive decisions.
So that was using modern technology. And then obviously, that's ten years
ago. And since then there's been a big take-off. So yes, the use of new technology made it much more possible.

And then your second point about analytical capacity is really fundamental. Government departments back then, often, they did have
analytical capacity but it was totally unconnected to the policy capacity.
And you still see that problem in many parts of the world. But the Delivery
Unit, the existence of a Delivery Unit required departments to connect
policy and analysis. I had a team of four or five completely wonderful bean
counters. They got called bean counters, and we celebrated that name. They
were fantastic data analysts. They would get data – we didn't collect our
own data. We got the data from the departments. And then we'd go back to
departments and say 'have you thought about this?' And they'd say how do
you know that, and we say we got it from your data, we just asked more
questions of it. So we were very persistent in getting people to ask questions.

I think there are three things that really matter. One is the data collection
which we've talked about. The second is the analytical capacity. And the third
and not to be neglected is the presentation of the data in ways that make it
easy for people to use. We had a lot of profound ethical debate in the Delivery
Unit about how you could make data simple enough for a Prime Minister
and a minister to use quickly without undermining the integrity of the data.
So all three bits, the collection, the analysis and the presentation, are equally
important in getting evidence-based policy to work.

JO: Do you have any reflections on the process of translation, if you like,
        of the data ... it sounds as though it's almost a set of stages: first of all
        mapping the landscape, establishing sound, reliable knowledge about
        the state of things in different public sector services. Then there's the
        extraction of advice on the basis of patterns in the data. Can you give
        examples, particularly from education, of how the interaction developed
        between a policy problem that a policy-maker has and the beginnings
        of patterning and then production of direction from the data?

MB: It's a good question. You could spend hours on it. I don't want to sound
        trivial but I'll just, for the purposes of brevity, talk about how we thought of
        it. Because we had some targets or goals that were public, we started from
        the targets. So we worked back from a target. So if you're talking about the
        patterns, we're looking for things that indicate we're on track or not to meet
        the target. The delivery unit, if you strip it down to the core process, all we
        ever did was say, what are you trying to do, i.e. what is your goal? How are
        you trying to do it, what's your plan? How do you know if you're on track?
        What's the data telling us? If you're not on track, what are you going to do
        about it? That's basically all we did. And so, at that simple level, when we
        got data from the Department of Health, what we want to know is are you

on track or not. And if you're not on track, how can we understand the problem better? So we didn't go into it with a kind of open research point of view where we say what are the many questions we could ask about this data. That's a perfectly valid thing to do but it wasn't our job. So we're going in with a particular perspective. Are you on track to meet the waiting times target or not? And we might then explore data, so we might say, It looks broadly as if you are on track, but what if we ask it by type of operation. And then you go through it and you find you're on track for every type of operation except orthopaedics. So what is the problem in orthopaedics? And then, we'd say, well, of the 200 hospitals, 180 are on track and 20 aren't. Why are 20 off track? So we explore the data from that perspective, going down the levels of analysis. And that's broadly how we did that. Because we were very focused on delivering the outcomes. So we had a set of government commitments that we were trying to deliver, we're in that sense totally focused. So there was lots of questions you could ask on the way that we were ignoring. They would be perfectly valid research questions but weren't our questions.

We don't just take the data at face value. We unlock the layers of it, until you get to an answer. When you get to the third question, if you're not on track, what are you going to do about it, you have to explore down to a deeper level to get the answers.

JO: Were you the person who pushed, who steered, who focused the direction of the analytical work that your bean counters were doing?

MB: The way I had the Delivery Unit organised in the last two-and-a-half years I was there, there was a health team and education team, a mainly crime and Home Office team and then a team for transport and other things. And those teams were in constant dialogue with the relevant departments. It became a very collaborative relationship. ...We turned the word 'bean counter' into a compliment because we just thought, we get dismissed as bean counters, we're doing this really important, vital stuff. And I had this debate with Richard (Olivier's son[3]) who runs Mythodrama, the people who do Shakespeare plays as management training. And he was saying to me, you know, Henry V didn't inspire people through bean counters, he did it through wonderful speeches. And I was saying yeah, but do you think when they left to go to Agincourt, they didn't check the numbers of bows and arrows and the amount of food and the march and the logistics. It was all sorted out. He could make the inspirational speeches because he had bean counters!

So that's what we were doing for Blair, effectively. Anyway, the point is, very often my teams in their dialogue with the relevant department came up with questions to which they needed answers. And then the analysts would find the answers for them or tried to. And my job, it was partly to keep asking questions, partly to set the ambition. So if we had a target, my job was to say we're going to meet the target. Maybe the department says this is too difficult or it's too complicated. They've signed up for it, we're going to do it. So don't ask the question, we can't do this, how should we retreat from it, ask the question what do we need to do to achieve the target. So it's keeping the level of ambition. Because it would have been very easy to get on to, oh, this is too difficult, let's moderate the target.

JO: And what kind of people were your bean counters? Where did they come from?

MB: They were government trained statisticians or operational researchers. They understood that they had a huge responsibility to take masses of data and present it to the Prime Minister in a way that was compelling and had integrity. And I said to them, you're the conscience of the Delivery Unit, so if you think that I'm traducing the data or misinterpreting it because I want to say something to the Prime Minister, you have to stop me. They were really good at that. So if we were going to present to the Prime Minister and the Minister of Health on health waiting times, I'd say I think the story is this, and they'd say I don't think you can say that. And then we'd debate it. It was a profoundly ethical role that they played as well. They thought about the data, the analysis, but they also thought about the presentation. And they had a big role on the integrity of the data, which was very important for our reputation, obviously. I think they invented a new role. They were very, very excited about it at the time.

I'm not deeply statistically trained but I got very good at looking at sets of data and trying to make sense of it. And we had a great, an endless debate. And actually, it's just as much fun debating why the trains are late as it is why children didn't learn. I think children not learning is more important but the fun of the debate about the data is just as much fun either way.

JO: I'm interested in your phrase about the profoundly ethical nature of the work that these people were doing. Does that ethical base come from the fact that it's government? Is it different in a commercial organisation?

MB: Obviously the circumstances are different. I see the ethical underpinning as being vital in both. But if I just refer to it in the government, we saw ourselves as having a responsibility to the British citizen. It sounds grand, but true. And the British taxpayer. Obviously there's a big overlap between those two things. For the British citizens, we were saying, we have an opportunity, if we can get this right, to have a big impact on the outcomes for British citizens. And from the taxpayer perspective of getting much better value for their money we can show them that the investment was worth making. And we didn't think, and we debated this a lot, we didn't think our job was to get Blair re-elected. What I said to the team is, Blair has got lots of people who can help him get re-elected, he's good at it himself. Our job is to make sure that the government delivers outcomes for the citizen and shows that paying taxes is worthwhile because you get significant benefits from it. And if you think of it, we were like 40 people, but we were influencing a lot of money. So, the ratio between the how much the government spent on us and the public expenditure we were influencing was 1 to 50,000. So a small percentage improvement in our performance had this big multiplier effect. We took our responsibility very seriously. And the data was absolutely vital to it. So, if we presented data that might please the Prime Minister but it was misleading, actually we were just completely undermining our own ethical base. So, it was important.

In the end, I think it's to do with the world we're in. There have been enough examples in the last decade of commercial organisations that have abused trust, misused data, withheld crucial things. And if you look at major institutions, whether it's the Catholic Church or government in general or parliament or the media, or business or banks in particular in business, all of those big institutions have been severely questioned in the last decade. So, if you're here and you're largely an education company, to me the only prospect for the future is to earn trust. And that means you have to demonstrate your impact on learners. Obviously you have to generate revenue and profit, but you have to demonstrate your impact. So we will have to show over time, Pearson will have to show over time that the products and services which it provides actually lead to learner outcomes. That's the way I think about it. And we'll see where that goes. Otherwise, I mean, there's no, to me there's no value in a commercial organisation that generates commercial return but doesn't actually change the world for the better.

JO: Do you see a shift from the time when you were working in the Delivery Unit and this was a way in which policy-making was altering, towards a new set of actors actually working in this space, in this field? Since 2005 when that kind of operation in government was established, do you see the commercial companies as almost catching up?

MB: I think there are two big changes. One is the quantities of real-time Big Data, which make new forms of analysis possible. That's accelerated dramatically since I left. I don't think I had even a glimmer of understanding what would be possible in 2005 that's possible now in 2013. And then the second thing is, there's a whole global megatrend towards transparency, which is everything from MPs' expenses to putting data out there. Last week, GlaxoSmithKline announced they were going to publish all the results of all the trials they've ever done. I mean, that's an amazing thing to do. I think we're all affected by those two things, whether you're a government or a commercial organisation. And governments are increasingly saying, not just here, that they can't do their data analysis themselves. They just kind of put the data out there and let other people do it for them. I think, what had started back in my time in government, was a health organisation called Dr Foster.[4] Do you remember that?

JO: Yes.

MB: I don't know if they're still going, but they were the beginning of that trend. Or they were the first I saw of that trend. And we quite liked them when we were in government, because they were sometimes very critical of us but they took the data and asked some pretty tough questions of the hospitals about it. I think those two things affect commercial and government organisations, I suppose that's what I'm saying. And I think, if I was commenting on academia, I think too much of academia hasn't caught up with that, so that its processes, some of which may be essential to the profession of being an academic, and I don't knock that at all, but some of them, the outcomes of the research are too slow to shape the debate.

JO: In this shift into the distribution of data, where does that leave professional expertise? Going back to government again, isn't there an argument that it's the responsibility of government to, if you like, organise the evidence rather than simply distribute it? How are people supposed to make sense of the enormous flows of information that are rocketing around? I'm interested particularly in the argument that knowledge gets distributed, and there's a democratising process in the distribution. But there's also surely a problem in terms of the translation, the understanding and the direction of this information. I'm just interested in how you see the interplay between these forces.

MB: That is a very difficult question because you could even, somewhat facetiously describe this as the postmodern condition, we're drowning in seas of data but making sense of it is really difficult. I don't think it's fair to think that that's a government responsibility alone to sort all that out. But it is the problem of our era. I think a lot of the way academia has developed (I'm not talking particularly about education here) over the last 30 or 40 years, is to get more and more specialised and deeper and deeper into smaller and smaller strands of knowledge simply because of the explosion of knowledge. I don't actually knock that. I think there's not just a value in it, it's probably necessary. But over and above that, then the synthesisers shall inherit the earth because they're the people that can connect these two things together. In a small way, the Delivery Unit, we were the connectors in government because we saw patterns in health data that helped us inform education policy or vice versa. So we were connecting across datasets, often at a quite practical level.

You do need people who are the synthesisers. And what those people look like is not entirely clear. But you see someone, I still follow developments in history for example, and you see some people who rise above the narrow confines of particular areas of history. There'll be somebody who can connect five or six great leaders and say they did this. Or five or six things about navies in the eighteenth century, and they did this.

JO: I see your argument. In a way though, you're relying on the data themselves to produce a synthesised knowledge with a bit of help from particular individuals who extract particular patterns and directions.

MB: Maybe. But I mean, the data is pretty raw stuff, isn't it. And it's open, there's normally more than one possible interpretation of data. So you bring your own perspective. There is, I mean, if you look at the commentary in *FT* and places like that, you'll see that seriously good data analysts are now becoming scarce resources and hard to find. So it's not, I don't think you're just relying on the data and then somebody tries to synthesise it. You need to create an intermediate set of skills about data analysis that can find the big patterns.

JO: I guess what I'm chipping away at is, who are these people with these intermediate sets of skills? If they're not politicians who have a public identification with particular directions from which choices can be made, then is this a sort of technocracy that's developing? If we look at OECD, for example, and the immense influence they have through their synthesising of data, and then their extraction of messages and their promotion of particular directions – are these the people who are going to steer education policy in the future? And is that a problem for democracy?

MB: Well ... there's something in the way you ask the question that just needs to be questioned itself, which is, it implies that if we look hard enough we'll find these people, that they're somewhere and we just haven't found them. But actually, anybody can, you know, it's not unanswerable, it's not like there's some mystery group of people that are doing this and if only we could find them, oh yeah, they're there, the OECD. I think anybody can do it. You can do it in the Oxford Department of Education or you can do it in Pearson or you can do it in the OECD. It's up to people to take those decisions. But the OECD has become very influential because it's now got a time series and it's got a reasonably reliable dataset, and around the world leaders of education systems understand that they need to improve their education system significantly for their citizens to succeed in the twenty-first century. And so the evidence-based insight is really helpful to them. And the OECD has been a leading provider of that. And as you know, in the McKinsey reports, we took their data and the TIMSS data and tried to a make a synthesis out of it. But that, anybody can do that. Anybody who wants to do that can do that.

JO: Anybody with the capacity, anybody with the resources.

MB: Yeah, but ... sure, anybody with the capacity to do it. Any university department that chose to could do that if it wanted to.

JO.   I'm interested in the way the knowledge changes. It's become comparative, essentially, hasn't it? I mean, we don't now look at data about performance without comparing with somewhere else.

MB: Right. It's certainly true that the targets that we, on the whole, we set in the early part of the last decade were within national confines. And you're right. We didn't do much benchmarking. Although we in the Delivery Unit started asking international benchmarking questions as one of the ways of solving problems. So you'd say, I remember vividly a conversation with the Department for Transport. We'd say, why couldn't you get to 90 per cent of the trains arriving on time. And they said nobody does better than 90 per cent. And I'd say, not even in France or in Japan. They say, yeah, apart from France and Japan. Then Switzerland and then we kind of go through a long list, and they start coming up with their excuses. International benchmarking was happening then but the targets were set internally. I think basically what's happening is globalisation. And it's affecting this like everything else. And I think it's an almost inevitable trend where, certainly once you've got benchmarking data being published, people are going to say, well, how do I do as well as Singapore or Finland or whatever it might be. And you need to get beneath those kind of shallow questions. It's a choice for a country to say, that's the only thing we care about, how well we do relatively. It's perfectly reasonable for a country to say, we wonder how well we do relatively but intrinsically these are the things we care about in Britain or in Scotland or in England or in Norway or wherever it might be. But you know, some of the people nowadays who I read, being critical of international benchmarking are the same people who have been advocating evidence-informed or evidence-based policy for years. And you can't really have it both ways. If you want evidence-informed policy, you've got to look at the benchmarking evidence. It doesn't mean you have to be driven by it. But you have to take it into account.

Just to reinforce one part of what you're saying – I mean, I don't spend as much time as I did looking at data on England and the performance of students in the school system. But recently, Geoff Whitty showed me some data which I hadn't seen at all, showing that Bangladeshi students have now overtaken the average in England, which is remarkable. You've got the average performance, using purely English data, which is my point, and then you see the Bangladeshi students overtaking the average. And the Pakistani students, coming from an even lower base, getting close to the average. And you think, I've missed that because I'm looking at the international benchmarking data. But the intrinsic data is showing something really significant which is missed and hardly ever mentioned – which is that England has done a really good job of narrowing the gap in the last ten years but nobody's noticed. It's not in the current government's interest to state that.

JO: Absolutely not, no.

MB: And oddly, it's not really an interest of a lot of the teachers because they'd rather grumble about education policy from successive governments rather than celebrate its successes, even though they're really their successes. And so, nobody's out there talking about it. But it's true. So one point, I suppose I'm agreeing with you that while the benchmarking, the international benchmarking is a definite trend and on the whole, I'm arguing, a good thing, it's not the only thing people should be looking at.

JO: It's interesting that you mentioned the teachers there. And yes, I couldn't agree with you more that the absence of celebration of considerable success is really depressing, particularly at the moment. This story of failure is quite hard to take, really. But one of the arguments about knowledge at the moment, particularly in relation to data, is, again, pursuing the sort of democratising argument, that with the existence of information, in a way, teachers ought to be conscious of this progress. They should be able to articulate this, push back against some of the pressures that are disrupting and fragmenting the education system (at least that's my particular perspective). But it doesn't seem to happen. I'm just, again, trying to pursue your thinking, as you are now thinking about how things are developing in terms of data, information, what one does with it, how one steers it, the ideas of co-production of this knowledge.

MB: I think that's a big question. You know, co-creation I'm in favour of, I think it's a really good principle. But let's just talk about that in a bit more depth. I think, there are two things that I'll mention. One is, on the teachers, I think one of the problems for quite a long time actually is that the people who speak on behalf of the teachers are obsessed with running a critique of government policy, when they should be looking above and beyond that and saying 'look what we're doing'. And they should be speaking to the public, teachers generally. Of course they have to think about government, but it's like a dialogue between the teacher leaders and the government, and they completely miss the communication to the public. So what the public hears is the government's claiming X and the teacher's union leader disclaiming X or refuting it with Y. It sounds like that. Whereas, they could, the Education Department [of the NUT] that you and I know well from long ago, they could have been doing wonderful data analysis now. And not focused on how we can get one over the government, but how can we show the public that Bangladeshi students are doing fantastically as a result of the efforts of teachers in Tower Hamlets.

JO: Is there a professional group that does this better, do you think?

MB: I don't know of one, but that might be my ignorance. So, my point is that the teaching profession should speak to its profession and the public more than it should just worry about the latest government announcement. So that's one thing. But then the other thing I was going to give you as an example on co-creation is, I don't know if you noticed, we published this thing with the EIU called the Learning Curve[5] in December.

JO: Yes.

MB: Which was the second most visited education topic on the BBC website last year. But in terms of co-creation, the hard work in that wasn't the writing of the report, the report is interesting but it's not the important thing, the important thing is, we put together in one location 60 global datasets. Lots of them about education inputs, class sizes and funding and teachers' salaries and all that, from international datasets. So they're there. And then, all the ones on outcomes, so PISA and TIMSS and PIRLS and graduation rates and literacy rates and all that. And then social outcomes, economic growth, employment, crime. So where you can get international datasets, we put them all in one place. And anybody can go in there and connect those bits together. So we've just done a really, really boring job that makes anybody like you able to do a job that would be more fun. I don't whether that's co-creation but it's creating the possibility of ...

JO: It's creating a resource, isn't it?

MB: Yeah. And we at Pearson are really going to look at doing that more and more with data, just making it available to people, so that people can see it.

JO: Why does Pearson do this?

MB: Because we want to have a reputation, a justified reputation for being a company that cares about improving the performance of education systems, and the students of various ages and stages who use Pearson products and services. And so we'd like to be part of the dialogue about how that works. So you could argue that in some very broad sense it has a commercial interest but we're not doing it to generate revenue. We're doing it because of what I just said. I don't know what you think but when I look ahead at the education system, I thought about this a lot before I came here, there's, obviously government systems and public systems are going to be a vital part of meeting the massive educational challenges of the next 20 years. And the more that can be done to improve and refine those, the better. But on their own, governments aren't going to solve those problems. It certainly isn't going to happen in the developing world. So then you think, well, where are the innovations going to come from? Where are the big changes going to come from? And a global education company seems like a plausible place to do that, if the values and ethics underpinning it were credible, which increasingly I believe they are. So that's why we're doing it. We'll see. The challenge of education in the next 20 or 30 years is absolutely huge, what needs to be done. And we're a long way short of it. And you can see in Pakistan, but it's also true in India or Africa, that the government sector alone can't solve the problems. But if you can get the right relationship between the government, the voluntary and the business sector, then you can make some progress.

Notes

1 Secretary of State for Health in the UK Government 1999–2003.
2 Secretary of State for Health in the UK Government 2003–05.
3 Richard Olivier, son of the famous Shakespearian actor Sir Laurence Olivier.
4 http://www.drfosterhealth.co.uk/
5 http://thelearningcurve.pearson.com/the-report

6   The World Bank and Higher Education Reform in Ethiopia

Knowledge Aid and Its Undesirable Effects

Tebeje Molla

Introduction

This chapter critically examines World Bank (WB) support for Ethiopia, specifically for its higher education (HE) system. It is now almost commonplace for support for developing nations from International Organizations (IOs) such as the WB to be the subject of analysis and critique. Reasons for this are not difficult to discern, particularly in relation to the WB's activities. This is because the WB is the largest external financial source for educational expenditure in developing countries in general and in Sub-Saharan Africa (SSA) in particular (Jones 2007). In fact, the Bank provides about a quarter of all external funds for education in low-income countries (LICs) (Domenech and Mora-Ninci 2009). In twenty years (1990–2010), the WB committed a total of nearly US$42 billion for education (Molla 2013b). Poor countries with low annual per capita income are eligible for the WB's financial aid, which includes concessional outright grants and interest-free long-term loans (World Bank 2007a).

Criticisms of WB activities typically focus on the conditions attached to the financial aid. For example, during the 1980s and 1990s, the WB imposed its Structural Adjustment Programs (SAPs) on aid-recipient countries as conditions to loans and grants. However, since the end of the 1990s, it has repackaged its neoliberal policy agenda in what are referred to as Poverty Reduction Strategy Papers (PRSPs), and the instruments of imposition have become softer, more subtle and (possibly) more effective. There is an increasing reliance on discursive dissemination to induce compliance to the WB's neoliberal policy prescriptions. It is these softer contributions of the Bank to Ethiopian HE that are the subject of analysis in this chapter, specifically its 'knowledge aid'.

In a particular policy field, knowledge can be an instrument of regulation in the sense that it can be used to influence the behaviour of policy actors through creating policy ideas and framing problems to be addressed. In this regard, the knowledge–policy nexus can be seen as an expression of a political use of knowledge. Power (be it political, financial or symbolic) is a capacity to control or withhold what others need and the object of monopoly can be ideas and meanings (Elias 2005). As such, control over the creation, dissemination and usage of knowledge for policy constitutes a basis for power. Debates over particular strategies and goals are power struggles over which knowledge is valued and hence legitimate to shape decisions. There is a power that comes with possessing knowledge. As Ozga suggests, 'Knowledge is (governing) power, and governance steers knowledge' (2008: 262). For Ozga, governing knowledge refers to 'the ways in which knowledge production and use is being governed (through steering and funding) and the ways in which that knowledge is increasingly used as a governing resource' (2008: 261). As much as codification of practice and production of valid knowledge that informs policy is defined by power, knowledge lends authority and legitimacy to a certain form of discourse that structures relations of power (Boswell 2009). In aid-recipient countries, the power of knowledge-based policy regulation lies in its apparently objective nature (evidence-based) and close association with funding.

Ethiopia is one of the main beneficiaries of WB financial aid. However, the impact of the WB's educational development aid for Ethiopia remains under-researched, if not neglected. This chapter seeks to shed light specifically on instruments and undesirable consequences of non-financial support of the Bank to the Ethiopian HE system. It tries to answer these interrelated questions: What sorts of knowledge-based policy regulatory tools did the WB use to influence higher education reforms in Ethiopia? And with what effects?

In addressing these questions I draw on critical policy analysis to review relevant policy documents from the Government of Ethiopia and the WB. Viewed from a critical policy analysis perspective, policy is not simply a text – it is a discursive process in which agents contest and struggle to construct and circulate their messages through various instruments, including research and consultancy (Ball 2005; Gale 1999; Ozga 2000). Agents, which may be located within and outside the state, struggle over meanings and priorities in the context of unequal power relations, and the influence of each agent is determined by his/her position (or capital) in the policy field (Mangez and Hilgers 2012). Those with the necessary resources (e.g., funding, knowledge, recognition and legitimacy) can define certain issues as valid policy concerns while neglecting or discrediting alternative problems and strategies. Therefore, a critical policy analyst should be conscious of both the power relations in policy-making and the role of the social setting in mediating the meaning of the policy and its implementation and effects (Codd 2007; Gale 2001). In other words, it is imperative to recognize the value-laden nature of policy, illuminate who is systematically privileged or excluded, and analyse the hidden structure of power in the discursive dissemination of policy ideas.

The policy analysis in this chapter reveals two major findings. First, the WB uses various instruments of discursive dissemination (e.g., research, consultancy, analytical reports and conferences) to induce compliance to its neoliberal policy prescriptions. Second, in Ethiopia, these knowledge-based pathways of policy influence have had undesirable consequences: it has weakened the nation's knowledge regime and it has established a condition of 'shared misrecognition' to impositions, which has enabled the prescriptions to go unchallenged through the national policy process. Also, the Bank's discursive influence on HE policy priorities and strategies has resulted in a misleading optimism about the 'knowledge economy' meta-narrative. These two findings are discussed in turn in the following two sections.

Knowledge-Based Pathways of Policy Influence

A sound policy decision requires coherently organized evidence on the problem to be addressed and alternative strategies to be considered. Knowledge that shapes policy decisions may come in the form of research findings, personal experiences of policy actors, and information on public attitude (e.g. through submissions, media reports and public discussion).

In the context of the global education policy field (Riziv and Lingard 2010), dis-cursive dissemination refers to the capacity of IOs 'to initiate and influence debates on policy issues' (Leuze *et al.* 2008: 8). It is about creating and communicating a body of knowledge that informs policy decisions and processes. IOs (e.g., the WB, the OECD and the UNESCO) discursively disseminate their policy ideas through gener-ating rankings, constructing benchmarks, identifying 'best practices', developing and clarifying concepts, analysing trends, evaluating policy impacts, and setting policy agenda and point of references for research (Schuller *et al.* 2006: 58).

Before committing funds to a particular project, the WB conducts sector reviews, produces project appraisals and commissions policy consultancy and research related to the sector in question. In the case of the HE sector, the WB has clearly stated that the appropriate mix of financial and non-financial aid is determined based on two key criteria: (a) the need to reform, and (b) willingness to reform (World Bank 2002). That is to say, the involvement of the Bank depends on the magnitude of the problem that necessitates reform and the political commitment of a government to accept and implement reform prescriptions (or policy options, as the WB prefers to call them). In practice, the need to reform is a result of an intentional construction of a policy problem by the WB. In its financial and non-financial involvements, the WB is proactive, not reactive. It contacts aid-recipient governments with packages of program loans and policy initiatives (Torres 2009). It commissions sector reviews and produces analytical works to show problems of a particular sector and outlines strategies to address them. It also indicates its interest to approve project or program funding if necessary. Against this backdrop, poor governments in Africa have little or no reason not to show willing-ness to reform. In other words, the WB uses its knowledge power to initiate interest for reform and uses its strong financial resources to implement the required reform in those countries. It creates *crisis* that needs to be averted and nominates itself – usually by virtue of its experience, knowledge and money – as a viable agent to deal with it. This supports what Naomi Klein (2007) highlights in *The Shock Doctrine*: there should be a reasonable 'shock' coupled with obedience of the aid-seeker as a necessary condition to induce neoliberal ideals into national public services.

In the case of recent Ethiopian HE reform, the WB's knowledge-based path-ways of policy influence can be categorized as (a) research and consultancy, and (b) analytical reports and conferences. These are discussed in turn.

Research and Consultancy

After decades of intentional neglect, in the late 1990s the WB expressed interest in getting involved in the restructuring of HE in Ethiopia. It commissioned a sector review and provided the government with policy consultancy services in the area of

HE reform and development. According to a former vice minister for HE who headed much of the reform process, the WB provided 'technical assistance' in the preparation of key policy documents, including the Higher Education Proclamation (No.351/2003) (Yizengaw 2005: 9). Its policy consultants were also involved in the preparation of the nation's first five-year education sector development program (MoE 1998).

The WB also commissioned expatriate consultants to devise a new HE financing system. It assigned Professor Bruce Chapman, the architect of an income-contingent HE charging system first implemented in Australia in 1989, as a leading consultant to investigate the possibilities and modalities of introducing user fees in public universities in Ethiopia. In his report, Chapman concluded, 'A charge is justified, and the best mechanism is collection depending on a graduate's income' (Chapman 1999: 11). Accordingly, the Bank activated its call for the introduction of user fees in HE and the issue came to be one of the policy priorities in the reform process in the early 2000s. In 2003, the parliament ratified the Higher Education Proclamation (No.351/2003; revised in 2009, No.650/2009) and introduced the cost-sharing scheme in public universities (FDRE 2009).

In 2003, before releasing the fund for its *Post-Secondary Education Project* (Ethiopia) (2005–2009), the WB conducted a sector review on the Ethiopian HE system and published its report entitled: *Higher Education Development for Ethiopia: Pursuing the Vision* (World Bank, 2003). In the report, the WB articulated problems and outlined its 'policy options' which included encouraging the private sector, introducing a cost recovery scheme, and decentralizing the governance of public HE. The government had to ratify the Proclamation (in June 2003) and show its compliance to these neoliberal policy elements prior to the WB's concept review (in September 2003), and subsequent approval of the Project (in September 2004).

To further consolidate the financing aspect of the reform, the WB commissioned a Washington-based HE policy organization, the Institute for Higher Education Policy, to 'design a workable budgeting formula' for Ethiopia (Merisotis 2003: 2). The consultancy report by the Institute recommended a simplified block grant budgeting system that enables the government to use policy-driven funding priorities to steer public HE institutions toward meeting specific goals and requirements. The proposed financing system was also thought to be instrumental in improving the performance of public universities and making them more efficient and competitive. In March 2004, the government commissioned a Committee of Inquiry into Governance, Leadership and Management of the HE system. In June 2004, the Committee (composed of HE managers and chaired by an expatriate consultant) finalized its report entitled: *Higher Education Systems Overhaul* (HESO) (Committee of Inquiry 2004). The report reaffirmed the WB's policy direction regarding the need for strengthening the steering role of the government in HE through performance-based budgeting and other regulatory frameworks.

It is worth noting that to study education systems and policies in SSA, the WB commissions expatriate experts who basically share its values and assumptions (Samoff 2005; Teferra 2004). Even when local experts are involved in such research projects, the terms of reference, benchmarks and indicators are set by the WB. These tend to reaffirm official views and positions of the Bank, and have little effect in presenting alternative views on the question in hand. Joel Samoff (2005) rightly notes that as the WB commissions sector reviews and task forces, it is inevitable that its 'assumptions, understandings, and expectations are embedded in the framing questions and the detailed terms of reference' (20). As a result, not surprisingly, findings and recommendations of commissioned knowledge production projects at different levels and localities in SSA conform to the WB's meta-narratives of market rationality and human capital formation. The process of knowledge production and dissemination is simply a way of 'manufacturing consent' on the Bank's policy priorities and agendas. Sector reviews and consultation services are, in the words of a senior official in the WB, 'primarily vehicles for selling projects' (quoted in Goldman 2005: 135).

Analytical Reports and Conferences

The WB globalizes its HE policies through producing and circulating categories/ discursive constructs, and supporting and organizing policy-learning platforms such as thematic conferences, workshops and seminars at international, regional and national levels (Shahjahan 2012). With a strong financial means at its disposal, the WB produces a large body of knowledge across a broad range of sectors and themes. In other words, it disseminates its policy ideas through publishing and circulating policy problems, proposals, best practices and comparative evaluation of performances of different countries in the field of HE policy and practice.

Since the early 2000s, as a manifestation of its renewed interest in HE in low-income countries, the WB has published several reports on HE. In addition to generic analytical works such as *Higher Education in Developing Countries: Peril and Promise* (2000), and *Constructing Knowledge Societies: New Challenges for Tertiary Education* (2002), the WB has produced a number of analytical reports specifically on HE in sub-Saharan Africa.[1] To increase their impact, the Bank circulates key publications for free (Altbach *et al.* 2004). Higher education experts within the WB believe that analytical and policy reports on HE have been produced and disseminated with the hope that they 'can serve as catalysts for initiating discussions and, ultimately, reforms' (Salmi *et al.* 2009: 109). That assumption appears to be true, at least in the case of Ethiopia where the WB's influence is evident both in content and language of key HE policy documents developed in the last ten years. The influence is marked in the endorsement of key reform prescriptions (e.g. cost-sharing and privatization) as well as the uptake of discursive constructs of the WB (as shown in the following section).

In its involvement in national policy processes of aid-recipient countries, the discursive functioning of the WB is expressed in the assemblage and dissemination of knowledge for policy. Its experts publicize major policy reports through regional and national conferences and workshops. In Ethiopia, technical assistance missions of the WB engaged in a series of dialogues with the government and set the terms of references for changes in the education system (World Bank 1998, 2004). The Bank team participated in in-country workshops and seminars purportedly to facilitate broad consensus on policy priorities and reform directions. The WB also supported the participation of government officials in thematic regional conferences organized in other African countries.[2]

The WB uses knowledge as an instrument of regulation through the setting of agendas and what it misleadingly calls 'knowledge sharing' or 'learning activities' (World

Bank 2002, 2007b). For the insiders, the WB is a 'knowledge-sharing institution' whose non-lending support to HE systems in developing countries is an act of helping 'governments *consider options* about possible higher education reforms' (Salmi *et al.* 2009: 106, emphasis added). However, this is a misrepresentation of the role of the Bank, to say the least. When policy ideas are entrenched in loan agreements (as attachments with a much needed fund), they become less *option* and more *imposition*. Again, as the policy idea mainly flows from the WB to national actors, it cannot be considered a *knowledge sharing* – it should rather appropriately be labelled as *knowledge aid*.

Undesirable Effects of the WB's Knowledge Aid

Arguably the concessional loans and grants of the WB are crucial for educational development in low-income countries. Even so, discursive practices that accompany lending services of the WB primarily serve to install the neoliberal ideology of unfettered market and limited government in public services, including education. The policy discourse imposes meanings and assumptions of the WB and rarely accommodates local realities and aspirations. In the case of Ethiopia, knowledge-based policy regulation instruments of the WB have resulted in dysfunctional discursive effects. They have weakened the national knowledge regime, misled the government to unreasonably commit to the 'knowledge economy' discourse, and established a condition of 'shared misrecognition' to the policy impositions. I will discuss these points in what follows.

Weak National Knowledge Regime

In the context of a policy process, knowledge regimes are directly linked with 'national ways of dealing with knowledge in public policy' (Mangez 2008: 111). A national knowledge regime can be broadly understood as the multiplicity and diversity of knowledge actors, and the possibility of their convergence and configuration to influence policy decisions. That is, a knowledge regime is not only about the diversity of knowledge actors but also the relations (e.g., struggles, partnerships and networks) among actors, and the possibility and degree of convergence for a common purpose – for example, to produce or challenge policy ideas (Gale 2003). Hence, at the centre of knowledge regime discussions are knowledge institutions (e.g. think-tanks, academics, research centres, networks of professionals and government agencies), and knowledge production and utilization trends.

In explicating the role of the WB in Ethiopian HE reform, it is necessary to address key questions such as: How do various actors interact in producing knowledge for policy? For example, who are the participants of policy inquiry committees and task forces commissioned by the government and the donors involved in the process?

In developing countries such as Ethiopia, independent policy think-tanks and professional networks are almost non-existent. Thus, the task of knowledge production through research is primarily the responsibility of universities. However, in Ethiopia, knowledge for policy comes mainly from donors. In the last ten years, crucial studies that informed HE policy reform were conducted by either WB staff (e.g., *Higher Education Development for Ethiopia: Pursuing the Vision*, 2003) or hand-picked non-expert political loyalists who had little or no knowledge and experience about the issue at hand (e.g., *Higher Education Systems Overhaul,* 2004). Even though there were well-established researchers with the relevant qualification and experience based in Ethiopia's 'national university' (Addis Ababa University, AAU), they were not consulted in the production of these crucial documents (Teferra 2004). Political loyalty seems to be more important than expertise. For example, during its formative period of reform and transformation (in the first half of the 2000s), Ethiopia's HE system was headed by a Deputy Minister graduate in Soil Sciences (not in education or any related field).

It is important to note that even though a lack of national resources for research and publication is an issue, the overdependence of the Ethiopian government on the WB's knowledge aid and the exclusion of local scholars cannot be explained by financial reasons alone. It has a political dimension as well. Due to the government's intolerance towards critics, domestic knowledge institutions and independent professional networks have been rarely involved in policy processes. According to an account by a veteran academic staff member in AAU, governments in Ethiopia, mostly due to their inimical relationship with the university, have not been in the right position to exploit its *intellectual resource* (Yimam 2008). In 1993, the government purged forty-two high-profile academic staff for their critical views on the policies and strategies of the government, and to silence critics, it banned university-based publications on current affairs (Yimam 2008: 57). In an article that questions the West's lack of interest to challenge the increasingly authoritarian behaviour of the current government in Ethiopia, *The Economist* (17 September 2011) reported 'heavy spying on universities'.

At first, the government used the WB's support as a way to escape from potentially disruptive dialogue from its vocal critics, mainly in the national university. Now, given that the government has succeeded in silencing its detractors, by draining the intellectual resources of the universities and other professional networks, it has no choice but to continue receiving knowledge aid from the Bank. The problem is cyclical. In the absence of active participation of local critical voices in public actions, educational development aid tends to 'lend legitimacy to corruption and repression' (Ashcroft 2011: para.40). Such a repressive regime does not support the development of a national knowledge regime and continues to seek knowledge aid. The consequence ranges from weak knowledge production and usage capacities to poor records of policy implementation.

The government relies largely on foreign expertise that has little or no attachment with the socio-economic and historical contexts of the policy problem it seeks to address. When local knowledge is systematically disregarded in a policy process, the consequence is detrimental (Crossley 2010). The decoupling of local knowledge communities from the policy idea creation leads not only to superficial (even flawed) representation of the policy problem but puts the legitimacy of the policy in question. This in turn undermines the effectiveness and impact of projects that are meant to translate the policy. The implementation of the WB's *Post-Secondary Education Project* (2005–2009) in Ethiopia is a typical case. The Completion Report by the Bank rated the project as 'moderately unsatisfactory' (World Bank 2010: i). Poor implementation of the project might in part relate to the marginalization of local actors in the initiation and development of the project.

Misleading Optimism about Knowledge Economy

Through its sector reviews, consultancy services and analytical reports, the WB elevates its key policy constructs to a position of significance, such that aid-recipient governments rarely question the relevance of the prescriptions to their respective contexts. In the policy documents of the Ethiopian government sampled for this study, it is easy to locate the uptake of WB's neoliberal discursive categories about the connection between knowledge and economic development, the role of market forces in the field, and expected economic returns to investment on education. Among the salient themes and conceptual constructs prevalent in the texts are human capital, knowledge-based economy, knowledge-intensive development, competitive economy, privatization and poverty reduction (FDRE 2009; MoE 1998; Committee of Inquiry 2004).

With the optimism of achieving knowledge-intensive development and ending poverty, HE has assumed a new level of importance in SSA countries, including Ethiopia. Poor performance in education is associated with disadvantages in economic productivity and competitiveness, and changes in the field of HE are closely associated with wealth creation and poverty reduction. In line with WB's long-held ideological disposition, human capital formation is viewed as a panacea for economic problems in Ethiopia. The government aligns HE development with the mission of fast economic growth to end poverty (MoE 2002; MoFED 2002). As a result, in a space of fourteen years the number of public universities has increased from two in 1999 to thirty-one in 2012. Full-time undergraduate enrolment in public universities jumped from about 20,000 in 1998/99 to over 246,000 in 2011/12 (MoE 2000, 2012). A costly public investment has made possible the fastest rate of HE expansion in Africa (Ravishankar *et al.* 2010). During this period of exponential expansion, the government spent more than 1.5 per cent of its GDP on HE, recorded among the top ten rates of expenditure in the world and the highest expenditure in SSA (UIS 2010).

The government's optimism about the economic growth effect of HE is misleading for at least four reasons. First, it is hardly possible to realize knowledge-based economic growth in a society where over 50 per cent of the adult population is illiterate and the HE enrolment rate is one of the lowest in the world (less than 6 per cent) (UIS 2012). Second, as a result of the ambitious expenditure on HE, public investment has been unfairly skewed to HE at the cost of other levels of education. Hence, the quality of education has considerably deteriorated which undermines the quality of university graduates (Semela 2011). Third, the government has failed to properly appreciate the degree of inequality in HE and to adequately appreciate its role in poverty reduction efforts. Social justice requires a strong notion of equity of opportunity and it needs active involvement of the government not only in widening access to HE but also in addressing structural barriers that constrain successful participation of historically and socially disadvantaged groups in the society. However, with the emphasis on efficiency through privatization and diversification of sources of income (following the prescriptions of the WB), the problem of social inequality in the HE system remains a secondary concern (Molla 2013a). Finally, by uncritically endorsing the knowledge economy discourse while at the same time tightening the its grip on political power, the government appears to have assumed that the economic productivity of a worker comes solely from his or her education. It overlooks such vital factors as political stability, freedom of the individual, cultural values of the society and availability of physical resources.

Shared Misrecognition to Policy Imposition

Clearly the WB is equipped with the necessary means of policy imposition. The symbolic capital it has acquired in the form of global legitimacy (as a special agency of the UN and subsequent position of impartiality), and recognition of its financial capacity and expertise (represented by its policy professionals and extensive field experience), have given the WB a symbolic power: 'the power granted to those who have obtained sufficient recognition to be in a position to impose recognition' (Bourdieu 1989: 23). Symbolism is a kind of power that exists as a result of the recognition and legitimacy afforded to other forms of power including economic, cultural and social. According to Bourdieu (1991: 170), symbolic power 'is defined in and through a given relation between those who exercise power and those who submit to it, i.e. in the very structure of the field in which belief is produced and reproduced'. In a policy network, symbolic power manifests when the dominant agent names and frames agendas and strategies, defining and thus justifying the pattern and object of relationship in the policy field (i.e. who should be included and why, and how agents in the field should interact and relate in the process, etc.). It is a power that provides the dominant agent with the capability to enforce its own classification and meaning. Gale (1994) describes this policy naming and framing work of symbolic power as *settling policy*.

Symbolic power is a power that is subtle enough to be overlooked as domination/ imposition and important enough to be recognized as a legitimate and hence acceptable relationship (Bourdieu, 1986). A key feature of such a power is the shared misrecognition that it manages to establish in the process of interaction between agents (Bourdieu 1990, 1998). In the context of the donor–recipient relationship, the shared 'categories of perception and appreciation' (Bourdieu 1998: 100) about the act of giving grants and 'free' knowledge-based services is instrumental in making the aid-recipients conform to the required policy prescriptions. In this interaction of donors and aid recipient governments, the shared misrecognition refers to the mutual denial of political and economic interests present in the interaction. The shared view (of the WB and national policy agents) that research and consultancy services are technical support of knowledge-sharing, illustrates the case clearly.

To further illustrate the point, during the formative period of HE policy reform in Ethiopia, the WB pushed its policy prescriptions with a forceful tone. In one of its sector reviews, the Bank clearly states its position:

> The Ministry of Education [of Ethiopia] and its higher education reform implementation team are therefore *urged to do all that is in their power to ensure that these essential policy and regulatory requirements* [diversification of revenue sources, formula funding, decentralised governance, etc.] *are put in place and effectively implemented*.
>
> (World Bank 2003: 81, emphasis added)

Accordingly, the government introduced the suggested changes through the Higher Education Proclamation and the Cost-Sharing Scheme, both ratified in 2003. Yet

HE policy experts within the WB insist that the technical assistance to aid-recipient governments is no more than a facilitation of policy changes and knowledge-sharing (Hopper *et al.* 2008; Saint 2004a, 2004b; Samli and Bassett 2010). More specifically, it is framed as a facilitation of 'the cross-fertilization of relevant regional experiences' (World Bank 2002: xxvii). In reality, knowledge aid by the WB serves as a means of agenda-setting, such that interactions between the WB and the government are largely linear: WB imposition, national compliance.

The subtlety of policy regulation instruments has enabled the WB to utilize powers of persuasion rather than sanction. They have helped the Bank exercise a veiled dominance in the policy process and avoid local resistance to its prescriptions. The shared misrecognition of the WB's imposition has also given the government grounds to claim strong ownership of policy ideas and to decline the influence of the WB in the reform process (Molla 2013b). Asked to comment on the relationship between the government and the WB on restructuring the HE system, a senior government official in the Ministry of Education preferred to emphasize his government's ownership of the reforms:

> HE reforms in Ethiopia do have Ethiopian premise. We have our own causes. It is part and parcel of the national development plan. We strongly believe that education in general and HE in particular is a key factor in the country's development and transformation. [...] our reforms are Ethiopian both in form and mission.
>
> (Interview, 23 October 2010)

Systematic domination of an agent over a social group or entity is possible partly through what Scott (1990) refers to as the 'hidden transcript of power' in which the dominant agent consciously keeps the rules of the game covered from the eyes and ears of outsiders, including the dominated. In this regard, by creating a relationship in which the dominated takes for granted the disguised/invisible imposition as a legitimate condition, the WB has created what Bourdieu (1989) refers to as symbolic violence. The violence (as expressed by the denial of imposition) has resulted in a calculated invisibility of imposed policy agendas that consequently has complicated research efforts to trace sources and effects of such agendas. For aid-recipient governments, denying external influence can be seen as a way of claiming a political legitimacy.

Conclusion

Notwithstanding the local rhetoric of ownership of reform agendas and processes, through its financial and non-financial instruments, the WB has played critical roles in system-wide and institutional restructuring of HE in Ethiopia. As argued in this chapter, knowledge-based policy regulatory instruments of the WB are not only a soft means of policy imposition but also impediments to the development and maintenance of the nation's knowledge production capacities. As Stehr (2005) rightly notes, 'the transfer of knowledge does not necessarily include the transfer of the cognitive ability to generate such knowledge' (307). In the knowledge-based policy regulation process, the product remains largely within the domain of the producer. In this regard, the codified knowledge underpinning the 'travelling policy' of the WB is not only ideologically contaminated with neoliberalism but undermines the tacit knowledge that is instrumental in translating imported policy ideas to reflect local meanings and needs (Ozga and Jones 2006).

With a weak national knowledge regime and under-developed economy, Ethiopia has very minimal *national capital* to take a gainful position in its interaction with global forces, and to access and use globally available knowledge. In other words, in order for externally imposed or imported policy ideas to be effectively and meaningfully implemented, they need to be filtered and localized. This, in turn, requires a strong national knowledge force that can adapt borrowed ideas, create new ones, devise realistic and justified policy frameworks, and hold public officials accountable for their actions and inactions. Such a functional knowledge regime requires, among other things, a substantial budget for research and publication and, most importantly, it needs a free political space that allows knowledge producers, policy actors and external experts to engage in dialogue and generate knowledge that informs public actions, including policies and strategies in the education system.

Acknowledgements

I would like to extend my deepest gratitude to Prof. Denise Cuthbert (RMIT University), Prof. Trevor Gale (Deakin University), Prof. Eric Mangez (University of Louvain) and Prof. Jenny Ozga (University of Oxford) for their valuable feedback and insightful comments on earlier versions of this chapter.

Notes

1   Recently published analytical and policy reports include: *Tertiary Education: Lessons from a Decade of Lending* (2002); *Improving Tertiary Education in Sub-Saharan Africa: Things that Work* (2004); *Higher Education and Economic Development in Africa* (2006); *Cost and Financing of Tertiary Education in Francophone Africa* (2007); *Higher Education Quality Assurance in Sub-Saharan Africa: Status; Challenges, Opportunities, and Promising Practices* (2007); *Funding Higher Education: The Contribution of Economic Thinking to Debate and Policy Development* (2007); *Higher Education in Francophone Africa: What Tools Can Be Used to Support Financially Sustainable Policies?* (2008); *Differentiation and Articulation in Tertiary Education Systems: A Study of Twelve African Countries* (2008); *Accelerating Catch-up: Tertiary Education for Growth in Sub-Saharan Africa* (2009).

2   In sub-Saharan Africa, the list of such events organized in the last ten years include, *Improving Tertiary Education in Sub-Saharan Africa: Things that work* (23–25 September 2003, Accra, Ghana); *Higher Education for Francophone Africa's Development* (13–15 June 2006, Ouagadougou, Burkina Faso); *Cost and Financing of Tertiary Education in Francophone Africa: Training Session* (2–4 July 2007, Cotonou, Benin); *African Union AMCOST (African Ministerial Council on Science and Technology) Meeting* (12–16 November 2007, Mombasa, Kenya); *International Conference on Quality Assurance in Higher Education in Africa* (15–17 September 2008, Dakar, Senegal); *Capacity Building Workshop on the Licence-Master-Doctorate (LMD) Reform for Francophone Countries* (19–20, September 2008, Saint Louis, Senegal); *The Partnership for Higher Education in Africa (PHEA) University Leadership Forum* (23–25 November 2008, Accra, Ghana); *12th General Conference of the Association of African Universities (on Sustainable Development in Africa: The Role of Higher Education)* (4–5 May 2009, Abuja, Nigeria); *Conference of Ministers of Education in Africa* (COMEDAF IV) (24–25 September 2009, Addis Ababa, Ethiopia); *National Conference on World-Class Universities* (27 September 2010, Abuja,

Nigeria); and *Workshop on Sustainable Financing and Governance of Regional Initiatives in Higher Education in Africa* (21 March 2011, Ouagadougou, Burkina Faso).

References

Altbach, P., Bloom, D., Hopper, R., Psacharopoulos, G. and Rosovsky, H. (2004) 'The task force on higher education and society', *Comparative Education Review*, 48, 1: 70–88.

Ashcroft, K. (2011) 'Africa: Dilemmas of development work', *World Universities News*, (African Edition), issue 0085, 16 Oct.2011, accessed from http://www.universityworldnews.com/article.php?story=20111014200731915

Ball, S. (2005) *Education Policy and Social Class: The Selected Works of Stephen Ball*, Hoboken, NJ: Routledge.

Boswell, C. (2009) *The Political Uses of Expert Knowledge: Immigration Policy and Social Research*, Cambridge: Cambridge University Press.

Bourdieu, P. (1986) 'The forms of capital', in J. Richardson (ed.) *Handbook of Theory and Research for the Sociology of Education,* Westport, CT: Greenwood.

Bourdieu, P. (1989) 'Social space and symbolic power', *Sociological Theory*, 7, 1: 14–25.

Bourdieu, P. (1990) *The Logic of Practice*, Stanford, CA: Stanford University Press.

Bourdieu, P. (1991) *Language and Symbolic Power*, Cambridge: Polity Press.

Bourdieu, P. (1998) *Practical Reason: On the Theory of Action*, Stanford, CA: Stanford University Press.

Chapman, B. (1999) 'Reform of Ethiopian higher education financing: conceptual and policy issues', *Economics of Education Series 2*, Washington DC: World Bank.

Codd, J. A. (2007) 'The construction and deconstruction of educational policy documents', in S. Ball, I. Goodson and M. Maguire (eds) *Education, Globalization and New Times*, Hoboken, NJ: Routledge.

Committee of Inquiry (2004) 'Higher education system overhaul', Report of the Committee of Inquiry into governance, leadership and management in Ethiopia's higher education system, Addis Ababa: MoE.

Crossley, M. (2010) 'Context matters in educational research and international development: learning from the small states experience', *Prospects*, 40, 4: 421–429.

Domenech, E. and Mora-Ninci, C. (2009) 'World Bank discourse and policy on education and cultural diversity for Latin America', in D. Hill and R. Kumar (eds.) *Global Neoliberalism and Education and Its Consequences*, New York: Routledge.

Elias, N. (2005) 'Knowledge and power: an interview by Peter Ludes', in N. Stehr and V. Meja (eds) *Society and Knowledge: Contemporary Perspectives in Sociology of Knowledge and Science*, 2nd edn, New Brunswick, NJ: Transaction Publishers.

FDRE [Federal Democratic Republic of Ethiopia] (2009) *Higher Education Proclamation* (No. 650/2009), Addis Ababa: Berhanena Selam Printing Enterprise/Federal Negarit Gazette.

Gale, T. (1994) 'Story-telling and policy making: the construction of university entrance problems in Australia', *Journal of Education Policy*, 9, 3: 227–232.

Gale, T. (1999) 'Policy trajectories: treading the discursive path of policy analysis', *Discourse: Studies in the Cultural Politics of Education,* 20, 3: 393–407.

Gale, T. (2001) 'Critical policy sociology: historiography, archaeology and genealogy as methods of policy analysis', *Journal of Education Policy*, 16, 5: 379–393.

Gale, T. (2003) 'Realizing policy: the *who* and *how* of policy production', *Discourse: Studies in the Cultural Politics of Education*, 24, 1: 51–66.

Goldman, M. (2005) *Imperial Nature: The World Bank and Struggles for Social Justice in the Age of Globalization*, New Haven, CT: Yale University Press.

Hopper, R., Salmi, J. and Bassett, R. M. (2008) 'Transforming higher education in developing countries: the role of the World Bank', in GUNI (ed.) *Higher Education in The World 3 – Higher Education: New Challenges and Emerging Roles for Human and Social Development*, New York: Palgrave Macmillan.

Interview with a senior government official in the Ministry of Education of Ethiopia, 23 October2010 (the interview was conducted as part of my doctoral research).

Jones, P. W. (2007) *World Bank Financing Education: Lending, Learning and Development*, 2nd edn, London: Routledge.

Klein, N. (2007) *The Shock Doctrine: The Rise of Disaster Capitalism*, New York: Metropolitan Books.

Leuze, K., Brand, T., Jakobi, A., Martens, K. and Nagel, A.-K. (2008) 'Analysing the two-level game: international and national determinants of change in education policy making', *TranState Working Papers No.72*, University of Bremen.

Mangez, E. (2008) 'Knowledge economy, knowledge policy and knowledge regime', in B. Delvaux and E. Mangez (eds) *Towards a Sociology of the Knowledge-Policy Relation*. (Know&Pol Literature Review, Integrative Report), retrieved on 7 October 2011 from http://www.knowandpol.eu.

Mangez, E. and Hilgers, M. (2012) 'The field of knowledge and the policy field in education: PISA and the production of knowledge for policy', *European Education Research Journal*, 11, 2: 189–205.

Merisotis, J. (2003) 'Higher education funding in Ethiopia: an assessment and guidance for next steps', Report prepared for the World Bank by Institute for Higher Education Policy, Washington DC), retrieved on 27 October 2011 from http://siteresources.worldbank.org/INTAFRREGTOPTEIA/Resources/merisotis_ethiopia.pdf

MoE [Ministry of Education] (1998) *Education Sector Development Program (Action Plan) I (ESDP I)*, Addis Ababa: MoE.

MoE (2000) *Education Statistics Annual Abstract 1998/99*, Addis Ababa: MoE.

MoE (2002) *Education Sector Development Program (Action Plan) II (ESDP II)*, Addis Ababa: MoE.

MoE (2012) *Education Statistics Annual Abstract 2011/12*. Addis Ababa: MoE.

MoFED [Ministry of Finance and Economic Development] (2002) *Ethiopia: Sustainable Development and Poverty Reduction Program*, Addis Ababa: MoFED.

Molla, T. (2013a) 'Higher education policy reform in Ethiopia: the representation of the problem of gender inequality', *Higher Education Policy*, 26, 2: 193–215.

Molla, T. (2013b) 'The neoliberal policy agenda of the World Bank and higher education reform in Ethiopia: the problem of inequality in focus', unpublished doctoral thesis, Monash University, Melbourne.

Ozga, J. (2000) *Policy Research in Educational Settings: Contested Terrain*, Buckingham: Open University Press.

Ozga, J. (2008) 'Governing knowledge: research steering and research quality', *European Educational Research Journal*, 7, 3: 261–272.

Ozga, J. and Jones, R. (2006) 'Travelling and embedded policy: the case of knowledge transfer', *Journal of Education Policy*, 21, 1: 1–17.

Ravishankar, V.J., Kello, A. and Tiruneh, A. (2010) *Ethiopia: Education Public Expenditure Review*, Department of International Development, UK, retrieved on 15 January 2012 from www.dagethiopia.org

Rizvi, F. and Lingard, B. (2010) *Globalising Education Policy*, London: Routledge.

Saint, W. (2004a) 'Higher education in Ethiopia: the vision and its challenges', *Journal of Higher Education in Africa*, 2, 3: 83–113.

Saint, W. (2004b) 'Prescriptions and antidotes, good intentions and misunderstandings', retrieved on 20 September 2012 from https://www2.bc.edu/~teferra/World_Bank_Study_Eth_High_Edu_Response.html

Salmi, J. and Bassett, R. (2010) 'Transforming higher education in developing countries: the role of the World Bank', in P. Peterson, E. Baker and B. McGaw (eds) *International Encyclopaedia of Education*, Vol. 4, Oxford: Elsevier.

Salmi, J., Hopper, R. and Bassett, R. (2009) 'Transforming higher education in developing countries: the role of the World Bank', in R. Bassett and A. Maldonado (eds) *International Organizations and Higher Education Policy: Thinking Globally, Acting Locally?* New York: Routledge.

Samoff, J. (2005) 'The pursuit of effective external support and persisting external influence – direct, indirect, and negotiated', paper prepared for the Nuffic expert meeting, *A Changing Landscape: Making Support to Tertiary Education and Research in Developing Countries More Effective*, The Hague, The Netherlands, 23–25 May.

Sassen, S. (2000) 'Spatialities and temporalities of the global: elements for a theorization', *Public Culture*, 12, 1: 215–232.

Schuller, T., Jochemes, W., Moos, L. and van Zanten, A. (2006) 'Evidence and policy research', *European Educational Research Journal*, 5, 1: 57–70.

Scott, J.C. (1990) *Domination and the Arts of Resistance: Hidden Transcripts*, New Haven, CT: Yale University Press.

Semela, T. (2011) 'Breakneck expansion and quality assurance in Ethiopian higher education: ideological rationales and economic impediments', *Higher Education Policy*, 24, 3: 399–425.

Shahjahan, R. A. (2012) 'The roles of international organizations (IOs) in globalizing higher education policy', in J. C. Smart and M. B. Paulsen (eds) *Higher Education: Handbook of Theory and Research 27*, Dordrecht: Springer.

Stehr, N. (2005) 'Knowledge societies', in N. Stehr and V. Meja (eds) *Society and Knowledge: Contemporary Perspectives in Sociology of Knowledge and Science*, 2nd edn, New Brunswick, NJ: Transaction Publishers.

Teferra, D. (2004) 'The World Bank prescription for Ethiopian higher education: the missing antidote in "pursuing the vision"', retrieved on 26 April 2008 from http://www2.bc.edu/%7Eteferra/World_Bank_Study_Eth_High_Edu.html

The Economist (2011) 'Human rights: the compass fails', 17 September.

Torres, C. (2009) *Education and Neoliberal Globalization*, New York: Routledge.

UIS [UNESCO Institute for Statistics] (2010) *Global Education Digest 2010, Education and Gender: Between Promise and Progress*, Montreal: UIS.

UIS (2012) *Global Education Digest 2010, Opportunities Lost: The Impact of Grade Repetition and Early School Leaving*, Montreal: UIS.

World Bank (1998) *Ethiopia – Education Sector Development Project* (Project Appraisal Report No.17739-ET). Retrieved on 25 May 2010 from http://www-wds.worldbank.org/servlet/WDSContentServer/WDSP/IB/1998/05/04/000009265_3980624142921/Rendered/PDF/multi_page.pdf

World Bank (2000) *Higher Education in Developing Countries: Peril and Promise*. Washington, DC: World Bank.

World Bank (2002) *Constructing Knowledge Societies: New Challenges for Tertiary Education*, Washington, DC: World Bank.

World Bank (2003) *Higher Education Development for Ethiopia: Pursuing the Vision*, Washington, DC: World Bank.

World Bank (2004) *Ethiopia – Post Secondary Education Project* (Project Appraisal Report No.28169-ET). Retrieved on 10 June 2010 from http://documents.worldbank.org/curated/en/2004/08/5069682/ethiopia-post-secondary-education-project

World Bank (2007a) *A Guide to the World Bank*, 2nd edn, Washington, DC: World Bank.
World Bank (2007b) *Building Knowledge Economies: Advanced Strategies for Development*, Washington, DC: World Bank.
World Bank (2010) 'Post-secondary education project – implementation completion and results report' (Report No. RICR00001285). Washington, DC: World Bank.
Yimam, B. (2008) 'Academic freedom at Addis Ababa University: an overview of its past and current experiences', in T. Assefa (ed.) *Academic Freedom in Ethiopia: Perspectives of Teaching Personnel*, Addis Ababa: Forum for Social Studies.
Yizengaw, T. (2005) 'Policy development in higher education in Ethiopia and the role of donors and development partners', paper presented at the international expert meeting, *Formulas that Work: Making Higher Education Support More Effective*, the Hague, The Netherlands, 23–24 May.

7 Expert-Consultants and Knowledge Production

'Teachers for EFA' in Brazil

Eneida Oto Shiroma

Introduction

The Education for All (EFA) World Conference held in Jomtien in 1990 and promoted by the World Bank (WB), United Nations Development Programme (UNDP), the United Nations Children's Fund (UNICEF) and United Nations Educational, Scientific and Cultural Organization (UNESCO) established goals and a global agenda for education. Since then, these International Organisations (IOs) have been constantly monitoring and comparing education systems. Furthermore, they coordinate actions and provide technical assistance for policy implementation around the world aiming to achieve the EFA goals: universal primary education, expanding early childhood care, meeting the learning needs of youth and adults, improving adult literacy by 50 per cent, gender equality and ensuring quality in education. As the global coordinator of EFA, UNESCO works with a wide range of networks in order to sensitise policy-makers and influence national processes of agenda setting. The global agenda for education faces political and legal obstacles in terms of its implementation in national settings, chiefly in terms of legislation, teachers' policies and union resistance. The tensions caused by government initiatives to implement reforms are softened by the activities of social networks aimed at building consensus in relation to educational reforms.

In this chapter I discuss a network of experts in charge of building knowledge about policies for teachers in order to provide the political and juridical basis for reforming teacher policies in Latin America. These experts mobilise other national networks with the aim of implementing global policies for teachers in Latin-American countries. Their attributes as experts and consultants tend to obscure the ideological and political dimension of their activities of knowledge production for policy.

This chapter analyses the process of knowledge mobilisation to implement this global agenda for education in Latin-American countries, particularly in Brazil.[1] I argue that regional networks play an important role as mediators in regard to the borrowing, lending and adapting of policy processes, transmitting and producing knowledge to support the reception of global policies and providing feedback about local settings to IO policy-makers. I have analysed a network of experts invited by UNESCO in 2011 to draw up policy guidelines for teachers in Latin America and the Caribbean that aim to achieve the EFA goals. Comparison of these guidelines to the education agenda of IOs reveals many similarities in arguments and recommendations, but also differences and adaptations. In order to explain the movement of ideas and how they are reshaped in national contexts, the role of experts in policy networks is the focus of the research reported here. These experts are more than the diffusers of ideas; they develop conceptual knowledge in order to promote educational reforms, drawing on their substantial experience as policy advisers to governments and IOs. I focus on the content and forms of implementation of policies for teachers suggested by IOs and performed by networks in order to discuss how the process of producing and disseminating 'knowledge for policy' constitutes a key resource for building the active consensus needed in governing.

The chapter is in four sections. The first discusses the IOs' interests in defining a global agenda for education and lists the main concerns about teachers expressed by the WB, OECD and UNESCO. The second section presents the regional strategy for 'Teachers for EFA' in Latin America and the Caribbean and the strategic partnership with a network of experts. The third section examines the activities of these experts in developing and disseminating the proposals of IOs for education in the region and in influencing national agenda setting. The fourth section is an analysis of the development of 'Teachers for EFA' in Brazil, identifying some proposals which have been implemented as well as others which are facing resistance from teachers and unions. The disputes around the policy of evaluation express the tensions between teachers, unions, and central and local governments. They reveal their strategies of partial adoption of the IOs' recommendations and consensus building, but also their drive to create alternatives to PISA delineated by the Mercosul[2] countries and to reinforce their sovereignty.

The Focus on Teachers of Global Agendas

The coordination of EFA requires the establishing of policy dialogue and communication initiatives through the media, meetings and events. UNESCO's activities encourage civil society organisations to engage in advocacy initiatives at national level including permanent policy dialogue with EFA partners – governments, parliamentarians and the private sector – and promoting the diffusion of ideas through workshops, websites, forums and publishing materials. These initiatives express the concern of IOs to use different ways of disseminating a 'desirable' interpretation of education data that will influence governments and public opinion to converge to the global agenda. In this context, establishing partnerships with research centres is extremely relevant because of their capacity to produce evidence and knowledge that give credibility to the proposed reforms and improve their acceptability.

In 2011, the coordination mechanism of EFA was revised in order to focus on the following priority areas: creating better synergies between national, regional and global EFA coordination; monitoring closely the delivery of commitments made by EFA constituencies; providing more strategic direction to the global EFA movement; strengthening the knowledge base and further promoting knowledge-sharing; and scaling up advocacy at the global level (UNESCO 2011).

The attentiveness of the IOs to education is related to economic interests and their concerns about the agenda for development. This is particularly evident in the report *Achieving World-Class Education in Brazil: The Next Agenda*, wherein the WB announced three paramount functions for education: developing labour force skills; contributing to poverty reduction, and transforming spending into educational results (Bruns *et al.* 2012: 18). According to the report, despite improvements, Brazilian educational indicators and workers' skills 'still lag behind those in other countries' (ibid.). The anxiety about improving the Brazilian workforce's education and skills led to some initiatives related to teachers.

In 2007, UNESCO estimated that 9.1 million new teachers were needed in primary education alone worldwide in order to achieve the EFA goals. An international task force – Teachers for EFA[3] – was created in 2008 at the Oslo EFA High-Level Group meeting.[4] It was the first alliance of EFA partners working together to address the global teacher shortage. In 2011, 1.9 million teachers were still required to realise universal primary schooling by 2015, with half of them needed in Sub-Saharan Africa (Nordstrum 2013: 32). The main concern is to supply these teachers without expanding costs. Arguing that 'teachers are expensive' (Bruns *et al.* 2011: 145), the WB consultants criticise job tenure for life, the rigidity of pay scales, the weak links between teachers' salary and performance, the very flat career progression and the absence of penalties for poor performance (Burns *et al.* 2012: 56). In the same spirit, OECD (2005: 7) has indicated several measures to increase the attractiveness of teaching careers and to make them and teacher training more flexible. The suggestions include: raising initial salaries; new criteria for teacher recruitment and selection; replacing the system of single salary scales with flexible payment such as Performance Related Pay (PRP), and rewarding 'effective' teachers with incentives or bonus schemes.

In spite of the discourse of 'performance and quality', however, the proposals of the IOs for education focus, paradoxically, on the reduction of teacher training costs. The OECD warns that 'it is not just a question of producing more of the same professional development' (Schleicher 2012: 76). It is argued that the teacher training provided by universities is irrelevant in dealing with classroom problems and in providing solutions in practice. The OECD recommends induction programmes for new teachers rather than increasing the length of pre-service education (OECD 2005: 11) and also suggests the provision of curriculum structures that enable trainee teachers to enrol part time or through distance education. They propose a remodelling of training that promotes socialisation into teaching in the workplace, as well as acculturation during the induction period when the new teacher can observe and be observed. In relation to teacher workforce remodelling, they recommend alternative avenues for mid-career entrants and hiring 'para-professionals' to respond promptly to schools' short-term needs (OECD 2005: 14).

A wide range of assessment methods are thus proposed to identify the talent to be rewarded and to identify poor performers who should be encouraged to leave the profession. The WB (2011: 56) proposes explicitly that governments should intervene, change teacher training through the implementation of a national curriculum, and review teachers' tenure and payment based on seniority. These internationally generated proposals boost and influence national agendas. However, the development of global policies in 'closed' meetings does not automatically generate global governance (Whitman 2009); acceptance in national settings is uncertain. Given the potential for conflict generated by these recommendations, consultants working for IOs suggest that governments make efforts to engage teachers and unions in the policy process. In addition, along with the world forums, conferences and official meetings of chiefs of states or ministers of education, IOs also promote other spaces of production and diffusion of knowledge about global policies for education.

Regional Strategies for 'Teachers for EFA'

UNESCO's Regional Bureau of Education for Latin America and the Caribbean (Orealc) work programme for 2008–2009 consisted of four major action lines: establishing the global leadership of the EFA movement; creating global frameworks and networks designed to strengthen the planning and management capacity of national education systems; promoting dialogue on policies, research and guidelines; and developing and providing technical support as a means of helping countries to attain the EFA goals. Orealc/UNESCO's strategies include mobilising actors and forging strategic partnerships, fostering social participation and collaboration with non-traditional educational actors, such as national parliaments, NGOs, social communicators, and business people. Many networks were created to catalyse EFA initiatives and stimulate the replication or adaptation of 'best practice' in the region. International consultants offer financial and technical assistance and technologies for implementing reforms, and in transmitting knowledge they can use regional and national networks, generating cooperation and synergy among actors both within and across countries.

The WB's strategy for the education sector for 2011 to 2020 is underpinned by the decentralisation of the policy-making process. The Bank works with consultants hired at regional headquarters because it is believed that analyses and reports from local experts are more likely to be compatible with local needs and more accepted by educators, unions and citizens. For example, the Systems Approach for Better Education Results (SABER) project, which is part of the WB strategy for this decade, is an initiative to collect, analyse and disseminate information about the top performing education systems. In collecting new data, the WB hires consultants based in the relevant country for some weeks to gather information for a country report (Vegas 2011). SABER compiles global education data, produces comparative analysis and uses user-friendly dissemination methods such as reports available on its website. SABER embraces other products, including papers, a conceptual framework, diagnostic tools, country reports, case studies and a knowledge base, thus filling a major gap in policy data and guidance (Vegas 2011). Aiming to identify the crucial elements of top performing and rapidly improving countries, SABER based their analysis on PISA results.

The broad diffusion of test results provides a rich resource for policy discourses and produces other effects (Ozga *et al.* 2011; Carvalho 2012). At the individual level, comparisons revealed by league tables constrain students and school teachers in times of performativity and accountability. At public policy level, alarming media headlines demand immediate responses from governments and explanations of 'what will be done'. Comparison forces governments to look for solutions and international experience may provide 'a much needed justification for introducing and accelerating fundamental educational reforms at home' (Steiner-Khamsi 2004: 8). Despite having the appearance of indigenous policies proposed by known regional experts, however, they are far from being *indigenous* and independently produced.

In 2011, Latin-American ministers of education were invited to a meeting promoted by UNESCO to debate the document *A New Agenda for Teachers' Policy in Latin America and the Caribbean: Critical Knots and Criteria for Action* (Cox *et al.* 2011). This event launched the Teachers for EFA programme in the continent and announced the partnership of UNESCO with the Centro de Estudios de Políticas y Prácticas en Educación (CEPPE) [Centre of Studies in Education Policies and Practices] to develop the Regional Strategic Project on Teachers.[5] The project aims to 'contribute with evidence-based *analytic categories* and a *prospective vision* to the development of policies for teachers' (CEPPE 2011a: 1). The group invited by UNESCO to run this project was composed of five researchers from Brazil, Uruguay, Chile, Mexico and Argentina. This team of experts was in charge of preparing a state-of-the-art report about teachers in the region, elaborating criteria and orientations for teacher policy in the region and organising a regional network of actors with policy-makers and teacher unions.

The group has published many documents related to teacher training, professionalism and career paths, criteria and guidelines for policy development, and their introduction in Latin America and the Caribbean and in teachers' organisations. Some aspects noted in the documents about the region include: the overwhelming predominance of female teachers, particularly in primary schools, with middle- or lower-middle-class backgrounds; the low salaries in comparison with similar professions; the unattractive career paths, in terms of opportunities for professional development and promotion; the low level of performance of entrants to the profession; the poor quality of teaching training programmes; insufficient regulation; and an absence of professional standards and assessments (CEPPE 2011a: 8).

Reflecting these concerns, CEPPE identified a 'critical knot': the tension between a school-centred and an academic approach to training. The main criticism is that university courses in pedagogy discuss theory, involving ideas that are seen to have little utility in improving the quality of education. To overcome this 'problem', they suggest fast and flexible training followed by the creation of a matrix of competencies to guide assessment and 'reform' teacher training. They note that performance is not much considered in the teaching career as it exists in most countries in the region because the decisive criteria for promotion are seniority and qualifications. Besides describing the situation of teachers and their organisations in the region, the team further identified the main challenges and proposed some policy criteria and guidelines for teachers in Latin-American countries aimed at overcoming them. Formulated in general terms, these guidelines demand significant effort if they are to be implemented in the different countries.

The CEPPE guidelines for policies for teachers in Latin America reproduce the recommendations of the IOs in the following ways, suggesting that governments: raise entry requirements; introduce entrance examinations; adopt more practical training based on competencies; implement a new career structure that uses PRP; base promotion on merit and end job stability; put pressure on teachers to improve results; use incentives based on students' results; and adopt certification and new mechanisms of regulation. Regarding teacher remodelling, they recommend changes in the teacher training provided by universities and present two controversial proposals: teacher residency programmes that introduce school-based training focusing upon classroom problems and solutions; and a national curriculum for teacher training in higher education. Those topics are sensitive, raising conflicts with the teacher unions, associations and universities, and these global ideas cannot be easily transferred to Latin-American education settings. Given resistance to these measures, CEPPE recommends that governments should involve teachers and unions in the debate because these groups usually have an important influence in shaping public policies. They argue that successful reforms require agreement between the principal actors – the Ministry of Education, training institutions and unions – about the standards to guide the reform of curriculum and certification. This requires the building of a consensus about 'good teaching' and the definition of standards to assess teacher performance (CEPPE 2011b: 15).

In the next section I analyse some of the activities developed by the experts in order to promote consensus and scrutinise their role as mediators of global policies in national settings.

Experts in Action

Some authors have observed that policy borrowing requires the reshaping of knowledge at the local level (Steiner-Khamsi 2004). Experts are highly qualified to drive that process. An analysis of the activities of CEPPE experts shows a long trajectory of teaching, lectures, consultancy, joint activities and co-publication. Because of their considerable experience of work within universities, research centres, IOs' management units and ministries of education, the experts act as policy advisers and provide capacity building to guarantee the sustainability of education reforms. The OECD also highlights that experts play important roles in terms of mediation, translation and dissemination in policy borrowing/lending process (Fazekas and Burns 2012).

Creplet (2001) distinguishes *consultants* from *experts*. In his analytic model consultants basically work with validated standardised knowledge, based on practical experience: they look for knowledge to solve problems and must meet their clients' expectations. On the other hand, experts create new knowledge. In practice, the boundaries are blurred but experts and consultants do circulate around the globe, join research projects, and attend meetings and conferences transmitting and receiving information. The emergence of this hybrid of expert/consultant and researcher produces changes in politics and in academia. In contrast to consultants, who are usually 'hidden participants' in the policy-making process (Kingdon 1995), experts are in the spotlight. Experts provide 'scientific advice' in political decision-making (Maasen and Weingart 2005) and their visibility and recognition are essential to the acceptance of policies. Evidence-based data combine with their academic legitimacy to develop a particular relationship between experts, policy-makers and the public. This is a symbolic function of expertise, and thus related to knowledge and organisational legitimacy.

The experts who produce alternatives, proposals and solutions also take part in other groups, boards, councils, task forces and networks, gathering information from diverse sectors. In order to provide scientific advice to policy-makers, experts and consultants need to access valuable information about government plans which improve their capacity to understand, analyse, compare and propose. This kind of networking promotes cooperation between 'different social worlds' (Carvalho 2012), which enables synergy and expands the possibilities of lobbying, advocacy and building consensus. Networks promote the know-how and 'know-who' that is essential to identifying the main actors in the policy process and articulating the various knowledges located in different places (Creplet 2001).

In networks, theoretical and practical knowledge from different areas and countries confront one another. Their expertise in researching and dealing with diverse audiences helps the co-production of a new interdisciplinary knowledge and promotes 'learning by interacting' (Crepelet *et al.* 2001). In addition, when working in networks, experts and other actors – IOs, government, NGOs, the media, private foundations, businesspeople, etc. – change one another. They exercise influence and are persuaded by others, which affects the 'content and form' of knowledge production and dissemination. This process affects their work as consultants and as researchers generating consequences in terms of both the production of knowledge 'for policy' and 'about policy' (Sibeon 1998; Ozga 2000).

In 2012, the papers produced by the CEPPE team were published and the experts themselves carried out the crucial function of the diffusion of ideas and proposals. They engaged in conferences, in training activities addressed to different target groups (i.e. teaching staff, school principals and university rectors), they provided technical support visits to the various countries in the region and meetings with their ministries, and participated in national seminars debating the proposals with policy-makers and authorities.

Reproducing the arguments of the IOs, the CEPPE experts argue that the agenda for education in Latin America should involve measures to develop the required competencies in defined times at a reasonable cost. In turn, the definition of costs and priorities demands the evaluation of the initiatives. Based on selective international experience of successful systems, they identified the key elements for national agendas as follows: schooling should begin as early as possible to develop skills in young children; teachers' selection and career progression should be based on student achievements; the leadership role of school principals should be strengthened; the curriculum should be more flexible; and there should be a reduction in 'freedom of choice of schools showing poor results, giving them a well-structured curriculum and support, and controlling their results through systematic evaluations' (Schwartzman and Cox 2009: 16). This proposal to restrict freedom indicates the trend towards heavy regulation of schools. They argue that these changes represent the dominant consensus among experts, but recognise that teachers and unions are resistant and assume that is fundamental to 'respect the adversary' in order to build consensus (Schwartzman and Cox 2009: 25). CEPPE experts highlighted that, historically, reformers in the region have avoided consulting teachers, meaning policies were proposed without the participation of those to be affected by the reforms. However, since 2000 there has been an assumption that education policies cannot succeed without the cooperation of teachers because they resist top-down reforms. Thus, policy-making is based on strategies of consultation and institutionalised through councils and others participatory forums (Palamidessi 2011: 9). The experts stress the necessity of changing national legal frameworks in order to deliver these agendas and advocate those ideas in papers, interviews in the media, newspaper columns, blogs, institutional websites, and conferences where representatives from the state and civil society organisations are debating the requirements for implementation.

This analysis reveals more than the creation of a network of researchers to support the education reforms; it is the constitution of transnational advocacy networks (Mundy 2007). Experts diffuse the ideas of the network in the countries of the region in partnership with the media, NGOs, research centres and private institutions, with the aim being to influence public opinion (Shiroma 2013). However, in parallel, they act as government consultants and support private sector lobbies which try to appoint particular candidates to key posts in the Ministry of Education. Both consultancy and transnational advocacy networks constitute low-visibility mechanisms of soft governance (Lawn 2006), and they are changing education policy in Latin America. The next section examines the attempts to implement these changes in Brazil.

'Teachers for EFA' Developments in Brazil

Brazil is a federation with 26 states and more than 5,560 cities; each of them has its own secretary of education, education system, curriculum, teacher's statutory regulations, salaries and career structures. Teachers in state schools are civil servants recruited by public tender and promoted based on qualifications and seniority. The states and municipalities have the autonomy to establish their education systems following national legislation defined by Congress and regulated by the National Council for Education. According to the WB, this decentralised basic education framework makes Brazil

> a natural laboratory for innovative education policies. Thousands of promising initiatives are launched each year across Brazil. In addition to government efforts, a significant number of private foundations are active in programme development and providing implementation support to states, the federal district, and municipalities.
>
> (WB 2011: 50).

IOs also develop projects and partnerships with some state governments, and international experts have an extensive agenda in Brazil including research meetings, interviews, lectures and consultancy to the Ministry of Education, secretaries of education of states and municipalities, and institutions of teacher training, among others. In these ways, international recommendations regarding policies for teachers have reverberated in the country.

In the last two decades, systematic attacks have been made on the university system of teacher training by experts who then promoted international recommendations for remodelling teacher training and careers. Other measures recommended by IOs such as performance assessment, the entrance examination and periodic re-certification have been implemented in Brazil. In 2006, the National Council of Education redefined the guidelines for teacher training curriculum and, in 2009, the Ministry of Education created a postgraduate Professional Masters Course in Education. These controversial proposals were promoted by CEPPE experts at major education events in 2011 to 2013 in Brazil, and were supported by private foundations, research centres and edu-business people. At these events, the Minister of Education, the National Institute of Pedagogical Research, the representatives of the councils of education, and the secretaries of education of states and municipalities are invited to speak and are exposed to the analysis and arguments of these international experts. An interesting example of their effects is the case of a secretary of education who, convinced by the speakers at a conference, declared that she would herself suggest to the Minister of Education the necessity of revising the current curriculum guidelines for courses of pedagogy and teacher training because they were not adequate to prepare teachers (Galvão 2008). This transmutation of an international recommendation to a proposal by a Secretary of State shows the active reception process and the outcome of active consensus building. As well as lectures and conferences, experts give interviews, provide courses for teachers and secretaries of education, and write materials – papers, policy briefs, books, etc. – which are used in teacher training in Brazil. They are engaged in regional networks and projects related to education reforms and in projects based in private institutions to reform public education. In sum, experts perform important functions in the internalisation and indigenisation process (Phillips and Ochs 2004), especially in relation to the diffusion of policy ideas and in influencing policy-making in national settings.

Many of the guidelines proposed by CEPPE experts for reforming teachers' policies are being implemented in Brazil, although most are facing strong resistance from teacher unions. Conflicts of interest emerge that reveal the importance of the 'transferability' issue. For example, in 2008, the creation of a national minimum salary for teachers was approved by the Brazilian Congress and defined by law. States or municipalities which could show that they could not afford the increased costs could apply for complementary funding from central government, and this was welcomed by the unions. However, at that time, six states refused to pay the national minimum salary and faced strong opposition in the form of long-lasting strikes. Currently, ten states do not pay the salary defined by the Ministry of Education, while some of them are trying to implement policies such as teacher assessment and PRP.

The principles of performativity and effective schooling have been implemented by the Brazilian Ministry of Education through the School Development Plan based on students' performance in national tests. In 2005, the central government implemented a national test called *Prova Brasil*, for evaluating the achievements of students at the end of primary and secondary education. The results of each school are published every two years and used to calculate the school's index of basic education development (IDEB) and the average of all schools' indexes in a city generates the IDEB of the city[6] and states. The target is to achieve a rating of 6.0, which expresses the quality of education in OECD countries, by 2015. This external assessment has forced some schools to adapt their curricula and introduce special classes to prepare students for this examination.

Poor results represented by a low index alarm the local authorities. For example, in 2007, the IDEB rating of Florianópolis led the secretary of education of that capital to create its own student examination, *Prova Floripa*, aimed at evaluating elementary and high-school student learning in a different way. Hence, in this city, students of municipal schools are submitted to two different annual external evaluations: one from the central government and another local one. The results of each student can be assessed in a database and function as a management tool for education managers implementing accountability. In 2011, a letter exposing the names of teachers with poor results was sent to all municipal schools of that city, causing embarrassment, shame and anger. Unions protested against the indignity. The local secretary of education published a clarification note explaining that the move was in fact an error.

As we can see, evaluations are source of conflict between teachers and principals, local and central government and unions. However, contradictorily, evaluations can also produce closeness between government and unions. In 2012, the ministers of education of Mercosul discussed PISA and the necessity of developing regional indicators to evaluate the quality of education in South America. In that meeting, the minister of Argentina argued that PISA compares incomparable realities: 'We are part of the group of countries that have found a more sovereign [i.e. independent] position to incorporate our own thoughts'. He suggested that South America countries should adopt shared criteria for evaluating education, including areas neglected by PISA. Union representatives participated in this meeting. Here the tensions related to performance comparisons at international level have produced a joint action on the part of teachers' unions and governments. The uncomfortable experience of being compared and doubts about the assessment criteria were felt by teachers, by secretaries and also by ministers of education, who thus decided to create regional indicators of evaluation.

Conclusion

Comparing CEPPE guidelines for teachers' policies with international recommendations and attempts at their implementation in Brazil, a complex process of harmonisation, translation and adaptation is revealed, serving the active reception of the global agenda. Despite the similarities in discourse – which express the movement of ideas – the analysis of the implementation of these policies demonstrated divergence, the resistance of social actors, disputes and adaptations, thus revealing that the policies that constitute ideas in movement are indeed reshaped in national settings.

Working in strategic areas – research, dissemination, advocacy and capacity development – experts act as mediators and have vital functions in the process of knowledge mobilisation, coproduction and reproduction. Bridging research and politics, experts and consultants are concerned with both agenda setting and implementation. More than the elaboration of proposals, their tasks involve influencing parliamentarians and decision-makers.

The crucial role played by experts in education reforms goes beyond the operational matter of designing policies and implementing methods. They do more than disseminate ideas: they develop the knowledge that produces conceptual change. Thereafter, experts act as active participants in the process of the indigenisation of policies. Beyond defining goals and strategies and designing policy plans, the networks of experts develop meanings, methods, interpretations and commitments. The process of producing and disseminating 'knowledge for policy' constitutes a key resource for building the consensus needed in governing.

The findings of this research reveal interesting questions about the content and form of the policy knowledge produced and disseminated by experts, as well as its constitution as a key resource for governing. However, this policy knowledge and its forms of production may have damaging consequences for the intellectual autonomy of new teachers and those who they will teach. The contradictions inherent in these new knowledge-based forms of governing education that are revealed here but eclipsed in the global agendas offer scope for future research.

Notes

1 The analyses that follow are based on the research project 'Policy Networks and Governance in Education', funded by CNPq-Brazil. I am very grateful to Jenny Ozga for her comments on earlier versions of this chapter.
2 Mercosul is an economic and political agreement established in 1991 between Argentina, Brazil, Paraguay, Uruguay, Venezuela and Bolivia.
3 http://www.teachersforefa.unesco.org/resources/All/Concept%20note_Bali_9%20Sept.pdf
4 The EFA High-Level Group brought together high-level representatives from national governments, development agencies, UN agencies, civil society and the private sector. Its role was to generate political momentum and mobilise financial, technical and political support towards the achievement of the EFA goals and the education-related Millennium Development Goals.
5 Cristián Cox, director of CEPPE, ex-Vice Minister of Education in Chile, consultant of OECD, IADB, WB and member of PREAL, was appointed leader of the UNESCO 'Technical Secretariat of the Regional Strategy of Teachers' for Latin America and the Caribbean.
6 The average of cities indexes generates the state IDEB and the average of all indexes creates the national IDEB.

References

Bruns , B., Filmer, D. and Patrinos, H.A. (2011) *Making Schools Work: New Evidence on Accountability Reforms*. Washington, DC: The World Bank.

Bruns, B., Evans, D. and Luque, J. (2012) *Achieving World-Class Education in Brazil: The Next Agenda*. Washington, DC: The World Bank.

Carvalho, L.M. (2012) 'The fabrications and travels of a knowledge-policy instrument'. *European Educational Research Journal* 11(2): 172–189.

CEPPE (2011a) *Estado da arte sobre políticas docentes na América Latina e Caribe*. [State of the art of teacher policies in Latin America and the Caribbean]. Santiago: CEPPE.

CEPPE (2011b) *Critérios e orientações para a elaboração de politicas docentes na região da América Latina e Caribe*. [Criteria and guidelines for the preparation of teachers policies in the region of Latin America and the Caribbean]. Santiago: CEPPE.

Cox, C., Beca, C.E. and Cerri, M. (2011) *Nueva agenda de Politicas docentes en America Latina y el Caribe: nudos críticos y critérios de accion*. [New educational policies agenda in Latin America and the Caribbean: Critical knots and criteria for action.] CEPPE-UC. Orealc /UNESCO Santiago. http://www.orealc.cl/informe-ept-2011/wp-content/blogs.dir/5/files_mf/nuevaagendaesp3web.pdf [accessed 13 October 2012]

Creplet, F., Dupouet, O., Kern, F., Mehmanpazir, B. and Munier, F. (2001) 'Consultants and experts in management consulting firms', *Research Policy*, 30(9): 1517–1535.

Fazekas, M. and Burns, T. (2012) *Governance and Knowledge*. Paris: OECD.

Galvão, F. (2008) 'Professores: vítimas ou culpados pela má educação?' [Teachers: victims or guilty of bad education], CGC Educação, São Paulo, 14 October. http://www.cgceducacao.com.br/canal.php?c=1&a=9947&i=0.

Kingdon, J. (1995) *Agendas, Alternatives and Public Policies*. New York: Harper Collins.

Lawn, M. (2006) 'Soft governance and the learning spaces of Europe', *Comparative European Politics*, 4: 272–288.

Maasen, S. and Weingart, P. (2005) *Democratization of Expertise? Exploring Novel Forms of Scientific Advice in Political Decision-Making*. Dordrecht : Springer.

Mundy, K. (2007) 'Education for All: Paradoxes and prospects of a global promise', in D.P. Baker and A.W. Wiseman (eds) *Education for All* (*International Perspectives on Education and Society*, Vol. 8). Bingley: Emerald Group Publishing Limited, pp. 1–30.

Nordstrum, L. E. (2013) 'A Sisyphean Complex? Economic and costs constraints in filling teachers quantity and quality gaps', in B. Moon (ed.) *Teacher Education and the Challenge of Development: A Global Analysis*. London: Routledge.

OECD (2005) *Teachers Matter: Attracting, Developing and Retaining Effective Teachers*. Paris: OECD.

Ozga, J. (2000) *Policy Research in Educational Settings: Contested Terrain*. Buckingham: Open University Press.

Ozga, J., Dahler-Larsen, P., Segerholm, C. and Simola, H. (eds) (2011) *Fabricating Quality in Education: Data and Governance in Europe*. London: Routledge.

Palamidessi, M. (2011) *Teacher Organisations*. Santiago: CEPPE.

Phillips, D. and Ochs, K. (2004) *Educational Policy Borrowing: Historical Perspectives*. Didcot: Symposium Books.

Schwartzman, S. and Cox, C. (2009) 'Las agendas pendientes d e la educación', in S. Schwartzman and C. Cox (eds) *Políticas educativas y cohesión social en América Latina*. [Educational policy and social cohesion in Latin America.] Santiago: Uqbar Editores.

Shiroma, E.O. (2013 under review) 'Networks in action: new actors and practices on education policy in Brazil', *Journal of Education Policy*.

Sibeon, R. (1998) *Contemporary Sociology and Policy Analysis. The New Sociology of Public Policy*. Eastham, Merseyside: Tudor.

Steiner-Khamsi, G. (2004). *The Global Politics of Educational Borrowing and Lending*. New York: Teachers College Press.

UNESCO (2011) *Guidelines of Global Teachers for EFA*. http://www.teachersforefa.unesco.org/resources/All/Concept20%note_Bali_9%20Sept.pdf [accessed 14 March 2013]

Vegas, E. (2011) *Saber- Teachers. Objectives, Rationale, Methodological Approach, and Products*. The World Bank Education Team, Human Development Department. http://siteresources.worldbank.org/EDUCATION/Resources/278200-1290520949227/7575842-1290520985992/SABER-Teachers_Framework.pdf [accessed 14 March 2013]

Whitman, J. (2009) *Palgrave Advances in Global Governance*. Basingstoke: Palgrave Macmillan.

World Bank (2011) *Learning for All. Investing in People's Knowledge and Skills to Promote Development*. Education Strategy 2020, Washington, DC: World Bank Group.

8 The Role of Knowledge in Scientific Policy Advice

Doing Knowledge

Alma Demszky and Armin Nassehi

Introduction

This chapter is about the role of knowledge in scientific policy advice. It is based on a particular perspective – that of Luhmanian system theory, and works with the idea that the social world is differentiated: that is it is made of distinct systems of communication. Drawing on this theoretical resource, we develop an argument that contrasts the functioning of political communication with that of scientific communication. More specifically, we seek to highlight and explain the process of translation that any message is subjected to when used across these distinct systems. We identify the type of function that scientific communication plays in policy systems, and we argue that scientific knowledge and policy-making are basically incommensurable, because science and policy in a functionally differentiated modern society belong to two different spheres: they follow their own norms, routines and claims to plausibility in their practice. The logic of knowledge production in the sphere of science is a logic of debating, doubting and rejecting knowledge claims. Thus, we suggest that science can never explore the final truth of the world – if this were the case, science would come to an end.

In our view, policy-making obeys a diametrically opposed logic. Policy is a practice of making visible and identifiable decisions that are supposed to change the social world. In such a context, the admission of doubt is fatal– a politician has always to be convinced of his or her position. Scientific policy advice tries to connect these two worlds with their different logics, so conflicts and misconceptions are inevitable. Yet despite this fundamental incongruity, scientific experts advise on policy and public decision-making appears to be more and more dependent on scientific evidence. Science legitimizes policy solutions in the way that tradition and religion used to do. Policy needs science – but their relationship is problematic.

In this chapter, we support our arguments through empirical findings drawn from the research project 'Knowledge and Policy' (KNOWandPOL).[1] These findings show convincingly the genuinely active aspect of knowledge in relation to policy: knowledge does not appear in the analysis as theoretical, but as practical as is any other form of social practice. This practicality is captured by our use of the term 'doing knowledge' which we discuss further below.

'Doing Knowledge' as a term does not refer mainly to a new definition or theory. Rather it is the result of empirical evidence of the changing role of knowledge in policy-making processes. As Karin Knorr Cetina emphasizes, it is an error to consider only the content and the substantial ideas of concrete knowledge forms. She argues that new knowledge-based practices can only be understood when social science is 'interested in the empirical question of how knowledge was produced' (Knorr Cetina 2007: 362). She does not have in mind the validity or the truth of knowledge but the practical aspects of how something gets understood *as* knowledge. This perspective is part of a 'demystification of science' (Reichmann 2011) in which ideals of 'truth' and of 'the autonomy of science' give way to 'social negotiations' (Evans 1999) and to practices of the condensation of knowledge. It may be, as Helmut Willke puts it, that in a knowledge society the relevance of knowledge rises while the relevance of the scientific system diminishes (Willke 2002). Knowledge in a differentiated society may become a problem instead of a solution, because knowledge gets trapped increasingly in problems of relevance and legitimacy due to clashing system rationalities (Engelhardt and Kajetzke 2010).

Knowledge – at least that knowledge relevant for making policy – is practice. But because of specific system rationalities, scientific or expert knowledge has to change its format when entering the world of politics. Put briefly, it has to expunge all doubts and take on the guise of unequivocal, mostly binary-coded arguments: yes or no, pro or contra, good or bad. The translation process of scientific knowledge into political arguments is one instance of the countless practices of 'Doing Knowledge'. This task is carried out by specialists called 'translators' who oscillate between the worlds of science and politics.

Defining Knowledge as Doing Knowledge

In the Western tradition, dealing with the difference between the object and subject of knowledge is the decisive problem. Even Plato distinguishes *episteme* from *doxa*, that is knowledge from meaning. The first is infallible and true, the second only plausible and therefore fallible. The most famous version of this distinction is Immanuel Kant's *Critique of Pure Reason* (Kant 2010). Kant distinguishes three modes of mentally representing reality: *meaning*, *believing* and *knowing*. Kant evaluates meaning as both subjectively and objectively inadequate. It can neither satisfy an objective examination, nor can it be subjectively appropriate. In the end, meaning is knowledge by pure chance. Belief is also objectively inadequate, but it is subjectively adequate as it stands for an authentic decision. Finally, knowledge is both objectively and subjectively adequate. Here Kant stresses the difficult issue of whether knowledge is a representation of the world with objective certainty for everyone. In this tradition the object that becomes represented by knowledge is imagined as an observed reality independent of the observer. The idea that knowledge is more a construct of the subject than an objective reality emerges in several theories of the twentieth century. One of the first sociologists of science, Robert K. Merton, identified science as an institution of a shared set of values and norms (Merton 1938). Kuhn introduced the notion of paradigm in science as an agreement concerning the rules of scientific praxis and as an outcome of the negotiation on social standards (Kuhn 1962).

Common to these approaches is a conceptualization of knowledge as a special representation of the world, a communicative form in which the content is claimed to be scientifically true. In knowledge societies (Stehr 1994) something can be used as knowledge if it is able to present itself not as a mere opinion but as objectivity. The legitimation of knowledge usually happens through institutionalization and scientification, and the role of knowledge for all fields of society, from everyday life to economics and politics is becoming vitally influential (Drucker 1993; Reichmann 2011). Knowledge communication gets attributed not only to the speaker but to something which exists independently of the speaker. Something works as knowledge when it asserts something about the 'real world'. At the same time the communication of knowledge creates the reality to which it refers, as MacKenzie and Millo put it with reference to academic economics: 'Economics does not describe an external "economy", but brings that economy into being: economics performs the economy, creating the phenomena it describes' (MacKenzie and Millo 2003: 108).

Knowledge creates the world which it claims to describe. It is a form of social practice just like any other kind of practice. 'Knowledge is constitutively social' (MacKenzie 1981: 225). Knowledge is that which works as knowledge. As Law puts it, knowledge practices

> become sustainable only if they are able to create knowledge (theories, data, whatever) that *work*, that somehow or other hold together, that are convincing and (crucial this) do whatever job is set for them. But then secondly and counterintuitively, they have to be able to *generate realities* that are fit for that knowledge.
> (Law 2009: 240 emphasis in original)

Knowledge is a form of praxis where the validity of knowledge is not a question of 'truth' but of practices of the social world summarized as 'connectivity'. Connectivity in this context means that other speakers or actors can connect to a speech act acknowledging its status as knowledge. The decisive criterion of knowledge therefore is its social success (Nassehi 2005). The notion of connectivity resembles what Knorr Cetina calls 'selectivity' inherent to science as an outcome of social negotiations situated in time and space rather than referring to universal rules. She points to 'indeterminacy and to contextual contingency – rather than non-local universality – as inherent in scientific procedure' (Knorr Cetina 1981: 152). The assertion that knowledge is a special communicative form in which the content is claimed to be true might be read at first sight as contradicting our earlier argument. However, we follow Niklas Luhmann (1990), who understands knowledge as a cognitive stylization of communication (1990: 138). For Luhmann, knowledge is a social reality which realizes itself within communication (Luhmann 1990: 68). This also means that scientific knowledge does not have real contact with reality, because it is itself a reality. Luhmann is not interested in the question of how to define knowledge or to sum up criteria which can characterize a special form of awareness or cognition as knowledge. His focus is on the question of how communication processes assume something to be knowledge. Knowledge, he says, is 'an implication of the communication process itself, a permanent assumption .... Like structures of language, knowledge has to be processed as an assumption and cannot be made completely explicit within the communication' (Luhmann 1990: 122; our translation).

Thus, for Luhmann, knowledge is unavoidable in communication, because all communication has to assume the idea of a shared knowledge about the world.

Communication always permits cognitive assumptions about knowledge. Knowledge therefore is not the precondition of communication and shared meanings. On the contrary: it is communication that produces knowledge implicitly and practically. What can be regarded as knowledge then, is a result, not a precondition of communication – that is true both for the implicit stock of knowledge and explicit forms of thematized claims for knowledge. But in both cases, the question of the truth of knowledge is a question of the praxis of communication. Both explicit and implicit forms of knowledge are dependent on the practical conditions of success. Knowledge therefore cannot exist beyond the practice in which it occurs. As Luhmann puts it, knowledge can be regarded as a 'condensation of observations' (Luhmann 1990: 123) – in other words, as a practical result of cognitive operations within communication systems. Knowledge therefore can be approached empirically only as 'Doing Knowledge'.

The proof of knowledge is, within this perspective, its practical success, dependent on the particular context and environment. This practical success is dependent on cultural prerequisites, constellations of power, on routines and tacit habits. Counter-intuitively and in contrast to naïve everyday expectation there is no fundamental epistemological difference between scientific and non-scientific knowledge, at least concerning the conditions of practical success. In both cases knowledge has to find its proof not outside or beyond its practice, but within its own social environment. The practice of knowledge creation within the scientific field is not more closely related to a 'reality' outside its practice than everyday knowledge – but it is able to observe itself as a practice of what we call *doing knowledge*. In Luhmann's language, the only difference between scientific knowledge and other forms of everyday knowledge is that scientific knowledge observes itself in terms of knowledge (Luhmann 1990: 192).

Laypersons are sometimes disappointed or surprised by the inability of scientific knowledge to provide more certainty than everyday knowledge and that there exist different versions of scientific knowledge about a given subject. However, the practice of scientific knowledge-making is a practice of bargaining, of competitive assertions and of battles for hegemony (Bourdieu 1975: 20). Such practices, as Bourdieu has shown for several fields of society, including science, are only possible because scientific knowledge does not produce a singular version of truth. The battle for hegemony is a specific practice to overcome the problem of different and contradictory truths. Therefore the sociology of scientific knowledge differs from a philosophical or epistemological perspective as it emphasizes the practical 'construction of scientific facts' (Latour and Woolgar 1986). The question then is not whether a particular statement is true or false, but whether or not it is acknowledged in a particular situation as knowledge. This is always an empirical and not a theoretical question.

Policy in a Functionally Differentiated Modern Society

The theory of public action as an explanation of policy-making in contemporary conditions stresses the multitude of actors involved in public decisions and de-centres the role of the state. Policy is no longer understood as top-down regulation but as involving a complexity of actors in different public and local arenas, conflicting and collaborating in the construction and shaping of the social world:

Faced with a vision based on giving precedence to governmental initiatives, State actions, and the actions of public authorities, by turning the concept on its head, we indicate the choice of an approach whereby the actions of the State institutions and multiple actors, both public and private, from civil society and the State arena, work together, with various interdependencies, at a national level but also locally and possibly at a supranational level, to produce regulatory structures for collective activities.

(Commaille 2004: 413)

In this approach, scientific knowledge has two different functions. On the one hand it can help to define problems, issues, and goals in fields of action. On the other, it is used as a tool to legitimize and defend practical interventions and to give them a special kind of power. This working definition implies a distinction that resonates with the idea of a functionally differentiated society.

To describe modern society as functionally differentiated is commonplace in some sociological theories of modern society (Alexander 1990; Colomy 1990; Luhmann 1997; Nassehi 2003, 2006, 2011; Chernilo 2002; Buzan and Albert 2010). According to this perspective modern societies are differentiated into functional subsystems that operate within their own logics. Acting in politics, economy, science, religion and art requires different logics of practice and different criteria of success. In everyday situations or even in organizations these different logics of action clash with one another and generate conflicts. Critics of functional differentiation attack the concept as being only a theoretical framework that hints at the coming together of different logics within the same situation (cf. Knorr Cetina 1992, 2000; Lindemann 2002, 2006, 2008). However, we argue that it is exactly the conflict of different logics of practice within the same situation that substantiates the existence of different fields of practice (cf. Nassehi 2005, 2006, 2011). What we want to emphasize is this: from the perspective of the theory of functional differentiation we have a theoretical and methodological tool to better understand the conflicts and the different orientations of actors in the field of public policy. A more scientific and a more political and practical decision-making orientation are the two triggers that bring public action into being. Hence knowledge and policy are different sources which have to be understood as an outcome of a functionally differentiated society. The differentiation of modern society in functional subsystems and in different spheres of practice was observed empirically at different points in the research by the German KNOWandPOL team. The short extracts below provide some examples of the evidence we found in the course of our analysis.

We have noted that the project KNOWandPOL dealt with basically different entities obeying different logics, and that the connection of these two worlds can therefore never be without conflict. One source of conflict is that policy is expected to rule fields other than political ones. Policy can handle only political formats – but citizens expect from politics the solution of all problems appearing in the social world, from education through economics to health. Policy-makers often experience this conflict vividly, and report on the resistance of particular fields to policy intervention, for example, in the quotation below, an advisor in the German Ministry of Health preparing the 2007 reform of the health-care system reports on the resistance of the private health funds to the attempts of policy-makers to regulate this field:

And even the reform of the private sickness funds was highly contested and they went much further in this reform than ever before, to regulate in this field, with all its own interests; it was hitherto unheard for them to intervene so strongly.

(I2: 415[2])

The formulation 'to regulate *in* this field' clearly illustrates the striving for independence of the particular fields, their resistance to control from outside, and the irritation in cases of intervention through politics.

The need for 'Translation' between different spheres of society

There is pressure for the legitimation of policy-making from outside the field, which creates many new problems. 'Scientization' reveals the need for legitimization through science at all levels of the social, on the individual, organizational and governmental level. The problem of legitimation is no longer solved through traditional means like religion, but through the myth of the rationality of scientific knowledge. Decisions both individual and governmental have to be backed by scientific expertise (Drori *et al.* 2003). This is often discussed in terms of a scientification of politics and policies and a politicization of science. In recent years, the emergence of Mode 2 epistemology (Hellstrom and Merle 2000) can be regarded as a response to a new border regime between politics and science. As mentioned above, cooperation between science and policy is not unproblematic, mutual disappointment on all sides is not unusual. We argue that misunderstanding and disappointment are not the result of failed communication but originate in the very nature of functionally differentiated modern societies. The different logics demand a translation process of contents when travelling from one sphere of society (in this case: science) to another (policy). The way in which this translation process proceeds will be outlined in the next section.

Knowledge in Policy: External Legitimation and Mutual Disappointment

In complex societies with democratic political systems political decisions and policy-making cannot be based on traditions and on unchallengeable stocks of knowledge. As Nico Stehr puts it, we can talk about a knowledge society precisely because knowledge has become less secure. He underlines the fragility of modern societies concerning their approach to decisions and knowledge routines (Stehr 2001). This fragility contributes to pressure towards 'evidence-based policy' and using 'best practice'. Legitimation of policy through parliamentary elections seems to need a supplement from other sources of legitimacy, which do not have a political format. One source of additional legitimacy is the support of policy decisions by expert scientific knowledge (Stehr 1994; Weingart 2001). Science has an aura of objectivity due to its cognitive stylization. In addition, decisions based on scientific insights are assumed to serve the general public and not particular interests, because the cognitive style of scientific knowledge can present itself as objective knowledge.

Ideas like 'evidence-based policy', 'knowledge-based regulation tools', 'knowledge society'(Stehr *et al.* 2009; Davies *et al.* 2000) deal with the problem of basing policy-making on 'facts' instead of beliefs and ideas in a more or less critical manner. Research promotion at supra-national level, for instance by the EU or OECD, is committed to the idea that enhancing research on policy and society will lead to 'better' solutions and the exchange between science and policy is only a question of better communication. Because of this expectation that differences and misunder-standings can be overcome through enhanced communication, researchers are exhorted to present their findings in 'easily readable, understandable und usable' forms (European Commission 2009: p. 10). The EU expects to produce knowledge from publicly funded research that will be useful for policy-making (Commission Staff Working Document 2007), reflecting the imperative that 'policy-makers and programme funders need to be clear from the beginning of the kinds of result they expect from the research they fund' (Nightingale and Scott 2007).

The growing tendency towards externalization in the justification of policies and towards 'scientification of politics' (Offe 1984) is experienced in many policy fields all over the world (Steiner-Khamsi 2003; Berenyi and Neumann 2009). Externalization 'functions as the last source of authority and it is invoked after self-reference falls short of its objectives' (Steiner-Khamsi 2003: 2). Decision-makers look for evidence to justify their actions: they seek 'ready-made and easy to sell evidence' (Berenyi and Neumann 2009). The public sphere and policy-makers mostly implicitly but some-times even explicitly raise the expectation that impartial and interest-free science should show the way to the 'correct' solutions to societal problems. Even politicians largely maintain the vision of science as a resource for impartial and objective knowl-edge able to support political decisions. Here an advisor in the German Ministry of Health explains that expert reports and research contracted by the government can support political decisions, because those research findings do not serve particular interests, but the interests of the public:

> For us of course all the reports, expert advice and statements that we our-selves provide or commission are relevant and important first of all. Because these are ordinarily, and there are exceptions here, not interest-oriented in the sense that they are supposed to get the best results for a certain association, but rather they attempt to pursue the public interest, to find the best solution and not a solution dominated by interests.
>
> (I2: 363)

The advisor quoted above refers to the possibility of finding 'the *best* solution' through the involvement of expert advice. As we will see later, policy-makers are very much aware of the problems of cooperation between science and politics and do not usually draw such an idealistic picture of expert advice. What we can see here is the pressure to satisfy the expectation of basing political decisions on expert knowledge – and through this, the expectation of the public that the best possible solution for all problems will be found. Although the naivety of this expectation is obvious, this mostly unspoken expectation is the reason for disappointment – on the part of politicians, citizens, the public sphere, and experts. Experts express their disappointment that their advice has not been implemented completely in the course of decision-making. For example, a member of a non-governmental organization describes his team's involvement in the legislative process and their disappointment at the end result: 'And then we brought in our ideas. And they were of course not all adopted by the ministry of education. And when it was finished, we said, well, we're somewhat disappointed' (I23: 442).

Both experts and citizens are often disappointed that although they are involved in the legislative process, their knowledge and experiences are not reflected to the same extent in the new regulations. Politicians, on the contrary, claim that experts are incapable of giving manageable advice for their decisions. In their view, scientists live somewhere in a world of ideas and theories, which do not fit to the complexity of reality, as this example of a state secretary's comments about scientists in general shows: 'And with some of them you get the impression that they really more or less live at the theoretical drawing board or in the ivory tower' (I13: 203).

Our analysis shows that this mutual disappointment is a misunderstanding which stems from the basic structure of a functionally differentiated society. We can, without exaggeration, term this an ontological misunderstanding. The importing of knowledge into policy cannot work without problems. Scientific insights can neither present the 'best' solution for a given problem nor set the agenda for policy-making. The first element in making policy remains the 'political will' to act; the knowledge of experts takes second place. In our interviews we asked a secretary of state whether or not new scientific insights could set the agenda for political decisions. The answer was, 'No, it definitely comes from politics, from social debates, without a doubt. But science and experts can make an important contribution, by giving the issue its contours (I5: 13–15).

Science can provide only the framing of topics and ideas to clarify political discussion. The perspectives of the different functional systems may react to the same semantic challenges on the same topics in public debates. But they react in fundamentally different ways. Functional differentiation in modern societies can be observed empirically through a particular kind of social order characterized by the limitation of interdependencies. Thus the idea of society as a whole, as a space of shared values regulated by political leaders, is deconstructed by the experience of practical multi-perspectivity: society appears differently because of the point of view from which it is observed (Nassehi 2011: 123–158).

In any attempted cooperation between political decision-makers and experts or even citizens there is a fundamental experience: they seem not to understand one another. To put it more sociologically: the political system is not able to handle any problems in non-political format, for example economic, scientific or medical realities. Political decision-makers are well aware of the limits of cooperation between science and politics and of the basically different way of functioning of these fields. Here is an illustration from a policy-maker:

> We want to make politics, we don't want to comment on scientific publications, right? This is a very basic question, and if we want to make politics then we do it according to our programme. [. . .] And we have to make politics actively, which means we have to try to realise these points. We

don´t wait until some university has written something and then start to make politics, but rather we have our central topics and around these topics we are searching for, if it makes sense, some professional assistance.

(I3: 321)

In a functionally differentiated modern society the relationship between the political and other parts of society, such as science, is a relationship that can be characterized as transformation of non-political contents into political semantics and language. We suggest that this transformation may be captured in the idea of translation.

Doing Translation

Translation, in our view, is never simple transfer. As linguistic and social sciences or ethnography have highlighted for decades, the translated content is re-interpreted in the new context in which it is compiled – first it is de-contextualized, than re-contextualized. The modern approach to translation breaks with romantic ideas of translation as an act of 'fidelity' that transports the 'foreign' into the familiar (Humboldt 1909; Herder 1990; Buden and Nowotny 2009). By the 1990s at the latest, the binary opposition between the 'original' and the 'translation' was disrupted, and translation was no longer seen as a transfer of content (Benjamin 1992). Translation was rather compared to the image of a tangent that touches a circle: they meet at one point and thereafter go their separate ways (ibid.). Parallel to this the social and objective context of translation became more and more important in the course of the so-called 'social turn' of translation studies: 'There is always a context in which the translation takes place, always a history from which a text emerges and into which a text is transported' (Bassnett and Lefevre 1990: 11).

From this point, translation is considered a 'socially regulated activity' (Hermans 2007) and a 'social practice' (Freeman 2009; Wolf 2007; Hermans 2007), which creates its own criteria of plausibility – as a form of 'rewriting' (Lefevre 1998), of 'invention' or 'construction' (Wolf 2007). In the course of the 'social turn' the social contexts, and not only language and culture, but also social relations, institutions, inequality and power, came into consideration. The variety of contexts comes into view, as well as the different rules for producing meaning and legitimacy which are not reciprocally representable (Geertz 1993).

Different contexts do not exist in harmony with one another, rather they must be linked with one another– and this is done not by 'translators' – people who oscillate between contexts. Nor can social scientists observe society and the translation between its different contexts from the outside, because 'we are always already translating when we start to think of translating' (Fuchs 2009: 25).

The project KNOWandPOL pointed to two substantial elements of translating from science to policy: first we can show scientific or expert knowledge becoming political argument, and second we uncovered the relevance of the actors (persons or institutions) doing the practice of translation. Below, we discuss how content changes in the movement of science to policy, and we then highlight the role of the actors we call 'translators'.

Translating Knowledge into Arguments

The need for scientific legitimation of political decisions, the 'scientification of politics' (Offe 1984), creates new problems for both science and politics. It is not as easy to make evidence-based policy as it sounds. A scientist we interviewed summarized the practice of making science as follows:

> So we always try to question that which is considered true. That's scientific progress. Scientific progress is, as we all know from Popper, the garbage heap of refuted truths. That is to say if something could be true, if we could produce truths, there wouldn't be science anymore, science would come to an end.
>
> (I38: 563)

Rejecting everything that is thought to be true is the main logic of making science. But as the interviewee goes on to say: 'such a way of thinking is of course fatal for a political system. One would never come to a decision' (ibid.). While science is debating and doubting, policy is making decisions. Policy-makers have to present themselves as undoubting deciders. The desire to pull science into the field of making policy is quite a paradoxical move. When scientific knowledge has a role in political decision-making, it has to change its format: knowledge has to become argument. This transformation does not happen at once, but bit by bit. In travelling from science to policy-making, knowledge changes its format through innumerable acts of translation. The first step in this transformation is described below by an expert from an institution dedicated to advising policy-makers: 'We received Professor Mandl to our facilities and said, so, how does one get from knowing to doing? What are the most up-to-date, best methods? What do you recommend?' (I42: 165).

Getting from 'knowing' to 'doing' conveys the process of transforming formats from theoretical knowledge into knowledge that is able to steer particular forms of practice. The first step of the transformation process begins with the question: How? Scientific knowledge is complex, it reflects the circumstances of its making and the limits of its validity. Making policy cannot reference all the complexities of reality, it has to make universally valid decisions. So a key process is the reduction of the complexity of scientific knowledge. As a scientist also working as a political advisor puts it:

> The answer has to be: yes, because! or: no, because! That is, you have to give an answer and subsume all the knowledge, which you would otherwise use to weigh for and against, under your decision. That is, you have to learn the decisional style. This has nothing to do with scientific intellectuality or meticulousness, but rather the task is to reduce complexity. And with an academic style you don't reduce complexity, there you expand the complexity, but that's not very helpful.
>
> (I38: 650)

In this scenario, scientific expert advice plays the role of making decisions visible and memorable. A decision which is not noteworthy as a decision is not viable in the political world. The scientific backing of a decision is thought to give the decision a legitimate appearance. But this scientific knowledge has to remove itself from its original format and take on the format of a politically practicable argument. An MP explains the way he gets information from his own facilitators:

> [A]t least to prepare the information in such a way, so partly also to write a summary or highlight it, then you throw 30 pages away because 'this is the decisive point,' and the delegates rely upon the important point actually being filtered out.
>
> (I42: 378)

Members of parliament or advisors in ministries rely on people who identify the two key pages of an expert opinion of over 300 pages. They need people who 'know' for them: 'to have a wonderful intern, who reads the 300 pages [laughs], and then tells me which parts I have to look at' (I42: 357).

Other researchers from the KNOWandPOL project made the same observation, about how the results of national or international enquiries, like PISA, are presented to the political audience:

> The results are then presented on press conferences and at high level meetings where statistical evidence leaves the scientific domain and gets translated to the easily digestible narrative of competition: the national average scores are presented in the 'league table of the nations.'
>
> (Berenyi and Neumann 2009: 44)

The quotation above introduces another easily practicable format besides yes or no, the logic of less or more: tables reducing the complex education system of a nation to a simple rank order declaring the Finnish education system to be better than the German are of practical use in political argumentation:

> The ranking and the league-tables of OECD – and IEA – type studies constitute a measurable and easily accessible, albeit often biased and abbreviated form of 'scientific rationality', which enables political stakeholders in education to appeal to the general public when planning or suspending a comprehensive reform.
>
> (Steiner-Khamsi 2003: 2)

Translators

Translating actors are either singular experts moving between different spheres of society, or institutions specializing in this task, for example in advising the research institutes of ministries. Translating experts play a very important role within the ministries themselves; they personally build bridges between scientific expert knowledge and decision-making, they prepare regulations and laws and advise ministers and state secretaries. These translators can fill the 'political will' of policy-makers with content. An expert doing this job describes his task as follows: 'My task really is at the interface between the executive and making the policy evidence based. The scientific foundation' (I19: 139).

These translators feel that they themselves and the environment they occupy is somewhere 'between' different worlds. The sociological idea of functional differentiation is most clearly apparent at system borders: people travelling between worlds, belonging to neither and where both are perceived as peculiar. Descriptions such as this are very numerous in our data: 'Professor Lauterbach is interesting, he's at the half-way point, on the one hand he is a scientist, on the other hand he is clearly identifiable as an SPD politician' (I54: 162).

In the last two quotations the term 'between' is used, and this characterization is common for other cases as well. But who are these translators and which competencies do they need? They have to move self-confidently in both worlds, and know the habitual norms and practices of both systems. They have to be able to reduce complexity and explain scientific insights not only comprehensibly, but impressively for bigger audiences or even the media. A policy-maker in a ministry explains what a policy advisor needs to be:

> It certainly also depends a lot upon the personalities and the people. One has to simply say, X is really someone who – ... – down here a press conference happened, the lodge was chock-full, and he could quite simply and very clearly explain the context, in a way comprehensible for anyone, at least for anyone with a bit of expertise – how he could bring something like that to the audience. There we can witness a working connection between theoretical background and practical know-how.
>
> (I21: 432)

Conclusion

In this chapter we have tried to demonstrate that the relationship of scientific knowledge and public action areas is not trivial. We have emphasized that the production of knowledge and its usage are different practices with different conditions of success, with different plausibilities, and with different habitualized forms of agency. The very simple expectation that knowledge formed at the scientific level and is then put into practice by users does not reflect the reality of the relationship of knowledge and policy. In a situation when more and more practices in society are becoming knowledge-based practices, knowledge itself suffers a loss of uniqueness and secureness. We argue that the reason for this is not in the structure of knowledge itself, but in the practices that use knowledge under their own conditions.

Our 'doing knowledge' concept is the result of research that has found that knowledge and its acceptance is a result of translation practices in which the conditions of acceptance cannot be presupposed but always have to be newly created. The term 'doing knowledge' underlines the constitution of knowledge as something ontologically practical and identifies some elements of this practice – which are surely countless in empirical reality. The practices of 'doing knowledge' are gaining in importance in making policy across the globe. Knowledge is becoming a direct source of policy and a resource of external legitimacy. The rise of 'big data' creates and boosts the impression of a governable and modifiable world. Data gained through international comparison seem to facilitate system knowledge. Social scientists observe the growing tendency towards (international) comparison as a basis for political action. The bigger and the more international the data the more they can conceal their constructedness. In their search for modernization and the achievement of world-class education, policy-makers seize on international data as a knowledge resource about other systems.

This volume offers detailed insights into the practice of making policy through data. This chapter has analysed some elements of this practice and pointed both to the changing of knowledge contents when entering the field of policy and to the role of people and institutions 'doing' knowledge. Translators are the actors who gain a constantly growing importance in the international shaping of education policy throughout the world. But we have still insufficient insight into how the practices of knowledge – 'doing knowledge' – work and how unelected national and international experts influence policy-making. This chapter offers some contribution to that enquiry.

Notes

1   This chapter has been published thanks to the support of the European Union's Sixth Framework Programme for Research – Citizens and Governance in a Knowledge-based Society theme (contract nr 028848-2 – project KNOWandPOL – for all research reports see www.knowandpol.eu). The information and views set out in this chapter are those of the authors only and do not necessarily reflect the official opinion of the European Union.
2   Due to issues of anonymity interviews are given numbers, the second number is the number of the lines within the transcribed interview.

References

Alexander, J. C. (1990) 'Differentiation theory: Problems and prospects', in Alexander, J. C. and Colomy, P. (eds) *Differentiation Theory and Social Change. Comparative and Historical Perspectives*, New York: Columbia University Press.

Bassnett, S. and Lefevre, A. (1990) *Translation, History and Culture*, London, New York: Pinter.

Benjamin, W. (1992) 'The task of the translator', in Schulte, R. and Biguenet, J. (eds) *Theories of Translation. An Anthology of Essays from Dryden to Derrida*, Chicago: Chicago University Press.

Berenyi, E. and Neumann, E. (2009) 'Grappling with PISA. Reception and translation in the Hungarian policy discourse', *Sisifo*, No. 10, 41–52.

Bourdieu, P. (1975) 'The specifity of the scientific field and the conditions of the progress of reason', *Social Science Information*, 14(6), 19–47.

Buden, B. and Nowotny, St. (2009) 'Cultural translation: An introduction to the problem', *Translation Studies*, 2(2), 196–219.

Buzan, B. and Albert, M. (2010) 'Differentiation: A sociological approach to international relations theory', *European Journal of International Relations*, 16(3), 315–337.

Chernilo, D. (2002) 'The theorization of social co-ordinations in differentiated societies: the theory of generalized symbolic media in Parsons, Luhmann, Habermas', *British Journal of Sociology*, 3, 431–449.

Colomy, P. (1990) 'Revisions and progress in differentiation theory', in J. C. Alexander and P. Colomy (eds) *Differentiation Theory and Social Change. Comparative and Historical Perspectives*, New York: Columbia University Press.

Commaille, J. (2004) 'Sociologie de l'action publique', in Boussaguet, L. *et al.* (eds), *Dictionnaire des politiques publiques* [Handbook of Public Policies], Paris: Presses de Science Po.

Commission Staff Working Document (2007) *Towards More Knowledge-Based Policy and Practice in Education and Training*, Brussels: Commission of the European Communities.

Davies, H. T. O., Nutley, S. M. and Smith, P. C. (2000) *What Works? Evidence-Based Policy and Practice in Public Services*, Bristol: The Policy Press.

Drori, G. S., Meyer, J. W., Ramirez, Fr. O. and Schofer, E. (2003) *Science in the Modern World Polity: Institutionalization and Globalization*, Stanford, CA: Stanford University Press.

Drucker, P. F. (1993) *Post-Capitalist Society*, New York: HarperCollins.

Engelhardt, A, and Kajetzke, L. (2010) 'Für eine Wissenssoziologie der Wissensgesellschaft', in Engelhardt, A. and Kajetzke, L. (eds) *Handbuch Wissensgesellschaft. Theorien, Themen und Probleme* [Handbook Knowledge Society. Theories, Themes and Problems], Bielefeld: Transcript.

European Commission (2009) *Scientific Evidence for Policy-Making*, Brussels: Commission of the European Communities.

Evans, R. (1999) *Macroeconomic Forecasting: A Sociological Appraisal*, London: Routledge.

Freeman, R. (2009) 'What is 'translation'?', *Evidence & Policy*, 5(4), 429–447.

Fuchs, M. (2009) 'Reaching out; or, Nobody exists in one context only. Society as translation', *Translation Studies*, 2(1), 21–40.

Geertz, C. (1993) *The Interpretation of Cultures. Selected Essays*, London: Fontana Press.

Hellstrom, Th. and Merle, K. (2000) 'Scientification of politics or politicization of science? Traditionalist science-policy discourse and its quarrels with Mode 2 epistemology', *Social Epistemology*, 14(1), 69–77.

Herder, J. G. (1990) *Über die neuere deutsche Literatur. Werke in zehn Bänden* [On new German literature], Bd. 1, Frankfurt a. M.: Deutscher Klassiker Verlag.

Hermans, Th. (2007) 'Translation, irritation and resonance', in Wolf, M. and Fukari, A. (eds) *Constructing a Sociology of Translation*, Amsterdam, PA: John Benjamins.

Humboldt, W. (1909) 'Einleitung zu Agamemnon' [Introduction to Agamemnon], in *Gesammelte Schriften*, Bd. 8, Berlin: B. Behr's Verlag.

Kant, I. (2010) *The Critique of Pure Reason* (translated by J. M. D. Meiklejohn), University Park, PA: Penn State University Press.

Knorr Cetina, K. (1981) *The Manufacture of Knowledge*, Oxford: Pergamon Press.

Knorr Cetina, K. (1992) 'Zur Unterkomplexität der Differenzierungstheorie. Empirische Anfragen an die Systemtheorie' [Under-Complexity of Differentiation Theory], *Zeitschrift für Soziologie*, 21, 406–419.

Knorr Cetina, K. (2000) *Wissenskulturen. Ein Vergleich naturwissenschaftlicher Wissensformen* [Cultures of Knowledge. A Comparison of Natural Sciences], Frankfurt a. M.: Suhrkamp.

Knorr Cetina, K. (2007) 'Culture in global knowledge societies: knowledge, cultures and epistemic cultures', *Interdisciplinary Science Reviews*, 32, 361–375.

Kuhn, Th. (1962) *The Structure of Scientific Revolutions*, Chicago: The University of Chicago Press.

Latour, B. and Woolgar, St. (1986) *Laboratory Life: The Construction Of Scientific Facts*, 2nd edn, Princeton, NJ: Princeton University Press.

Law, J. (2009) 'Seeing like a survey', *Cultural Sociology*, 3(2), 239–256.

Lefevre, A. (1998) 'Translation practice(s) and the circulation of cultural capital: Some Aeneids in English', in Bassnet, S. and Lefevere, A. *Constructing Cultures. Essays on Literary Translation*, Clevedon and Philadelphia: Cromwell Press.

Lindemann, G. (2002) *Die Grenzen des Sozialen. Zur sozio-technischen Konstruktion von Leben und Tod* [The Borders of Society. The Socio-technic Construction of Life and Death], München: Wilhelm Fink.

Lindemann, G. (2006) 'Die Emergenzfunktion und die konstitutive Funktion des Dritten. Perspektiven einer kritisch-systematischen Theorieentwicklung' [The Emergence and constitutive function of the Third. Perspectives of a critical theory], *Zeitschrift für Soziologie*, 35, 82–101.

Lindemann, G. (2008) 'Theoriekonstruktion und empirische Forschung' [Construction of Theory and Empirical Analysis], in Kalthoff, H., Hirschauer, S., and Lindemann, G. (eds) *Theoretische Empirie. Zur Relevanz qualitativer Forschung*, Frankfurt a. M.: Suhrkamp.

Luhmann, N. (1990) *Die Wissenschaft der Gesellschaft* [Science of Society], Frankfurt a. M.: Suhrkamp.

Luhmann, N. (1997) 'Funktional differenzierte Gesellschaft' [Functionally differentiated society] in *Die Gesellschaft der Gesellschaft* [Society of Society], Vol. I, Frankfurt a. M.: Suhrkamp.

MacKenzie, D. A. (1981) *Statistics in Britain 1865–1930: The Social Construction of Scientific Knowledge*, Edinburgh: Edinburgh University Press.

MacKenzie, D. and Millo, Y. (2003) 'Constructing a market, performing theory: The historical sociology of financial derivates exchange', *American Journal of Sociology*, 109, 107–145.

Merton, R. K. (1938) 'Science and the social order', *Philosophy of Science*, 5, 321–337.

Nassehi, A. (2003) *Geschlossenheit und Offenheit. Studien zur Theorie der modernen Gesellschaft* [Closure and Openness. Studies on the Theory of Modern Societies], Frankfurt a. M: Suhrkamp.

Nassehi, A. (2005) 'Organizations as decision machines: Niklas Luhmann's theory of organized social systems', in Campbell, J. and Rolland, M. (eds) *Contemporary Organization Theory*, Malden, MA/Oxford: Blackwell.

Nassehi, A. (2006) *Der soziologische Diskurs der Moderne* [The Sociological Discourse of Modernity], Frankfurt a. M: Suhrkamp.

Nassehi, A. (2011) *Gesellschaft der Gegenwarten. Studien zur Theorie der modernen Gesellschaft* II [Societies of Parallelity. Studies on the Theory of Modern Society], Berlin: Suhrkamp

Nightingale, P. and Scott, A. (2007) 'Peer review and the relevance gap: ten suggestions for policy-makers', *Science and Public Policy*, 34(8), 543–553.

Offe, C. (1984) *Contradiction of the Welfare State*, London: Hutchinson.

Reichmann, W. (2011) 'Institutionalizing scientific knowledge: The social and political foundation of empirical economic research', *Sociology Compass*, 5(7), 564–575.

Stehr, N. (1994) *Knowledge Societies*, London: Sage.

Stehr, N. (2001) *The Fragility of Modern Societies. Knowledge and Risk in the Information Age*, London: Sage.

Stehr, N., Bechmann, G. and Gorekov, V. (2009) *The Social Integration of Science*, Berlin: Edition Sigma.

Steiner-Khamsi, G. (2003) 'The political league tables', *Journal of Social Science Education*, 1. http://www.jsse.org/2003/2003-1/pdf/khamsi-tables-1-2003.pdf

Weingart, P. (2001) *Die Stunde der Wahrheit? Zum Verhältnis der Wissenschaft zu Politik, Wirtschaft und Medien in der Wissensgesellschaft* [The Moment of Truth? On the Relation of Science, Economics and Media in a Knowledge Society], Weilerswist: Velbrück.

Willke, H. (2002) *Dystopia. Studien zur Krisis des Wissens in der modernen Gesellschaft* [Dystopia. Studies on the Crisis of Knowledge in Modern Societies], Frankfurt a. M.: Suhrkamp.

Wolf, M. (2007) 'Bourdieu's 'Rules of the game': An introspection into methodological questions of translation sociology', *Matraga*, 14(20), 130–145.

9   Modernizing Education in Pakistan

Networked Governance, the Role of Consultants and the Prevalence of Data

Sajid Ali

Introduction

This chapter takes stock of recent developments in the educational context of Pakistan which are purportedly leading the project of modernizing education in Pakistan. The focus of the chapter is on a number of inter-linked developments. The first is the changing nature of education governance that reflects the more widespread shift in governing from directed, rule-following bureaucracies to more fluid, networked forms – in other words – from government to governance (Rosenau 2000). In discussing this development, the chapter draws on the examples of the development of Pakistan's National Education Policy 2009, the work of the Task Force on Education Policy Implementation and the preparation of the Provincial Education Sector Plan. In each of these examples the role of wider 'consultation' with various stakeholders including donors, non-governmental organizations (NGOs), the private sector and academia is very apparent. The other significant development in all of these cases is the utilization of 'consultants' to spearhead the development of policy and plans. All of these developments illustrate the growth of networked governance and the influence of expertise derived from consultants and experts in decision-making by the government of Pakistan.

Another development is the role of data and knowledge resources in education governance. In relation to this topic the chapter will focus on the increased importance of various national and international datasets, comparative statistics and knowledge resources. The specific examples of datasets and statistics produced by the United Nations Educational, Scientific and Cultural Organization's (UNESCO) Global Monitoring Report (GMR), the Annual Status of Education Report (ASER) and knowledge resources such as 'What Works in Education in Pakistan' and the 'Learning and Educational Achievement in Pakistan Schools (LEAPS) report' will be considered. Attention will also be paid to the increased appetite of the government for data in its decision-making through such data resources as the National Education Management Information System (NEMIS), the Provincial Education Assessment Centre (PEACE), the Examination Commission and Education Atlas. The discussion will focus on the effect of these changing forms of governing technologies on the decision-making ability of the state and on its overall performance in reaching its educational objectives.

These phenomena – networked governance, the role of consultants and the prevalence of data – are closely interconnected. New public management (NPM) doctrine suggests that the state should manage its affairs through 'steering' rather than 'rowing' to symbolize a hands-off rather than hands-on approach to managing state affairs (Clarke and Newman 1997). The distance that is created between the state actors and the field of practice triggers the need for policy-makers to devise means of knowing the system. That need is apparently fulfilled through the supply of all sorts of data on various aspects of the system. Thus, for example, in the education sector the need to create new schools demands initial knowledge/data about existing schools, which is made available through a database created and maintained by the Ministry.

The Context of Education Governance in Pakistan

Pakistan is located in South Asia, neighbouring India in the East, China in the North, Afghanistan and Iran in the West and the Arabian sea in the South. The total area is 803,940 sq. km. The current population is around 180 million. The country possesses a rich variety of geography and has the second highest mountain peak – K-2 – in the north, fertile plains in the centre, and desert and sea in the south. The country is divided into four provinces: Sindh, Punjab, Baluchistan and Khyber Pakhtunkhwa (KP). Other regions included in Pakistan are Azad Jammu Kashmir (AJK), Gilgit-Baltistan (GB) and the Federally Administered Tribal Areas (FATA). Pakistan came into being in 1947 after the departure of the British Raj from the sub-continent. At independence British India was divided into India and the separate state of Pakistan which comprised mainly the Muslim population. In 1971 the eastern part of Pakistan separated from the federation to form Bangladesh. During its sixty-five years of independence, Pakistan has experienced three military coups and subsequent military regimes interspersed with brief intervals of democracy. The government which came into power after the elections in 2008, was the first ever democratically elected government to have completed its full five-year tenure of office and to hold elections in 2012 in which another democratically elected government took office (I. Hussain 2011). As a result of weak democratic traditions and military dictatorship the administrative structure of the state is quite weak and without established traditions of public service and stable institutions. Two other important features of the governing context that need to be noted are the existence of a strong feudal class and the aftermath of 9/11 and the so-called war on terror. During the British Raj the feudal class was established and strengthened to provide a useful administrative indigenous ruling class that enabled control of the population, and this class maintained its power after the independence. The weakness of democratic norms and prevalence of corruption are some of the consequences of the continuation of a feudal mentality (Lieven 2011). The war on terror launched in neighbouring Afghanistan post 9/11 has had serious implications for Pakistan. The rising militancy in various parts of Pakistan, particularly those bordering Afghanistan, has created an ideological polarization between the radical and liberal elements in the country during the past decade (Z. Hussain 2011) and has led to or aggravated various divisions – ethnic, linguistic, religious sectarian – already existing within the society.

Because of these unstable politics, the threat of terrorism and internal divisions, education as a policy field has increased in importance, as it is geared not simply towards educational or economic imperatives but also towards strategic imperatives (Khan and Yusuf 2011). Education is seen by the government as a way of combating extremism, building national harmony and strengthening the economy (Pakistan Ministry of Education 2009). This project, however, is compli- cated because of the existence of parallel provision of education – public, private and *madrasahs*[1] – in the country. Students in these different forms of provision are exposed to different curricula and quality of education, which in fact further entrench divisions (Rahman 2004).

Moving to the educational context the record shows the difficulties of the context. The current adult literacy rate is 56 per cent (Pakistan, Federal Bureau of Statistics 2011) while around 5.1 million children of primary school age are still out of school (UNESCO 2012). Yet despite this missing population, there are, at primary level (both public and private) 25.45 million children in primary schools (Pakistan, Ministry of Professional and Technical Training 2011). To cater for this enormous population there are 154,641 primary schools with 436,928 primary teachers. At higher education level, there are 135 universities with an enrolment of 1.12 million. There has been a recent increase in the share of the private sector in education at all levels. A census carried out by the Ministry of Education in 2005–06 revealed that the private sector's share of education provision was more than 33 per cent (Pakistan, Ministry of Education 2006). While the public sector is still the largest provider at primary education level, that reduces at secondary and tertiary levels.

In 2010, the Government of Pakistan introduced the 18th Constitutional Amendment to give more power to the provinces, and as a result the education sector was also devolved from the federal to the provincial level. In each of the provinces there is an Education Ministry which is assisted by a very large administrative machine. At the head of this administration is the Secretary of Education with various departments under his office at the provincial level; below the provincial level there are districts, *talukas*[2] and union councils. The district is headed by District Officer of Education who is in charge of the huge platoon of educational officers at district, *taluka* and union council level. To give a little sense of the scale, in Sindh province alone there are around 2,000 supervisors who are supposed to visit schools to carry out inspections and offer support (figure quoted by Sindh Education Secretary Fazalullah Pechoho in a Seminar held in Karachi on 31 January 2013).

Despite this elaborate hierarchical structure, the depressing educational stand- ards cited above indicate the poor performance of the public education system. Over the years the government has failed to achieve its stated objectives in numerous policies (Ali 2006). The recent education policy documents highlight implementa- tion as a serious policy challenge and acknowledge the inability of the government to tackle these problems single-handed (Aly 2007; Pakistan, Ministry of Education 2009). There is a growing tendency to involve private sector, non-governmental organizations and donor agencies in various policy initiatives.

The Changing Form of Education Governance – Networked Governance

There is a growing trend towards the adoption of networked governance of the education sector by the government of Pakistan, which is revealed in analysis of three significant policy examples: first the formulation of National Education Policy in 2009 (Aly 2007; Pakistan, Ministry of Education 2009); second, the work of the Task Force on Education Policy Implementation (2009–11 minutes of the meetings); and third the preparation of the Provincial Education Sector Plan (2012–13 minutes of the meetings, presentations and personal experience). The two most important elements of this new mode of networked governance – the use of processes of public consultation to draw new actors in policy-making (Reddel and Woolcock 2004), and the use of consultants/technical assistance in order to construct new knowledge for policy – will be elaborated later in the chapter.

The current National Education Policy of Pakistan, NEP 2009, was formulated following an unprecedented policy process which lasted for around four years during 2005–09. The final policy document, NEP 2009, was preceded by various preparatory policy documents – Green Papers, Thematic Papers and the White Paper. Elsewhere I have analysed the policy process preceding the NEP 2009 and observed that it was unprecedented and heavily committed to consultation (Ali 2009). A National Education Policy Review (NEPR) team was established towards the end of 2005 to spearhead the process. The team comprised independent national consultants and was supported by the staff of the Ministry of Education's Planning Wing. The NEPR team laid down a three-stage policy formulation process – a diagnostic stage, prescriptive stage and policy development stage. The NEPR team and the Ministry of Education (MoE) were very positive about the extensive consultative process that informed the development of NEP 2009, as exemplified in this extract from the MoE website:

> The NEPR team embarked upon a comprehensive process of consultation and pursued a structured methodology. To ensure that the policy review document is owned by all stakeholders, far and wide it was intended to make the review process intensively and extensively.
>
> (www.moe.gov.pk, accessed 20 April 2009)

The NEPR team was anxious to demonstrate the widest possible representation from various stakeholders from all provinces and from different layers of the government, i.e. provincial, district and sub-districts (Ali 2009). One of the MoE officials heading the review process commented: 'We have consulted teachers, students, educationists, retired people, journalists . . . you name it. We talked to everybody. There were workshops held, there were visits to the districts, 35 districts were visited (F-MoE18, quoted in Ali 2009, pp. 193–194).

These consultations were aimed at developing understanding of education issues for the NEPR team, generating recommendations for future policy and most importantly building ownership among government and non-government stakeholders, who were thus engaged as co-producers of the policy. The consultation process was an indication of the government's commitment to using more networked, less bureaucratic governance mechanisms to not only modernize the policy process in Pakistan but to manage the various tensions that the government is increasingly facing as a result of globalization. The second example of networked governance is apparent in the working of the Pakistan Education Task Force (PETF), which was created to improve the implementation of NEP 2009. The PETF was established in 2009 through a joint agreement between the governments of Pakistan and the UK government. The PETF was co-chaired by Sir Michael Barber and Ms Shahnaz Wazir Ali. Ms Ali was the Advisor to the Prime Minister of Pakistan on the Social Sector; Sir Michael was a consultant at McKinsey and was contracted by the UK Department for International Development (DFID) for the Task Force. He had previously been head of the UK Prime Minister's Delivery Unit, when Tony Blair was PM. Describing the mandate of the PETF, Sir Michael said:

> The role of the Task Force is first of all to offer advice on the implementation of education policy …. Two, try to get some kind of shared view of the future of Pakistan's education system … the Task Force is a kind of a national voice for education and in the current fiscal circumstances in Pakistan, somebody needs to be the voice for education, why education should be the priority for Pakistan … and the third is building a shared agenda among donors, not just the British but the other donors – the World Bank, the Americans and a number of other smaller donors.
>
> (Barber 2011)

The Task Force was a high-powered federal entity which had membership from all provincial education secretaries, representatives of NGOs, academia, industry and donor agencies. During 2009 and 2011 the PETF held around eight meetings discussing various policy options and action plans for the provinces. Towards the end of 2010 the government introduced a constitutional amendment popularly known as the 18th Amendment (Government of Pakistan 2010) which devolved the education sector to the provinces. Since the passing of that constitutional amendment that activities of the PETF gradually diminished and eventually became dormant without any clarity about its future status.

An analysis of the minutes of the PETF suggests that it was concerned with issues such as performance score cards for provincial education, the establishment of funds for low-cost private schools, supporting provincial education sector plans, media campaigns for education emergency, textbooks and curriculum issues.[3] The minutes also reveal that the role of the Task Force was more advisory than executive. Dialogue with various stakeholders was a key mechanism to both raise the political importance of education and in building consensus on various educational issues including coordination among donors:

> Most times when I am there, I talk to the World Bank, the Americans, other donors. We have done some coordination of donors around the Baluchistan Action Plan, which emerged during the middle of last year. I have chaired a couple of meetings among donors for Baluchistan. So we have had lots of dialogues with donors.
>
> (Barber 2011)

The work of the PETF demonstrates the critical role played by various consultants in providing technical assistance. Professor Marshall Smith, former Dean of the School of Education at Stanford joined the PETF as an international expert. Various experts made presentations to the Task Force, for example the Institute of Social and Policy Sciences (I-SAPS – a non-profit organization based in Pakistan) made a presentation on private schools and an evaluation of the work of the PETF by independent consultants. The PETF minutes illustrate the centrality of this issue:

> The presentation on 'Private Sector Education: Mapping made by the Institute of Social Policy and Sciences (ISAPS)' gave a comprehensive picture of the private sector. Members of the PETF were cognizant of the fact that though the private sector suffers from quality issues, yet it displays good models/practices, which could be strengthened and built upon for improved service delivery. The meeting, however, expressed the need to be clear and realistic about the role and nature of Public Private Partnerships (PPPs); and the role of the State in the provision of education in the future-raising the critical question of scaling PPP's. The presentation on private schools highlighted the issue of regulation and the need to revisit the Private School Regulatory Law.
>
> (Minutes of the meeting, 25 October 2010)

Here we see consultants influencing policy and promoting discussion on changes in regulation. A more recent example is the preparation of Education Sector Plan (ESP) by one of the provinces. Since 2011–12 all the provinces have been developing their education sector plans following the same broad strategies. One province launched its ESP strategy in 2012 with the intention of seeking funding for the support of the plan. The provincial education department convened a group of stakeholders in order to consult them for their input into the plan; the group consisted of representatives from NGOs, academia, media, development partners and private sector. It was referred as a local education group (LEG). I was included in this group and my observations here are based on that experience. The funds for the consultation and ESP formulation were provided by a multi-lateral donor agency. A group of national consultants were recruited to assist the Ministry in carrying out the consultation and developing the plan, which was also supported by two international consultants whose presence was supported by a donor agency. The Department of Education convened the initial meetings of the stakeholders and apprised the members of the development of ESP and their possible contribution. From the outset it was clear that the Ministry wanted to develop the ESP in order to be able to apply for funding from an international donor and that the consultants were hired to support the Ministry to develop the plan. Eventually, the consulting agency took over the development of the ESP and convened several meetings with the stakeholders to formulate various segments of the plan. During these meetings, rather than leading the process, the government officials simply participated and received the outcome. The consulting agency continued to discuss the development of the plan with the government and other stakeholders, however, they seemed also to be in the position of making decisions or speaking on behalf of the government.

Reflecting on this experience, it appears that the role of the government was more as a facilitator and manager of resources rather than that of authoritative executive. This illustrates the repositioning of the state in circumstances that require different forms of coordination and cooperation mechanisms (Pierre and Peters 2000). The government officials drew on and managed various financial and knowledge resources. The financial resources were generally provided by the donor agencies, while knowledge resources came in various forms, provided by various stakeholders to different effect. The consultants provided expertise in the consultation process itself and in the drafting of plans. The representatives of the LEG served as critical assistants to the government officials in scrutinizing the influence of consultants and donors.

Consultation and Consultants

All the above examples are taken from significant policy instances where at least two things are quite visible, first a growing importance of consultation as a policy technology, and second the involvement of consultants in the policy process itself. Both of these elements are important feature of new forms of governance which are becoming more apparent in the education context in Pakistan.

In modern public policy discourse the consultation process precedes almost any policy decision and it is considered an essential element of public policy formulation. Stewart (2009, p. 15) suggests that in modern democracies the government engages various stakeholders for a number of reasons such as:

- improving information flows;
- seeking a diversity of views;
- obtaining early warning of problems;
- tapping into community resources;
- political management.

This engagement of new partners in a joint governing 'project' is not always benevolent. Engaging potentially critical groups in the consultation helps government manage dissenting or critical voices in private settings, and may be a form of co-option of critical groups. Indeed the consultations discussed above were designed to achieve various objectives. As I noted in my earlier work (Ali 2009) the consultative process helped the NEPR team in understanding basic educational issues pertaining to policy and building ownership among the stakeholders. The PETF allowed for the airing of different views while remaining more concerned with the political management of the education sector. The development of the sector plan attempted consultation because it was a precondition of the funding agency and because it provided access to information and resources possessed by non-governmental and private sector actors in education. During the deliberations I personally witnessed strong dissenting voices, which were managed through various strategies, for example by asking for submission of written proposals, reminding the group of the need to complete its deliberations in the limited time available, or defusing criticism by promising to incorporate suggested changes in future drafts of the plan.

It is also quite apparent that these forums were not decision-making forums, though the public voice was heard and noted. Consultations generally provided an immediate form of feedback on the policies that government was attempting to introduce. They worked for the government as early warning mechanisms and also provided the opportunity to manage any potential irritants by giving them some sense of participation and voice. Consultation, in these examples, emerges as a major technology employed to make networked governance possible in the context of Pakistan. At the same time we can also observe that the government is trying to draw more people and interest groups into the processes of governance.

The doctrine of consultation and involvement of various stakeholders can be traced to the work of the international agencies in Pakistan, particularly the World Bank. During the 1990s, the World Bank started raising the issues of 'governance' and 'good governance' and at the same time increased its support to the work of NGOs (Williams 2008, pp. 66, 69). This development reflects the way the World Bank started to redefine the role of the state from big government to small government, from provider to facilitator (World Bank 2002). The preferences of the World Bank and other international agencies affected the workings of the government of Pakistan. The participation of stakeholders was encouraged and pursued by the international development agencies and thus became a prerequisite for the work of the government. Thus we also see the shift in the way the government of Pakistan does policy work now – through networked governance.

These examples also highlight the role of consultants. In the work of National Education Policy review, a team of national consultants was employed to carry out the review and prepare the policy document. The example of the Task Force on Education shows that Sir Michael Barber, then at McKinsey, was appointed to co-chair the work. Another US-based consultant, Professor Marshall Smith, also supported the work of the Task Force. Sir Michael Barber described his work to me as follows:

> So when you are asking what my job is: it's to help with implementation, it's to help with explaining the story of reform, it's to help make the case for more money for education, but above all it's is to convince people that they can succeed.
>
> (Barber 2011)

Later in the interview Sir Michael also referred to one of his co-authored publications at McKinsey, which draws from a global knowledge pool of best practice. He said:

> the report McKinsey published in December, on improving schools systems … looks at systems everywhere, from Madhiya Pardesh in India through to Korea, Singapore, Finland – which are among the best systems in the world – and looks at how they improve. There is a growing amount of knowledge that can be brought to bear in situations like Pakistan, where is 10–15 years ago we were basically guessing how to improve systems. Each country had its agenda, now there is a common knowledge base about what we need to do. And that can be brought to bear in Pakistan like everywhere else.
>
> (Barber 2011)

Consultants also play an important role in the third example of sector planning, where a national consulting firm was hired to develop the sector plan, which was further supported by two international consultants. In the case of Pakistan, the experiment of sector planning borrows heavily from the Global Partnership for Education toolkit where similar sector plans for other developing countries are displayed.

These observations suggest that there is growing intrusion of the private sector into public provision through such contract and consultancy work (Ball and Junemann 2012). The involvement of consultants has also brought a cultural shift in the attitude of government bureaucrats, who find it convenient that someone else does their work for them. The government officials keep themselves busy in their bureaucratic routines and consultants continue to do the planning work. As there are frequent transfers in the educational bureaucracy in Pakistan, the national consultants are often the most stable personnel and thus the most knowledgeable. The consultants are also trained to fulfil the demands of the international organizations and speak their language. Thus they perform to the requirements of the funding agency that lend their services to the government. This, although it may appear convenient, has a devastating effect on the overall capacity of the government officials, who continue to decline in number and this results in a further weakening of the government system.

The Role of Data and Knowledge Resources

The growth of education data of various sorts and its increasing importance in education discourse is a recent phenomenon, but while data are important, other knowledge-based resources, particularly high impact research reports, have also been gaining considerable importance.

As far as the data resources are concerned the UNESCO's Education For All (EFA) – Global Monitoring Report (GMR) is of major importance in the Pakistani context. For example the GMR 2012 report shows that Pakistan has the second highest number of primary school age children out of school (5.1 million) and that Pakistan is going to miss the EFA targets for 2015. This has led to substantial criticism of the government internally and externally. The GMR is an international report that benchmarks all countries on various educational indicators that were part of EFA targets agreed by member states in Dakar in 2000. The 2012 GMR report produced by UNESCO places Pakistan at 113th position on the EFA Development Index (EDI), because of the poor performance of Pakistan on basic education indicators including the net enrolment rate, the adult literacy rate, gender parity and the retention rate to grade five. A UNESCO-based expert who worked on the GMR commented on its effects:

> The first obvious effect is that it becomes a resource. And I suspect it gets a lot more used by academics and students in the first place, because it has all the information you need .... I think the second effect it has on the country ... is which I call the politics of league tables. It has what is called the 'Education Development Index' which is constructed, based on four of the six quantifiable goals, and countries get obsessed annually every year whether they are number one, two, three, four, five .... The third effect is that it is used by different people for advocacy purposes. NGOs would pick up the literacy report and say look how bad the state of world's literacy is ... so they use it as a way of providing evidence for the advocacy position or justification for the advocacy position.
>
> (Interview, 24 February 2012)

Such data and indicators, then, become part of policy discussions and create policy effects.

Another statistical report with policy effects is the ASER (Annual Status of Education Report) survey (ASER-Pakistan 2012 2013). The first ASER report was launched in 2009 and the main organization behind this survey is the NGO *Idara-e-Taleem-o-Aagahi* (Centre of Education and Consciousness). The ASER survey provides an annual snapshot of various districts of Pakistan in terms of basic education indicators such as enrolment, children out of school, physical facilities at school, qualifications of teachers and qualifications of parents. The most important estimate is the learning status of children in basic subjects such as the local language, the English language and arithmetic. Each year the report is launched with a huge fanfare at the federal and provincial levels and influential education experts are invited to comment on the findings and government officials are asked to take note the major findings and recommendations. ASER surveys the performance of the private as well as the public sector so that a dataset on the performance of the education sector as the whole is emerging. The survey also constructs a provincial score card measuring the performance of various provinces and providing some basis for public naming and shaming.

As well as data, some research reports especially the LEAPS (Learning and Educational Achievements in Punjab Schools) report, have had an impact on policy. The LEAPS report was prepared by US-based scholars of Pakistani inheritance, and was funded by the World Bank. The report uses detailed quantitative methodology to illustrate the learning achievements of low-cost private schools in rural Punjab compared with their government counterparts. The report apparently demonstrates that the low-cost private schools are charging lower fees, providing better management and despite the lower salaries and qualifications of their teachers, produce better attainment results. These findings support the current World Bank strategy promoting low-cost private schools in Pakistan with financial aid by the government.

In contrast a report prepared by education scholars in Pakistan received much less publicity. *Education in Pakistan: What Works and Why* (CQE 2007) used various successful case studies to draw common messages for policy-makers. This NGO- and academia-led report used a qualitative methodology, illustrated the complexity of reform and did not provide numerical formulae for success – all of which may help explain its lack of impact.

The growing prevalence of data and knowledge resources has increased the appetite of policy-makers for data and supported the demand from various donor agencies for data demonstrating performance on a variety of indicators. The government assiduously gathers basic education data from all its schools through an Educational Management Information System: data are collected by provinces and compiled at the federal level. Other data sources established recently include data on students' assessment at elementary level (grades five and eight) in Punjab province along with the Provincial Education Assessment Centres (PEACE) and Education Atlas. Invariably these databases are supported by various donor agencies, the World Bank being prominent among them.

Conclusion

Networked forms of governance are becoming apparent in the policy contexts of developing countries such as Pakistan. Ball and Junemann (2012) discuss research that has emerged in the UK, USA and Europe: based on the discussion here it may be noted that the new governing technologies are now becoming visible in the context of developing countries, though with their unique contextual peculiarities. The spread of networks – as an example of policy borrowing (Steiner-Khamsi 2004) is an example of a policy technology making its way from global into national space. Consultants act as conduits to such transfers of knowledge and ideas, replicating best practice from one context to others. But international ideas do not simply get replicated (Ozga and Jones 2006), they mutate while embedding in the local context. Thus we have seen that the ideas generated by the Task Force on Education co-chaired by Sir Michael Barber were taken up in the Pakistani context, at least initially. However, devolution through the 18th Constitutional Amendment in Pakistan made the very constituency addressed by the Task Force void. Disjuncture is created in the embedding process, a contextual feature that presents not only in Pakistan but in other countries that experience a fragile political situation.

In relation to the growth of consultancy, the appointment of consultants by the government is portrayed as a way of ensuring transparency and openness. The expertise of consultants is seen as adding credibility to the process, and counters the general perception of the lack of capacity in the government bodies in Pakistan. These preferences have to be seen in the light of the 'good governance' discourse of the international donor agencies such as the World Bank (2002) and UNESCO (2009). The UNESCO report of 2009 explicitly highlights the need for good governance in education. The same report and its subsequent version shows that Pakistan is at the lower end of performance in education indicators and thus not only needs to improve its performance, but has to do so through ensuring good governance. Thus consultation and the involvement of consultants seem to be fulfilling that requirement from government's perspective.

However, consultation hides the agenda-setting efforts of policy-makers and the manoeuvring towards a pre-selected outcome. The government continues to politically manage the process and its outcome and may also co-opt dissenting voices and present the outcomes as consensual (Stewart 2009). Moreover, although consultants bring expertise to the system, they in effect weaken the intellectual capacity of government officials by denying them opportunity and responsibility for development and for increasing their knowledge base. This is an intellectual hollowing out of the state (Jessop 2002).

Consultants, particularly international ones, act as a group of people who carry a shared repertoire and toolkit – a kind of magistracy – with which they devise solutions which often yield similar policy outcomes (Donn and Al Manthri 2010, p. 156). This highlights the issue of external solutions versus indigenous knowledge resources and draws attention to the powerful role of data and particular, selective knowledge resources. Various datasets (GMR, ASER, NEMIS) and knowledge resources (LEAPS and What Works) are visible in Pakistani education policy context and have effects. These datasets and knowledge resources are used differently by governments and by the consultants. While the government seems to use them as resources to know the system and manage it, consultants use the same data for promoting policy solutions. Thus, for example, the LEAPS study, which was sponsored by the World Bank and which favours public–private partnerships in education (Ali 2012), was utilized by consultants and donor agencies to support the promotion of PPP policy. We have thus seen the work of PEF and SEF being supported by the World Bank finances.

Within this context, the broader question that I conclude with is the role of state in the modernizing of education in Pakistan – is it in charge in the traditional way, and if not, in what ways has its authority been challenged and reshaped? In certain aspects the state seems to be losing its authority, in other cases it is gaining more authority – the decentralization and centralization processes go hand in hand. In addition, it is also not correct to assume that networked governance has abolished the old bureau-cracies and hierarchies – it is a fluid process evidencing complex and sometimes contradictory features (Jessop 1994). The cases presented here also demonstrate this complex reality. Although there are national imperatives for devolution, in line with so-called 'good governance', and evidence of networked governance being experi-mented with in and by Pakistan, the involvement of international consultants and donors brings the weight of global imperatives into the same reforms. Pakistan's mod-ernization of education is a mix of local and global imperatives, reflecting weak 'national capital' (Bourdieu 2003), where government is steering some of the pro-cesses, while at times being steered by global forces.

Notes

1 Religious schools.
2 Geographical administrative unit between district and union council.
3 Minutes of the meetings accessed through internet from www.petf.gov.pk in February 2011.

References

Ali, S. (2006) 'Why does policy fail? Understanding the problems of policy Implementation in Pakistan – a neuro-cognitive perspective', *International Studies in Educational Administration*, 34(1), 2–20.
Ali, S. (2009) *Governing Education Policy in a Globalising World – the Sphere of Authority of the Pakistani State*. University of Edinburgh, Edinburgh.
Ali, S. (2012) 'Education policy borrowing in Pakistan: public-private partnerships', in G. Donn and Y. A. Manthri (eds) *Education in the Broader Middle East: Borrowing a Baroque Arsenal* (pp. 23–40). Oxford: Symposium.
Aly, J. H. (2007) *Education in Pakistan a White Paper Revised – Document to Debate and Finalize the National Education Policy*. Retrieved 14 March 2007 from http://www.moe.gov.pk/nepr.
ASER-Pakistan 2012 (2013) *Annual Status of Education Report 2012*. Lahore: South Asian Forum for Educational Development.
Ball, J. S. and Junemann, C. (2012) *Networks, New Governance and Education*. Bristol: The Policy Press.
Barber, S. M. (2011) Interview with Sir Michael Barber by the author, 15 February. London.
Bourdieu, P. (2003) *Firing Back: Against the Tyranny of the Market*. London: Verso.
Clarke, J. and Newman, J. (1997) *The Managerial State: Power, Politics and Ideology in the Remaking of Social Welfare*. Thousand Oaks, CA: Sage.

CQE (2007) *Education in Pakistan: What Works and Why*. Lahore: Campaign for Quality Education (CQE).

Donn, G. and Al Manthri, Y. (2010) *Globalisation and Higher Education in the Arab Gulf States*. Oxford: Symposium.

Government of Pakistan (2010) *Constitution (Eighteenth Amendment) Act, 2010*, 20 April. Karachi: The Deputy Controller Stationery and Forms.

Hussain, I. (2011) 'Retooling institutions', in M. Lodhi (ed.) *Pakistan: Beyond the 'Crisis State'* (pp. 149–168). Karachi: Oxford University Press.

Hussain, Z. (2011) 'Battling militancy', in M. Lodhi (ed.) *Pakistan: Beyond the 'Crisis State'* (pp. 131–148). Karachi: Oxford University Press.

Jessop, B. (1994) 'Post-Fordism and the state', in A. Amin (ed.) *Post-Fordism: a Reader* (pp. 252–279). Oxford: Blackwell.

Jessop, B. (2002) *The Future of the Capitalist State*. Cambridge: Polity Press.

Khan, S. and Yusuf, M. (2011) 'Education as a strategic imperative', in M. Lodhi (ed.) *Pakistan: Beyond the 'Crisis State'* (pp. 251–266). Karachi: Oxford University Press.

Lieven, A. (2011) *Pakistan: A Hard Country*. New York: Publicaffairs.

Ozga, J. and Jones, R. (2006) 'Travelling and embedded policy: The case of knowledge transfer', *Journal of Education Policy, 21*(1), 1–17.

Pakistan, Federal Bureau of Statistics (2011) *Pakistan Social and Living Measurement Survey (2010–11) – PSLM 2010–11*. Islamabad: Government of Pakistan, Statistics Division.

Pakistan, Ministry of Education (2006) *National Education Census 2005 – Pakistan*. Islamabad: Academy of Educational Planning and Management, Statistics Division Federal Bureau of Statistics. Government of Pakistan.

Pakistan, Ministry of Education (2009) *National Education Policy 2009*. Islamabad: Government of Pakistan.

Pakistan, Ministry of Professional and Technical Training (2011) *Pakistan education statistics 2010–11*. Islamabad: NEMIS, AEPAM, Government of Pakistan.

Pierre, J. and Peters, B. G. (2000) *Governance, Politics and the State*. London: Macmillan Press.

Rahman, T. (2004) *Denizens of Alien Worlds: A Study of Education, Inequality and Polarization in Pakistan*. Karachi: Oxford University Press.

Reddel, T. and Woolcock, G. (2004) 'From consultation to participatory governance? A critical review of citizen engagement strategies in Queensland', *Australian Journal of Public Administration, 63*(3), 75–87.

Rosenau, J. N. (2000) 'Governance, order, and change in world politics', in J. N. Rosenau and E.-O. Czempiel (eds) *Governance Without Government: Order and Change in World Politics* (pp. 1–29). Cambridge: Cambridge University Press.

Steiner-Khamsi, G. (ed.) (2004) *The Global Politics of Educational Borrowing and Lending*. New York: Teachers College Press.

Stewart, J. (2009) *The Dilemmas of Engagement: The Role of Consultation in Governance*. Canberra: ANU E Press.

UNESCO (2009) *EFA Global Monitoring Report 2009 – Overcoming inequality: Why Governance Matters*. Oxford: Oxford University Press and UNESCO Publishing.

UNESCO (2012) *EFA Global Monitoring Report 2012 – Youth and Skills: Putting Education to Work*. Paris: UNESCO Publishing.

Williams, D. (2008) *The World Bank and Social Transformation in International Politics: Liberalism, Governance and Sovereignty*. London: Routledge.

World Bank (2002) *World Development Report 2002: Building Institutions for Markets*. New York: World Bank and Oxford University Press.

10 Big Data and the Politics of Education in Nigeria

David Johnson

Introduction

This chapter argues that 'big data' have the potential to transform access to services, including education, and the quality of life of the poorest communities in the developing world. This is not to suggest that the mining of data, big or small, or their application are unproblematic, and I am sympathetic to the arguments (there are many in this volume alone) that an increase of 'knowledge-based technologies' and a proliferation of 'networks of experts' have combined to compete for national policy and governance space. Indeed, the relationships between data, politics and education policy are complex and constrained by the competing interests of a variety of actors both within and outside government. So the question whether big data and their associated technologies have altered the basis of governance is timely. In order to answer that question, and especially how it concerns low-income African countries, this chapter suggests that the notions of *demand* and *intent* are critical to the debate, and it addresses the following questions: what is the nature of big data, what are the demands for data and what are the intentions for their use?

In relation to the new buzz words 'Big Data for Development' I suggest that it is reasonable that if a particular country has a specific requirement for data, for example, on where to build schools in war-torn south Sudan, then school mapping through geographical information systems (GIS) is essential to planning and resource allocation and that given the nature of the exercise, so is the need for a network of experts. Equally, if a country such as Kenya is prone to post-election violence, the consequences of which are the widespread displacement of school communities or a significant loss of learning and teaching time (Johnson *et al.* forthcoming), then real-time data are critical for an 'early response' in respect of where and how displaced students and teachers are accommodated. It is also reasonable to argue (and any European tax payer would be incensed to be told it is not) that data are necessary to monitor the returns to education (or development more broadly) of 'aid dollars'. Here, the locus of demand shifts from national government to international donor partnerships. But, by the same token it would be entirely right for a government that has invested its own resources to ask the question too. In my view it would also be difficult to argue with South Africa's decision to participate in international comparative surveys of educational achievement such as TIMMS or PISA: South Africa is a middle-income country with a share of youth that see their competitive futures as tied to the global economy. In the same way, countries such as The Gambia, Nigeria or Zambia, with similar aspirations, are entitled to participate in regional surveys of educational achievement.

The point here is that the demand for data in all the scenarios above is both legitimate and high, but the intended application of data to planning and policy is different for each case. Though not an exhaustive list, there seem to be at least three areas in which the demand for data for education decision-making is high. First, there exists a demand for big data to enable governments to respond quickly to the educational implications of development shocks such as armed conflict or drought. These data are collected in real time and rely on advances in mobile phone or GIS technology. Although traditional surveys have useful things to add, they are too cumbersome and expensive to scale up to the point that they can function as an effective and proactive basis for decision-making and solutions to global shocks. The second area is the demand for more traditional forms of data, in order to monitor progress towards an education development goal – for example that the world's population of children of school-going age all have a school place. These data can take time to be collected, processed, verified, and eventually published and ideally form an integral part of a country's official statistical data generation mechanisms, such as the educational management information system (EMIS). Sadly, there are a large number of developing countries where the EMIS is dysfunctional, and which have to rely increasingly on surveys carried out by donor agencies, but these in turn invest substantial resources in building such systems. The third area reflects a growing appetite in a number of middle-income countries for an understanding of their educational standards and how the country 'measures up' to more developed nations. The intention here is to understand the potential of a country to compete in the global knowledge economy. South Africa, Brazil, Mexico and India have all participated in international comparative surveys of educational achievement and this is potentially where the greatest confusion arises in the literature in respect of *intent*. Do these countries participate because the intention is ultimately to adopt wholesale the educational 'policies' of more developed countries? Indeed, does the UK on the basis of its PISA ranking want to emulate the culture of pedagogy in Finland or Germany? Or more to the point, are new policy technologies that include data systems (Lascoumes and Le Galès 2007) intended to construct policy problems and frame solutions beyond and across the national in the remaking of Europe (Ozga 2012)?

My sense is that the intent of countries where there is a demand for comparative data of this kind is less for a standardisation of 'policy', whatever that means, and more a means for understanding the returns to investment in education relative to other countries. There will be education policies and practices in those countries that do well in the rankings that appear attractive to those who do less well (Phillips and Ochs 2004) and that may well be borrowed, but these borrowings will always be constrained and mediated by a country's particular political and policy trajectory. For example, the rapid transformation in educational attainment achieved by South Korea in the last 10 years and the concomitant growth of its economy will not escape the attention of South Africa, Brazil, Mexico or India, but it is naïve to think that any one of these countries would seek to adopt South Korea's 'education policies'. More realistically perhaps, and where their resources allow, they may experiment in certain areas. But their core policy goals, of inclusiveness, gender parity and rights, born out of political struggles around race, gender, caste and ethnicity, are unlikely to alter significantly.

I am making two arguments here. The first is that it is necessary to consider more carefully why big data are important, and indeed particularly crucial for low-income countries, and the second is that it is necessary to recognise that data are not politically neutral and the manner in which they are used is mediated by different political interests. In order to treat these arguments, the chapter is divided into three sections. First, it discusses the nature of big data in low-income countries and argues that as many of these countries are prone to volatility they have come to rely on geo-imaging technologies for development planning. It looks in some detail at the uses of big data in low-income African countries. Second, the chapter looks at a recent large-scale study of teacher knowledge in Nigeria and teases out the questions of demand and intent. It looks at the promise that the data offer in respect of policies on teacher recruitment, deployment and professional development, but also the threat that the data, because it is 'high stakes', poses to a variety of political interest groups. The study shows that the demand for data, legitimacy notwithstanding, can stand or fall on the question of intent – i.e. what politicians say the data are intended for and what other political actors think the intentions are. The chapter concludes with the thought that big data are the new oil, but like oil, work best when they are refined, and by this I mean in terms of the legitimacy of demand, and the honourability of intent.

The Uses of Big Data in Low-Income African Nations

Though it is not a feature unique to them, many low-income African countries are forced to contend with 'development traps' such as being landlocked with bad neighbours (Collier 2007) or indeed 'development shocks', such as armed conflict or drought, and because of their increasing connectedness to the global economy, to the current financial crisis in Europe or the USA. The impact of such shocks on the political, social or economic lives of the most vulnerable people is far-reaching and often irreversible, and the problem for development planning is that by the time data on the effects of a shock become available through normal survey methods, it is often too late to make decisions that are meaningful.

According to the OECD, global volatility is unlikely to abate:

> [d]isruptive shocks to the global economy are likely to become more frequent and cause greater economic and societal hardship. The economic spill-over effect of events like the financial crisis or a potential pandemic will grow due people, goods and data travel.
>
> (OECD, 27 June 2011, cited in UN Global Pulse 2012: 11)

It is precisely as a result of global uncertainties that the demand for big data has increased. A major challenge for the well-being of children in Africa is ensuring that limited supplies of life-saving medicines are distributed to the health facilities where they are needed. But, according to a report in the *MIT Technology Review* (2013), the demand for drugs is unpredictable and depends on outbreaks of one disease or another. To ensure that the right distribution is achieved, in the right places, real-time data are needed. In Tanzania, a pilot programme called SMS for Life persuaded front-line workers from every clinic to send an SMS (text message) with their stock count each week. As soon as coordinating staff had access to these figures, they were able to accurately target restocking of the clinics. The results were dramatic: the proportion of health facilities with no stock of one or more medicines fell from 78 per cent to 26 per cent, and stock-outs were virtually eliminated by week 8 of the pilot (*MIT Technology Review* 2013).

In Kenya, according to a report in the *MIT Technology Review* (2013), a team engaged in a project aimed at controlling the spread of Malaria monitored the movement of people through their use of mobile phones. It is important to stress that the researchers did not tap or listen into people's calls or read their text messages. Rather they monitored patterns of use. They found that people making calls or sending text messages originating at the Kericho tower (a mobile phone satellite that was being monitored) were making 16 times more trips away from the area than the regional average and were three times more likely to visit a region northeast of Lake Victoria that records from the health ministry identified as a malaria hot spot. Satellite images revealed a significant waypoint for transmission of malaria (*MIT Technology Review* 2013).

Also in Kenya, in the sphere of education the large-scale displacement of communities and the traumatisation of children following the 2007 elections had prompted government and non-governmental organisations to find ways of establishing an 'early warning system' to enable a more timely response to election- related violence in schools. Working with the Kenyan Primary School Head Teachers Association (KEPSHA), UNICEF, and a local mobile phone network, Johnson (2013) developed an SMS-based survey designed specifically to monitor the physical safety and security of schools in real time – immediately before, during and immediately after the elections, establishing whether they reopened in time, the rate at which children were attending and the levels of their participation. Using the KEPSHA membership of over 20,000 headteachers spread across 47 newly devolved counties, the researchers were able to map in real time the levels of security in schools before the elections. The areas outlined in in Figure 10.1 show the counties with a higher percentage of respondents indicating that they considered their schools insecure during the time of the election.

The final example of the use of big data in low-income African countries is the development of a GIS school mapping initiative in Sudan. School mapping is the art and science of building a geospatial database with relational databases of educational, demographic, social and economic information for educational administrative authorities. The GIS school mapping data set in Sudan shows school locations and other significant geographic features such as road networks, administrative boundaries, distribution of settlements, public utilities, river systems and other geographic features.

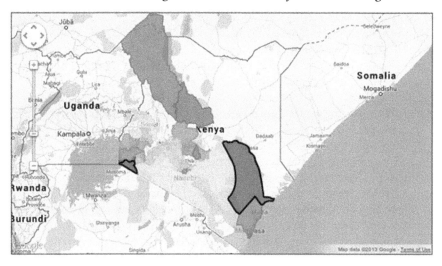

Figure 10.1   Screen grab of the online SMS dashboard analysing Head Teachers'
perceived levels of insecurity expressed by SMS two days before the
elections on 4 March 2013, organised by county (KEPSHA 2013).

Hite and Hite (2004: 23) maintain that GIS in school mapping provide for

> expanded "holistic" representation and exploration of the contexts of
> schooling through the direct and dynamic use of multiple sources of influ-
> ential data such as those found in census, transportation, utilities, health
> care, land use and agricultural databases which are otherwise very difficult
> to include in educational planning and management.

These examples show some of the ways in which rapid advances in the application
of geographic information system and geo-imaging technology for educational
purposes have transformed educational planning and decision-making.

Having discussed some applications of big data in low-income African countries,
I return to the concepts of demand and intent. Using a large-scale study of teacher
professional knowledge in Nigeria, the chapter now discusses how demand for data
arose, the intentions of government in how these data would be used, and the political resistance that followed in some parts of the country though not in others.

Data and the Politics of Education in Nigeria

Demand and Intent

In 2008 the Commissioner for Education and the Governor of the state of Kwara
expressed concern that a significant share of the education budget in that state was
being spent on teacher in-service development but that it was unclear what effects
this has had over the last decade or so, given that data suggested that student
learning achievements had stagnated during this period. Given the debates about

the relationship between teacher knowledge and learner achievement, the state commissioned a study of the professional knowledge of all primary school teachers. The original intention of the state was that the weakest teachers would be purged from the system. The following quotation from the Commissioner (published in the *Punch* newspaper) makes this point:

> [T]he most important factor that would determine whether the children could produce the results expected of them is the quality of teaching that the child will be able to receive. In auditing these different factors, we ask ourselves whether the teachers are capable of teaching them to achieve the results. Since the entry point into upper primary is primary four, we now said a teacher who will teach primary four should be able to know what a primary four child was being asked to do. What you don't have, you cannot give. Secondly, I am not an educationist but I understand policy. All our teachers cannot be on the same level of incompetence, all of them can also not be on the same level of competence. We need to know scientifically, how many of those teachers are very good, how many of them are not so good, how many of them are manageable and how many are totally bad.
>
> (*Punch* 2008)

The Commissioner goes on say that it very quickly became clear that the proposed high stakes nature of the data on teacher performance had antagonised a number of political actors, including teacher trade unions:

> When I first came up with the idea many people argued that it would not work. I almost received a slap from some senior civil servants in the ministry during a management meeting when the matter came up for discussion. They argued that such a policy could not work because of the political situation in the state. I insisted that we would do it and that the worst was that the policy would fail then we would have learned an important lesson that it could not be done.
>
> (Ibid.)

A number of meetings ensued and eventually a compromise was reached. The state agreed that teachers would not be dismissed as a result of their performance on the test: 'We had promised that the results won't be used to sack any teachers that failed but that anyone who refused to write the exams would earn an automatic sack' (ibid.). However, the state continued to argue that it was important to profile teachers in order to offer a more targeted professional development training programme. The Commissioner stated that:

> The essence is to categorize them and design the kind of training suitable for each category because if you don't do that, we won't be able to determine the categories and the proficiency of the teachers. That was why we conducted the assessment.
>
> (Ibid.)

It was clear from the outset that the demand for data was high and that the intentions of the state in how the data would be used were clear. The state was determined to purge the system of 'weak' teachers, with some possibility for redeployment. One reason advanced was that weak teachers absorbed, with no evidence of any benefit, scarce resources. The second, and perhaps more crucial reason for the proposed purge was the view that teachers with insufficient subject knowledge and professional capabilities weakened the quality of learning outcomes. The state was keen to act on findings from studies that showed unacceptably low levels of student achievement in literacy and mathematics. The state also recognised that feelings ran high about corruption in the employment and deployment of teachers, and wanted to take steps to ensure that those who held posts merited such positions. It was also clear that there were those who benefited from corruption and that there were many groups and actors, all with different interest and the ability to exert influence and power. Such 'actors' included teacher trade unions, and while they cannot be accused of corruption, they often have interests different from those expressed by the state in respect of teacher rights and responsibilities.

It was clear that trades unions would not agree to an assessment of teachers if one of the consequences might be the dismissal of teachers. This revealed the first challenge to the state's claim on the legitimacy of the data needed for policy-making. But in Kwara State, the political reaction was managed and the tests did go ahead, with far reaching consequences. *Punch* (2008) ran the following story:

> Early last week, the Kwara State commissioner for education, science and technology, Malam Bolaji Abdullahi, made a shocking revelation. Out of 19,125 teachers, including 2,628 university graduates, who took a test designed for primary four pupils, only seven passed. Two hundred and fifty-nine teachers, including 10 university graduates, scored zero in the test which was in English and Mathematics. This is the barest manifestation of the utter decay in our education system.

Indeed, that the story ran at all offers a sharp insight into the politics of educational decision-making. The Commissioner of Kwara State went on record in an interview with *Punch* and revealed the following:

> We were confused. We contemplated whether to kill the result or publish it because we were concerned with the image of the state and how it would portray our educational system. We invariably decided to publish it so that other state governments would know that there was a problem in their own educational system because Kwara is one of the leading states as far as the standard of education is concerned. We then called all the stakeholders in the education sector and announced the result. Everybody was shocked.
>
> (*Punch* 2008)

As the quotation above shows, the state took a brave decision to make the data publically available. This set in train a number of interesting events. First, international donor partners rallied to the support of Kwara State and set in motion a number of interventions that had been recommended in the research report. These included projects aimed at increasing the literacy levels of teachers, to enable them to read for information more effectively and to use information more efficiently in their teaching. Second, the Federal Government made more resources available to the state and took steps to institutionalise the teacher test. In a short time Kwara State had begun to show results in the improvement of teacher standards and this stimulated the curiosity of other state governments, many of whom commissioned the study for their states.

It is perhaps useful to pause here to offer something of an insight into the diagnostic potential of the data and what attracted other states to the study.

The study was carried out in Lagos State in 2010. As in Kwara the entire population of primary school teachers was assessed.

The Study

In the absence of published teacher standards, consultative groups were established in the states in which the study was conducted and the following was agreed as a fair expectation of what teachers should be able to do.

Teachers should be able to mark accurately at least 80 per cent of items on a mathematics test paper as answered by 10-year old children; they should also be able to mark accurately at least 80 per cent of an English language paper that contains a reading comprehension test and other aspects of language such as word meanings and vocabulary, and correct for form, content, and punctuation a number of sentences and a letter written by a 10-year-old child. Teachers themselves should be able to write a friendly letter that takes into account purpose (who the letter is intended for), that is grammatically correct, and that is relatively accurate in spelling and punctuation, such that it might be used as a model for teaching children to write such letters. In addition, teachers achieving the desired professional working knowledge threshold should be able to extract information from a variety of short information giving texts and use this to write short notes, such as that which might be expected in outlining the content of a lesson that they would teach to primary school children. It is expected that teachers would master at least 80 per cent of such reading material, and demonstrate the ability to summarise it accurately such as they would in writing notes on the chalkboard for children to copy into their exercise books. Finally, teachers should be able to do simple arithmetical operations such as calculating averages and percentages and interpreting simple graphs, and use the information to comment upon and track the progress of individuals or groups in the classes. Further, that they should be able to use a marking guide to assess the quality of student's writing and to discriminate between writing produced by different students, in so doing demonstrate their own understanding of children's learning. Again, it is expected that teachers achieve this up to 80 per cent of the time.

The Data

Rather than discuss the results of the components of the test, it suffices here to show the diagnostic potential of the data when it was presented. The results were presented for each Local Government Area (LGA). Figure 10.2 shows that there were several LGAs in Lagos that fell below the overall mean score achieved by all Lagos teachers. Of the 20 LGAs, nine performed only slightly above the mean, although it is interesting that the variation in scores between LGAs was not significant. The immediate value of the data was that they pinpointed for the state those LGAs in which teachers required more or less attention in further professional development. The highest performing LGA was Lagos Island. Teachers there achieved an average percentage score of 46.2 per cent. The profile of teachers in Ikeja was very similar. Teachers in these two LGAs achieved scores nearly two percentage points above the mean. Lagos Mainland, Ibeju Lekki and Amuwo Odofin were the worst performing LGAs. Teachers in Ibeju Lekki scored over four percentage points below the mean. However, the variation in test performance between LGAs was not statistically significant.

There was also significant variation in the test performance of teachers within each LGA. Figure 10.3 shows how the scores were distributed. It is interesting to look at the outliers in each case: a number of teachers in each LGA did very well in every test, but it is also clear that a significant number of teachers were bunched at the other extreme. Those outliers marked by a dot denote individual teachers who achieved scores of between 1.5 per cent and 3 per cent above the interquartile range. Those outliers marked by a star denote teachers who achieved scores more than three times the interquartile range. Figure 10.3 shows that in 14 out of the 20 LGAs a small number of teachers achieved scores of 80 per cent or over. But, in every LGA there are significant numbers of teachers who achieved very low overall scores, the lowest scores in each case being zero. The highest-performing teachers were in Eppe and Mushin.

In summary, the results for Lagos were not very good; teachers achieved an overall mean score that fell over 35 percentage points short of the desired achievement benchmark. As suggested above, I am less concerned here with an analysis of the results, and

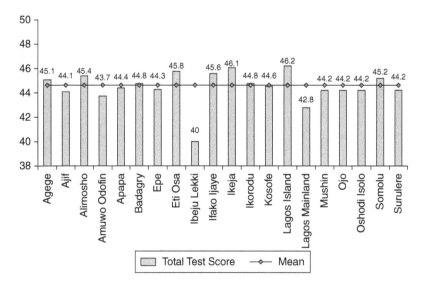

Figure 10.2   Mean percentage scores by LGA: total test.

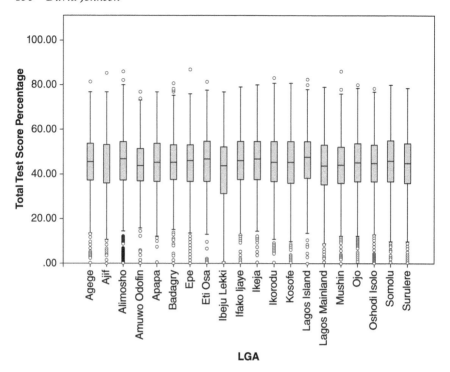

Figure 10.3   Distribution of test scores by LGA.

more with demonstrating the diagnostic potential of big data for policy and planning. Using the profiles in Figures 10.2 and 10.3, the state can target more efficiently its resources, or make decisions about the recruitment or deployment of teachers, or the use of the best-performing teachers as a resource to support the development of others.

The Politics of Resistance

Lagos State like Kwara State was able to manage resistance to the teacher assessment and the study went ahead. But there were a number of states where they tests did not go ahead because political resistance was too strong. In Ekiti State, the Governor established the demand for data but was also clear on the intentions of their use. Teachers boycotted the tests in the belief that they would be dismissed if their results were poor. *The Nation* newspaper carried the following story:

> [T]eachers, acting on NUT [Nigerian Union of Teachers] platform boycotted most of the 39 test centres across the state, leaving invigilators, security agents and consultants from various universities waiting endlessly.

> Governor Kayode Fayemi and others accused them of sabotaging government's efforts to sanitise the education system.

> (*The Nation* 2012)

Interestingly the state convinced the NUT of the legitimacy of the study, but teachers broke ranks with their union and continued to boycott the tests.

> After meeting with the national leadership of NUT, the governor said the teachers had agreed to write the tests, though a new date has not been fixed.
>
> The Ekiti teachers are not happy with the NUT leadership for making such commitment on their behalf. They opposed the national body, which they said never consulted them before accepting a decision they 'see as a matter of life and death'.
>
> (Ibid.)

It is interesting that the teachers did not trust the intentions of the state; one teacher at Emmanuel Anglican Primary School maintained that 'government is actually planning to sack some of us', adding: 'We don't know government's intention now. Principals who sat for it earlier are now regretting it' (ibid.). Another teacher commented:

> We will sit for the test if we are clear regarding the intentions of government. No one fears tests. We also test our pupils. But, really no one can be sure about the real intentions of government. That's why we don't want to have anything to do with it.
>
> (Ibid.)

Having lost the backing of their union, teachers turned to the National Parent-Teacher Association (NAPTAN):

> At a meeting in Mary Immaculate Secondary School, Ado-Ekiti, NAPTAN accused the "government of taking such a serious decision without first consulting with other stakeholders; especially the PTA".
>
> In a communiqué jointly signed by its Chairman, Pastor Sunday Isikalu; Secretary, Mr Biodun Famoroti and Public Relations Officer, Mr Oke Gbenga, the association warned that the issue might assume worrisome dimensions if not carefully handled.
>
> NAPTAN advised the government to organize seminars and workshops for teachers to sharpen their skills as an alternative to the test.
>
> (Ibid.)

In Bayelsa State, the government also set out its arguments for data on teacher knowledge; and it was uncompromising in its statement in how the data would be used. The Governor Seriake Dickson said:

> The exercise is part of government's plan to make drastic changes in the education sector in line with its free and compulsory education policy. A total of 5,119 teachers and 541 headmasters from public primary schools in

the state are expected to be trained, retrained and be tested on the skills acquired at the end of the exercise.

(Ibid.)

As was to be expected, the NUT came out against sacking any teachers who failed the test.

Conclusions

The study discussed above provides interesting insights into the political dilemmas associated with the demand for and the intent of data. It also shows that potential diagnostic potential of big data and the extent to which that may allow a government to plan more efficiently.

To take the second point first, the data allow the government to build theoretical policy models. For example, the government of Lagos might ask whether the academic abilities of aspirant teachers are adequate when they enrol for initial teacher training. There is as yet no definitive answer to that question but it is highly likely that they are not. It would, therefore, be a sensible policy option to use the tests developed here to screen applicants as they enter initial teacher training and through a similar method of profiling achievement, to put in place a series of academic support programmes. If the profile suggested by the tests discussed here is similar when applied to those enrolling for initial teacher training, it is likely that a significant proportion of applicants would be rejected on the grounds that they have insufficient basic literacy. At least half of all applicants might have to dedicate a good proportion of an academic year on specifically designed courses to improve their basic literacy and numeracy.

The data also point to other areas for research. It suggests that pre-service teacher training is ineffective in increasing teacher subject and professional knowledge. But the extent of the problem has not been fully investigated, and given limited data, researchers have not been able to tease out differences between that knowledge necessary for teaching a subject such as mathematics, and that necessary for carrying out professional classroom administrative tasks which rely on a basic knowledge of arithmetical operations, or similarly, the knowledge that is needed to teach a subject such as English, or in the language of English, and that necessary to read basic texts and extract from these information necessary to prepare teaching notes or lesson plans. The benefits of the study discussed here in providing reliable knowledge to direct the construction of the initial teacher training curriculum are significant.

It is also the case that when the quality of teaching is weak, the typical response of many governments and their international development partners has been to place their faith in policies for in-service teacher development. But the question rarely asked is, can in-service teacher development programmes remedy the effects of low entry standards and increase the academic and professional competencies of teachers, both those who hold teacher qualifications and those who do not? There is very little research on the effectiveness of in-service professional development on such basic teacher knowledge and capabilities. Anecdotal evidence suggests that it has little significant effect, but it would be unthinkable for it not to feature prominently as a teacher policy in the education plans of many developing countries.

More to the point, if in-service teacher development is not the panacea it is often made out to be, how should those teachers with unacceptably low professional capabilities, and this study shows that there are many, be supported? There is no doubt that the majority of teachers need some form of continuous professional development. But it is clear from the data that one size will hardly fit all. The way forward could be to target, with programmes more specifically tuned into the needs identified in this study, specific groups of teachers. It is clear that a sizeable proportion of teachers could improve with specifically developed materials to scaffold their reading and writing literacies. Better still if this was integrated with an approach that placed more emphasis on literacy in the classroom.

The most challenging policy decision for the government is what to do with the large numbers of teachers who fall a long way short of achieving acceptable norms in their knowledge of subject or pedagogy. It seems that the governments of Lagos and Kwara may have to experiment with more innovative ways in which to actively employ these teachers in professional tasks that do not immediately require, those levels of competence described here.

Good information systems are also crucial to monitoring and evaluation. A big concern at the moment is that there are no reliable baselines against which to measure the efficacy of teacher professional development programmes. Also, it would not be possible to track, over time, what progression if any individual teachers are making against their own professional development profiles. On this hinges important questions about teacher pay and reward policies, teacher deployment and career progression. Good information is also vital for policies on teacher dismissal, if after time, those teachers have not responded well to professional development activities.

To return to the first point, the study reveals the political dimensions of the demand for data and the intentions that lie behind data use. I illustrated how Commissioners of Education in four Nigerian States established the demand for data on teacher knowledge. In the States of Kwara and Lagos, the governments were able to mediate political resistance to the demand for data largely through softening the intent. The tests went ahead in these states. It was different in Ekiti State and Bayelsa State where the demand for teacher data was resisted.

The chapter has made the case that big data are important and frequently serve a vital function in low-income countries. But the chapter also shows that unless the demands for data are strong and credible, and that the intention is shared, and importantly, as demonstrated in the case of Kwara, that the political will to use the data is strong, its development is likely to die in the stranglehold of political interest groups.

References

Collier, P. (2007) *Why the Poorest Countries Are Failing and What Can Be Done About It.* Oxford: Oxford University Press.

Hite, S.J. and Hite, J.M. (2004) *Geographical Information Systems in Education Planning and Management: A Training Module Created for the IIEP/UNESCO.* Paris: IIEP/UNESCO.

Johnson, D., Datoo, A. and Cunningham, A. (forthcoming) 'Elections, education and social cohesion in Kenya', *Journal of East African Studies,* 7(4).

KEPSHA (Kenyan Primary School Head Teachers Association) (2013) *Survey of School Safety and Security.* Nairobi: KEPSHA.

Lascoumes, P. and Le Galès, P. (2007) 'Understanding public policy through its instruments. From the nature of instruments to the sociology of public policy instrumentation', *Governance,* 20(1), 1–21.

MIT Technology Review (2013, April) http://www.technologyreview.com/featuredstory/513721/big-data-from-cheap-phones/

Ozga, J. (2012) 'Governing knowledge: data, inspection and education policy in Europe', *Globalisation, Societies and Education,* 10(4), 439–455.

Phillips, D. and Ochs, K. (2004) 'Researching policy borrowing: some methodological challenges in comparative education', *British Education Research Journal,* 30(6), 773–784.

Punch (2008, 8 December) http://www.punchng.com/opinion/the-menace-of-unqualified-nigerian-teachers/

The Nation (2012, 31 August) http://thenationonlineng.net/new/education/states-teachers-tango-over-test/

UN Global Pulse (2012) *Big Data for Development: Challenges and Opportunities.* New York: United Nations.

11 Governing Through Feedback

From National Orientation Towards Global Positioning[1]

Maarten Simons

Introduction

It is striking to notice how during the past decades it has become increasingly important to come to understand oneself through comparison. This is not only the case when it comes to the self-understanding of regions in a global world or to member states in the European Union. The comparative dimension is also evident in, for instance, how schools understand their position in a national educational system, how teachers and students are asked to understand themselves, and how academics and scholars come to know themselves. The gaining of self-knowledge through comparison seems to include that this knowledge is mainly about *positioning* oneself: where do I or we stand in relation to others, or in relation to my or our past position? These and similar questions not only orient today's modes of self-understanding but are clearly part of our self-government as well: the 'will to know through comparison' is at once about a 'will to improve' continuously one's position as a region, EU member state, school or teacher. Far from all this being something that is enforced or imposed, comparative knowledge and related forms of monitoring increasingly appear as something vital, that is, it seems to be part of who we are and what we want. It feels as 'we' are permanently in need of information in order to position ourselves and to improve that position.

The aim of this chapter is to argue that the evident need for and exchange of comparative information should be regarded as a symptom of a new mode of governing that installs less-evident power relations. The approach is taken from Foucault who analyses governing as a form of 'conduct of conduct' or a more or less calculated and rational attempt to direct human conduct by applying specific technical means (Foucault 1982: 237). The thesis is that the current 'conduct of conduct' takes shape as 'feedback on performance', and which logic can be summarised as follows: what is of strategic importance today is the circulation of *feedback* information, and as far as the actors involved in education come to understand what they are doing as a *performance*, feedback information is experienced as indispensable. Hence, in line with the literature on 'governing by numbers' (Rose 1991; Grek 2009; Ozga 2009) and 'governing by comparison' (Nóvoa and Yariv-Mashal 2003), the chapter first aims to focus on mechanisms of 'governing through feedback', and specifically to examine how educational policy and state authorities increasingly rationalise (and justify) their role as collecting and offering feedback information. Within the scope of this chapter, the argument is developed while focusing in particular on the role of feedback information for Flemish educational government. Hence, the focus is limited to Flanders – being a community within the federal state of Belgium responsible for educational policy. Second, the objective of the chapter is to come to an understanding of the new power mechanisms that spread through today's modes of governing. It is argued that instead of the power of surveillance (in the panopticon) and the power of examples/exceptions (in the synopticon), it is 360° feedback that offers a paradigmatic articulation of new forms of power today.

A Government in Need of Feedback

In many countries information from the well-known *Programme for International Student Assessment* (PISA) and *Trends in International Mathematics and Science Studies* (TIMMS) has come to play a role at the level of national educational policy. Belgium, and particularly the Flemish community, is no exception. The subtitle of the policy declaration (2004–2009) of the previous Flemish Minister of Education (Vandenbroucke 2004) was very instructive in that regard: 'Today champion in mathematics, tomorrow also in equal opportunities'.[2] Based on the good results of international, comparative studies, the document claims that it is the task of educational policy to 'consolidate and stimulate' the high quality of education in Flanders, as well as to focus on the weaker performance with regard to 'equal opportunities' in education. Concerning the latter, and drawing on the 2003 PISA report, the policy document highlights the strong influence of socio-economic status on the performance of students in Flanders compared to the average in other OECD countries. As a result, this information, combined with national statistics, is used to identify and justify problem areas for policy intervention in a specific way. Educational policymakers in Flanders see it as their task to enhance the quality of education, and moreover 'quality education' is now framed as 'international performance' (Vandenbroucke 2005). In a similar way, yet at the level of European Union, these approaches are in evidence.

   In the European context, educational policy is still claimed today to be the responsibility of the member states (justified by the principle of subsidiarity). The European Union is therefore required to limit its contribution 'to the development of quality education by encouraging cooperation between member states and, if necessary, by supporting and supplementing their action' (Maastricht Treaty 1992). In this context, the Open Method of Coordination is used, and in order to meet the goals of the Lisbon strategy, benchmarks or 'reference levels of European average performance' have been introduced regarding education and training (Lisbon European Council [LEC] 2000: §37). It is claimed that although these reference levels are based on comparable data, they should 'not define national targets'. Yet the Council (2003: 4, see also 2005) expects that these benchmarks will be used by national governments to orient their educational policy. With regard to Belgium/Flanders, and similar to the results of PISA, this is indeed the case.

An example was the benchmark introduced relating to the number of early school leavers: 'By 2010, an EU average rate of no more than 10% early school leavers should be achieved' (Council 2003: 4). This benchmark was used as well at the level of Flemish educational government to identify weaknesses in the performance of the Flemish educational system and to formulate policy measures (Vandenbroucke 2004: 14). Another example was the benchmark concerning lifelong learning. Participation of the adult working age group in lifelong learning of 12.5 per cent by 2010 was put forward as a target (Council 2003: 5), and used by the Flemish government (Vandenbroucke 2004: 14) to assess their present performance and to take initiatives for its optimisation. The use of similar benchmarks – as part of the follow-up programme *Education and Training 2020* – continues today.

'Europe' thus enters the policy context of Flanders through the development of educational quality standards that are being expressed in data on performance indicators, and additional information on best practices. As a result, domains as well as objectives of educational policy increasingly have a European, comparative dimension. Moreover, as the case of Belgium/Flanders clearly indicates, this global and European framework of educational quality was welcomed and even perceived as a necessity. For instance, the minister of education (Vandenbroucke 2005, 2006) in Flanders stressed:

> An information-rich environment […] is notwithstanding essential for educational policy in Flanders. […] Are enough data, indicators and benchmarks available at the level of central policy to shape central government and to monitor local policy? [...] Are we able to check our policy based on the best practice of other countries?

Although the minister (Vandenbroucke 2005) argued that Flanders has made great progress in what he calls the 'professionalisation of educational policy' based on 'international stimuli', he stressed that more data are conceived to be indispensable. It is important to understand, however, what kind of policy and what kind of state/agency perceives 'professionalisation through information' as vital. Or to reformulate this in Foucault's approach of an ontology of the present: who are we (today), we for whom a particular kind of information has become necessary in order to govern ourselves and others? In order to answer that question, a more detailed analysis of current processes of governmentalisation, and the implied modes of conduct of conduct, is required.

Processes of Governmentalisation

Although the main interest is the role of national policy (Flanders, in Belgium), the focus first is on some features of the current role of Europe, in particular relating to education. As mentioned earlier, the European Union conceives its task as one of developing educational quality. However, the EU limits its governmental actions by claiming to respect the responsibility of member states. As such, the EU (LEC 2000: §41) rationalises this limited role as 'a catalyst' in order to establish 'an effective framework for mobilising all available resources for the transition to the knowledge-based economy'. Within the scope of the Lisbon strategy this limited role is an *economic* role in three different ways (Foucault 2004: 253). First, it is economic for it reflects upon its own governmental practices in economic terms, i.e. governmental interventions are 'economised' by taking into account and using existing governmental practices (member states). Second, it is economic for it conceives of these practices in economic terms as resources that should be 'managed' in a particular way in order to reach the strategic goals. And as far as these strategic goals are themselves to a large extent economic (e.g., the knowledge economy), also at this level a kind of economic government can be noticed.

This catalyst or enabling role is exemplified very well in the Open Method of Coordination, through which member states, and all other partners that are mobilised for these strategic goals, come to understand themselves as 'calculative' agencies being part of 'calculable spaces' (Haahr 2004: 219). As such, the freedom and responsibility presupposed in the principle of subsidiarity is of a particular kind, that is, a freedom that encompasses the responsibility to calculate and mobilise resources and the virtue to optimise one's performance in view of common targets. Furthermore, part of this role of Europe is the construction of a new identity of the European Commission: 'an institution capable of legitimately and authoritatively passing out grades to member states, thereby establishing their relative forwardness or backwardness in terms of virtue' (Haahr 2004: 223). The Open Method of Coordination hence opens up the space to reflect upon the role of the Commission in 'managerial' terms with one of its main tasks being the management of information on performance.

Instead of regarding Europeanisation as a gradual process of integration ultimately resulting in a kind of 'nationalisation of Europe', the developments mentioned above help to understand it in terms of a 'governmentalisation of Europe' (Masschelein and Simons 2003). The emergence of a managerial mentality and procedure reconfigures the role of Europe as well as the entities to be governed. What takes shape is an 'art of European government' that constitutes the European Union, its institutions and experts, as central 'agencies of coordination', i.e. of managing the conduct of member states (Barry 1994). It would be more precise to approach this as the *managementalisation* of Europe.

In order to have a clearer understanding of these processes, it is important to discuss the specificity of the 'calculable spaces' in which member states frame their national system of education. As the title of the earlier cited policy declaration in Flanders – 'Today champion in mathematics, tomorrow also in equal opportunities' – suggests, the Flemish educational system is ranked with other (European, OECD) systems related to its performance. As a consequence, policy in Flanders affirms that educational systems are commensurable, can be compared and measured on a single scale of performance or output. In this context of 'performativity', as Lyotard (1979) discussed some time ago, the criteria of efficiency and effectiveness become of central importance. 'Good education' is framed as effective and efficient performance with respect to specific indicators (e.g., achievements relating to mathematics) and calculated on the basis of

European/global average performance (Commission 2006). A particular kind of information becomes indispensable if one is positioned within such calculable spaces of efficiency and effectiveness: that is, comparative information on one's performance in relation to a specific norm, average or past performance. This kind of evaluative information is defined by Wiener (in cybernetics) as feedback and its function is to control the operation of a system 'by reinserting into it the results of its past performance' (Wiener 1950/89: 61). As calculating agents, member states, and in particular the Flemish government, come to experience this kind of feedback as essential at two, related levels.

On the one hand, comparative information evaluates the performance of a state's past and present educational policy and can be used to re-orient educational policy and to optimise its performance. As such, information generated through the European coordination method and other international assessment instruments is welcomed in Flanders in order 'to have a better understanding of one's own educational policy' (Vandenbroucke 2004: 25) and it is perceived as a kind of stimulus for the 'professionalisation of educational policy'. Clearly, this process of professionalisation has a particular focus: the activity of educational policy itself is framed as performance in an international, competitive environment and it is perceived as engagement in a 'process of competitive self-improvement' (Haahr 2004: 223). On the other hand, feedback on the performance of national educational systems justifies and reinforces the role and tasks of national government in terms of performance management. The issue of 'equal opportunities' for example is used as an indicator of the system's performance, and information on this indicator evaluates whether resources are mobilised in an optimal way. As such, central policy in Flanders seeks to become a kind of 'performance targeted policy' (Vandenbroucke 2006) in an international/European, competitive environment. At this level, feedback is crucial to inform the management of processes of competitive self-improvement of an educational system. And the urgent need for additional performance indicators and a rich information environment, expressed by Flemish policymakers, should be regarded as a logical outcome of this managerial attitude.

Thus, as far as (optimal) conduct is conceived as (optimal) performance, both at the level of educational policy and the educational system, feedback is needed in order to direct this conduct. In short, governing, or what Foucault approaches as the 'conduct of conduct', takes the form of 'feedback on performance' in the practices being discussed, and the collection and distribution of feedback information becomes a powerful steering mechanism (Bröckling 2006). Moreover, it is exactly within this configuration of governing that new centres of monitoring and calculation take shape and, drawing on Callon (1986), start to function as 'obligatory passage points': European benchmark reports, and international studies such as PISA, become increasingly indispensable for (member) states to know themselves in view of improving performance (see also Grek *et al.* 2009; Nóvoa and Yariv-Mashal 2003). Furthermore, the emerging *will to know* and *will to perform* of these actors actually reinforce the authority of these reports and studies, amplify their visibility but also (and therefore) 'black box' their production mechanisms and the organisations and experts 'behind' them (Latour 1987). As the Flemish case exemplifies, what is put centre stage, or more precisely, what is inscribed as a reality, is that educational quality is about performance, that the educational system is champion when it comes to mathematics, and that Finland – the example of best performance – shows it is possible to become champion as well in equal opportunities.

The Good Conduct

The current mode of governing through feedback helps to understand the emergence of new 'policy virtues' as evidenced in the conduct of the Flemish government in its role as calculating agency: (1) a readiness to learn from comparison; (2) to benchmark and look for examples, to collaborate in order to compete; and (3) to be proactive or reactive.

1 Feedback is needed for national government in order to position itself within a competitive environment, but primarily it seeks to feed the process of ongoing self-improvement. Here 'learning' enters the scene: '[A]ll actors in the education and training process have to be ready to learn; and mutual learning, as implicit within an "open method of co-ordination" is a way of increasing the quality of service delivered to the citizen' (Council 2001: 16). Yet it is important to keep in mind that this 'readiness to learn' is from the very beginning framed within a competitive environment where learning outcomes are derived from the best performing policies and educational systems. What is at stake is learning from comparison and learning for the optimal organisation of input, process and output or the optimal mobilisation of resources. As a result the 'need for feedback' and the 'need for learning' reinforce each other. The policy declaration of the Flemish minister of education (Vandenbroucke 2004: 25) – in need of feedback, as mentioned earlier – uses for instance the notion of 'policy imitation' or expressions such as 'learning from others to make progress in achieving one's own objectives, learning from the successes of others, as well as from their failures'. In its staging as a competition state (Yeatman 1993), the Flemish government not only frames the task and object of government in managerial terms, but also discovers *learning* as the fundamental force or resource to re-orient and optimise performance, that is, as a solution for innovation and improvement within a competitive environment. Furthermore, (mutual) learning is not only perceived as a process to secure the optimal performance of each (member state), but at the same time to secure the overall economic (and social) performance of Europe (in comparison with the USA and Japan, for instance). Hence, learning based on feedback on performance plays a kind of strategic role for it brings about a 'double bind of individualisation and totalisation' (Foucault 1982: 232). Learning is regarded as what constitutes optimal performance of one individual member state (Belgium/Flanders), yet at the same time links this individual performance with a totality (Europe). Due to this double bind, questioning the importance of (mutual) learning becomes a vice, and actually comes down to disconnecting oneself from the European strategy.

2 The combination of the 'need for feedback' and the 'will to learn' in a competitive environment helps in understanding the importance of benchmarks and examples of best practice (Arrowsmith *et al.* 2004: 315). The former minister-president of Flanders (Leterme 2006) explained the governmental importance of benchmarking very well:

> Our Flemish welfare is in the year 2006 more than ever a relative issue in space: we are a high performing, open economy in an increasingly globalised world with open borders. Therefore, the Belgian horizon cannot be our benchmark. Our most important trade partners and competitors have done radical conversions [...]. We were down in too many international classifications.

What is clearly assumed is a spatial, or rather ecological, understanding of Flanders (and its economy) in a global, European environment and commensurability at the level of (economic) performance: 'Where do we sit in relation to others?' (Larner and Le Heron 2004: 227). A typical feature of this ecological reasoning is that 'good conduct' (with regard to education or economic policy, for example) is no longer about acting in accordance with general principles or norms, and for instance in accordance with a country's historical mission or traditional identity. Contrary to modern, historical reasoning, ecological (self-) understanding involves mobilising one's resources that are available here and now in view of an optimal performance in comparison with the performance of others. Hence, specific targets or benchmarks are needed as 'global positioning systems' and in order to set a momentary level of optimal performance. The benchmarks or 'reference levels of European average performance' with regard to education and training are illustrative here.

Based on these benchmarks, and statistical data on performance indicators, a table with the 'best performers in the five benchmark areas' as well as information on progress of each performer (member state) is distributed in order to stimulate 'learning from best performance' (Commission 2006). Benchmarking here functions as a kind of calculative 'practice of comparison' (Larner and Le Heron 2004: 218) that satisfies the need for feedback (at the level of Flemish government, for example). But it also reinforces the idea of learning being a fundamental resource in the process of competitive self-improvement.

> Considering that a number of EU member states are already achieving world-best performances in a number of areas, whereas others are faced with serious challenges, there is real added value available in exchanging information on best policy practice at European level.
>
> (Commission 2006: 9)

What has to be learnt first and foremost is to understand why some are better performers, i.e. why and how some manage in a more optimal way the mobilisation of available resources. As a result, the calculative practice of benchmarking leads to the identification of so-called 'best practices', and more specifically the willingness to know 'background variables' and 'context' that explains the 'added value' (Desjardins *et al.* 2004: 2 and 90). What is assumed, as part of this ecological reasoning, is that all, despite the so-called 'cultural differences', are actually doing the same – performing in a challenging environment – and hence, everyone in principle can be an example for and learn from everyone else. Thus what is installed, and continuously reinforced, is a very specific 'space of equivalence' (Desrosières 1998). Part of this space is that the criterion for truth claims is 'what works' or what has proved to perform better or worse given the set indicators or benchmarks. This criterion in fact results in a situation where each truth claim on performance is at once a normative claim for measures of improvement. In sum, the prevailing message today is no longer 'look back' or 'remember your history', but 'look around' – both in order to know how you perform and to find examples for better performance.

3 Finally, global positioning of performance and mutual learning through benchmarking involves a managerial virtue that combines in a particular way an attitude of collaboration and competition. The information exchange, and mainly the information on benchmarks and good practices, functions as feedback information for each of the member states so that they can orient themselves in an international environment and assess and re-orient/consolidate their performance. But in order to maximise this competitive environment, at the same time member states collaborate with each other: as partners in order to formulate common objectives, as suppliers of information to calculate averages and best performance, and as peer reviewers. Thus collaboration is needed in order to have feedback information at one's disposal and in order to be able to monitor, assess and optimise one's own performance. A combination of collaboration and competition works as a procedure of 'coopetition' (Brandenburger and Nalebuff 1996), and this procedure is closely related to a shift in general (political) attitudes at the level of national government.

Broadly speaking, the distinction between 'conservative' and 'progressive' was used to classify political attitudes and policies in the welfare state. What both labels presuppose is a temporal or more specifically, a historical understanding of society, that is, the classification in terms of progress or conservation includes a linear time conception. However, the current mode of governing primarily involves a spatial, ecological understanding of society as an environment and stresses the 'here and now', that is, the time of opportunities, the instant moment or, as Beck (1992: 135) suggests, the 'eternal present'. Permanent monitoring becomes the ideal and correlates with the establishment of global performance indicators in order to answer the typical ecological, and not historical questions, on where we are or how we perform in relation to others. This ecological and global understanding of educational policy in the competition state seems to give birth to new political attitudes: a distinction and tension between a reactive/defensive and a proactive/offensive attitude. The policy declaration of the Flemish government, for example, stresses the importance of a 'proactive stance' of Flanders and of a 'European and international strategy' in order to use the support of Europe in developing and collecting suitable performance indicators (Vandenbroucke 2004: 25). This is clearly a political message of the minister of education to those who hold a kind of reactive and even defensive attitude towards Europeanisation and globalisation. And more specifically, the spatial, global frames of reference also allow for new nationalist and culturalist repositioning, for instance of Flanders against the 'less performative' community in Belgium.

The Power of 360° Feedback

Without the ambition to make any universal or epochal claims, it is striking to notice that patterns of governing through feedback described at the level of (member) states and Europe are also visible elsewhere: government, for instance, seeks to steer schools through offering them feedback on their past performance, feedback becomes a strategy to govern teachers as part of modes of performance appraisal, and increasingly personalised learning trajectories of students seem to correlate with permanent monitoring and feedback systems (Simons and Masschelein 2008). Moreover, questions like 'Where are we?', 'What is our position?', 'How did we perform?' today are treated no longer as symptoms of lack of self-confidence or trust, but appear as legitimate concerns and hence self-evident for good conduct. Drawing on this observation, the challenge is to identify the dominant form of power in the present regime of feedback on performance. This will be done by differentiating it from other power mechanisms identified by Foucault. First, two paradigmatic forms of power – panoptical and synoptical power – will be discussed and illustrated in order to propose '360° feedback' as a third modality of power suited to articulate power relations at work in governing through feedback today.

Typical modern power mechanisms, according to Foucault (1997), seek to discipline human beings through the normalising gaze of experts. Like inmates in a prison, pupils in a school, labourers in a factory and patients in a clinic come to understand themselves in terms of normality and normalised development under the normalising gaze of experts (teachers, managers, doctors) and their examinations and inspections. The paradigmatic articulation of disciplinary power – 'the diagram of a mechanism of power reduced to its ideal form' – is for Foucault (1977: 205) the panopticon, designed by Jeremy Bentham in 1791 as a specific architectonic model of an inspection house. It works according to a logic where the few in the middle of the circle continuously observe the many, but without the many necessary having to know whether there is actually someone observing (Figure 11.1). The ambition, Foucault (1977: 201) argues, is to arrange so that 'surveillance is permanent in its effects, even if it is discontinuous in its action'.

Today, the 'power of surveillance' can be noticed in classic practices of school inspection. Here indeed, the few (i.e. school inspectors) observe and control the many (i.e. schools or teachers), often without the latter knowing when to expect the visit of the inspection. The surveillance is not permanent, yet part of this form of power is to give the impression that inspection can take place at any moment. The inspection, furthermore, works through the judgement of examined cases in view of a fixed set of norms or standards. These function as stable

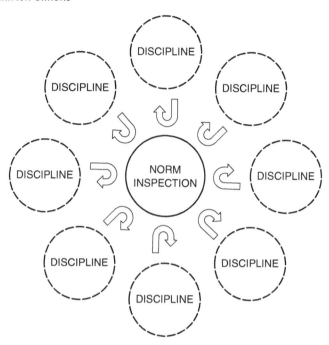

Figure 11.1   Panoptic diagram: norm (instrument); discipline (mode of subjection); inspection (technique).

orientation instruments for both the inspected and inspecting agencies. In the case of the inspection in the Flemish community, the 'attainment targets' – that is, the minimal requirements expected from schools to achieve with their students – operate according to this logic. As fixed and uniform reference levels beyond the empirical realm, they can function as norms or standards that offer a permanent point of orientation, and hence discipline the conduct of for instance schools. It is expected that when references to normality or standards become part of the school's self-understanding, the circle closes and the power machinery runs.

Although disciplinary power clearly has not disappeared today, it no longer seems to be the dominant form of exercising power. It is striking to see, for instance, that in Flanders the school inspection and its normalising judgement is strongly criticised for not being sufficiently objective. An evaluation of the inspectorate by the Court of Audit, for instance, mentions: 'As the school inspection doesn't have a sufficient number of well-established performance data, there is a risk that the inspection focus may not be representative. There is not always evidence that the inspectors found their judgments on performance data' (Court of Audit 2011: 2). The point being made is that professional judgement is insufficiently objective, at least in contrast to objective testing and measurement of school/student performances. Instead of looking at this discussion as merely a matter of validity or reliability, we can look at it as a symptom of changes in governing, including changes in justified forms of power exercise and modes of knowledge production. This should become more clear when elaborating on synoptic power first in order to attempt to identify the diagram of power in governing through feedback afterwards.

Disciplinary power is quite different from the power mechanisms of the spectacle (Foucault 1977). In the spectacle of public punishment, as well as in the theatre for example, the many observe the few and this observation is meant to control the masses (cf. Mathiessen 1997: 219). The synopticon is the paradigm of power of the rule or the law: the many observe the few in the middle of the circle whose punishment or gratification is set as an example, and this observation of the example/exception is aimed at reinforcing submission to the rules or laws. Through exemplification or gratification – and hence by governing through the staging of consequences – the (sovereign) power of rules and laws is re-affirmed, and what is hoped for is further submission.[3] It could be called the 'power of (the) example/exception' (Figure 11.2).

This rather old modality of power is very visible today. An obvious example is the teacher who seeks to govern students through setting an example – a gratification or punishment of someone in front of the whole classroom. But also the PISA reports and other international or European rankings offer images of performance or 'best practice' and organise a kind of (mass) spectacle. The arena of education, and its performance, is rendered visible to all. These public reports operate as a kind of *mass media* that allow the many (schools, states) to watch and observe the few (cf. Vinson

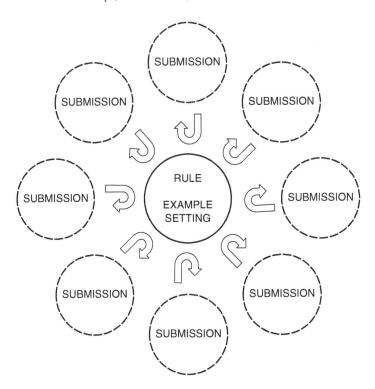

Figure 11.2   Synoptic diagram: rule (instrument); submission (mode of subjection); example setting (technique).

and Ross 2001). What is being watched in this synoptic diagram is a spectacle or arena of the best performers or those representing in an exemplary way optimal performance or 'good conduct'. The spectacle or championship of performance puts states, but also schools or teachers, into a position in which they long themselves to become an image of good performance, to be part of the happy few being watched and admired by the many, and to be a champion themselves (or avoid becoming seen as a loser). The title of the Flemish policy declaration (2004–2009) is perfectly clear in that respect: 'Today champion in mathematics, tomorrow also in equal opportunities.' The Annual Progress Reports on European benchmarks – naming the top three 'Best EU performers' and those making 'Most progress' – and the exchange of 'good practices' among European member states express a similar logic. In Flanders, the synoptic diagram is also visible in the public presentation of 'good practices on school innovation' that are derived from successful so-called 'testing grounds' and that are expected to inspire other schools (Vandenbroucke 2004). Another case in point are the numerous national or European (s)elections of teachers or schools of the year.

A basis synoptic mechanism is the steering in the absence of direct control, that is, power occupies the time in between two public events. Different from the random discontinuity of surveillance and panoptic power, synoptism includes an ideal of regularity and hence allows for purposeful preparation and targeted submission. Current synoptic practices are clearly distinct from their classic predecessors. Whereas classic synoptic power works according to so-called impartial judgement and the reinforcement of law and order, the current power of best performances or good practices is based on so-called accurate and reliable measurement. What is assumed, and constantly reinforced, is what could be called the 'law of performance', framed for instance as, the most efficient and effective use of resources, the best mobilisation of competencies, the highest outcomes. The arena or scaffold thus is replaced by public rankings or by the presentation of practices that are de-/re-contextualised in such a way that they can function as either a good or bad example. As soon as one focuses on the ranking or the example, the circle of power closes: the joined submission to a common law or rule is affirmed, one thinks and acts in its presence and behaves accordingly.

Panoptic and synoptic power diagrams, however, only partly make the exercise of power in today's governing through feedback intelligible. Enabled by new digital information and communication technologies, public stages or constructed frames of reference have become a permanent setting today. They function in such a way that they are the place and time for each and all to become observed and more particularly, to become real. When the Flemish minister of education (Vandenbroucke 2004) argues for the construction of an information-rich environment for Flemish government and for schools, it is exactly about the construction of a data-based stage where the visibility for others is the condition for becoming visible for oneself as government or school. When looking at oneself as performing in a staged environment, the main concern is a kind of permanent 'reality check', that is, monitoring the balance between how one is seen and how one sees oneself. What takes shape as the correlate of permanent monitoring is a kind of 'data-based self' (Simon 2005); the self becomes a collection of multiple (performance) indicators and flows of data that can be monitored. In other words, performance no longer only refers to some exemplary measured and staged quality, but becomes a way of life and hence an instrument to be noticed or to be seen; to be, is to be seen or noticed, and hence to perform. While rules ask for submission and norms invoke discipline, performance necessitates monitoring. This is again very precisely phrased by Wiener (1950/89: 30 and 24) when he argued that feedback is about 'the property of being able to adjust future conduct by past performance' and that it requires agencies that 'perform the function of tell-tales or monitors – that is, of instruments that indicate a performance.' It is not at random inspection or regular example setting, but permanent, data-driven feedback that enable the, for instance, self-monitoring school and member state to perform.

A practice that articulates this logic is the 'school feedback report' offered by the *Center for School Feedback* on payment to Flemish schools with information on the school's 'added value' (as the difference between the 'factual means' and the 'expected means').[4] This 'fast, automated feedback' is produced by the school delivering test scores (and other contextual information) and comparisons with reference groups of similar schools (and records of previous test scores). What takes shape is a 'data-based school', and Flemish school life becomes real as staged performance and subject to monitoring. Another practice is the *Education and Training Monitor*, a follow-up of the EU progress reports but now drawing on a Joint Assessment Framework, and published yearly to monitor progress towards the *Education and Training 2020* objectives and benchmarks (European Commission 2012). Since it does not install a permanent feedback stream this new practice includes elements of the synoptic diagram, but it moves beyond that for it allows member states to become real at a common reference stage and in relation to common indicators and feedback. The mode of subjection is not about disciplining oneself in view of norms or submitting oneself to certain rules, but monitoring oneself in view of performance (Figure 11.3).

The diagram of today's power then is not the synopticon nor the panopticon, but is to be found in the technique of 360° feedback. As a management tool, 360° feedback puts the employee in the middle of a feedback circle composed of all relevant actors in the employee's environment: managers, subordinates, friends, family, customers …. The ideal situation is when the employee's self-evaluation coincides with how all others evaluate her performance. It promotes a kind of self-government that includes a staging in the centre and where one submits oneself permanently, voluntary and openly to the gaze of others – and actually installs a dynamic in which one's own gaze and that of others merge.

The diagram of 360° feedback takes elements of both the synopticon and panopticon, but its logic of operation is different. It is not about the impression of continuous surveillance, but actual and permanent monitoring; not about watching the examples or exceptions in the arena, but staging or positioning oneself in the middle of the circle in order to be seen and receive feedback on the observed performance. What is installed is a permanent and multiple gaze while staging oneself in the middle of the arena and turning one's life or organisation into a performance in need of an audience to

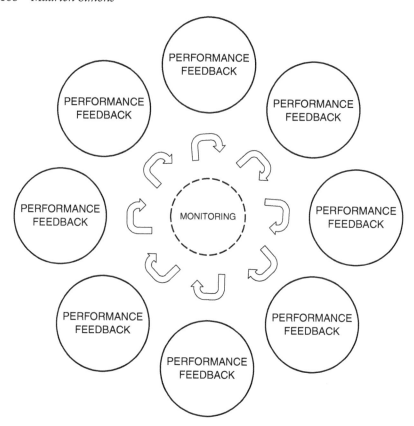

Figure 11.3   360° feedback diagram: performance (instrument); monitoring (mode of subjection); feedback (technique).

become real. Applause, as Wiener (1950/89) already noticed, is the first, basic form of feedback. The driving logic of the 'power of feedback', that is, the moment when feedback actually turns into a power mechanism and the circle closes, is when applause, so to speak, decides on who and what one is and wants to become (as a country, school, teacher, student, etc.). And that means that one no longer knows what to do or how to behave without feedback. Without feedback and monitoring one is lost – which means that feedback actually works as a global positioning system. Within this feedback diagram, there is one thing that is more threatening than a low ranking or negative feedback: not to be seen, or not being able to stage oneself, and not being successful in having recognised what one is doing as a performance.

Conclusion

This chapter has tried to clarify that governing in education today is not only about surveillance or regulation and legislation, but the organisation of feedback loops and related monitoring apparatuses. The main mode of governing is no longer about orientation based on stable, institutionalised points of reference, but about a permanent positioning in space and drawing on flexible performance levels; no longer mainly or only about a linear, historical time conception, but a conception of instant time and opportunities available here and now. Because power is involved in the governmental regime of performance and feedback, this is not necessary bad. But without doubt, it is potentially dangerous (Foucault 1984: 386). It is especially dangerous because the message indeed becomes: 'perform, or else' (McKenzie 2001; Lyotard 1979), and because it becomes very difficult for us, in how we reflect upon ourselves and upon education, not to be part of it. In other words, the mechanisms become powerful when feedback on performance turns into an indispensable navigation tool. This attempt to identify the type of power at stake could be regarded as a modest counter-act, or an attempt to 'enhance the contestability' (Rose 1999) of the regime that seeks to govern us. Is that kind of critical analysis sufficient? In line with Latour (2005), this analysis can be regarded perhaps as a critical gesture that includes a movement of 'making things public': an attempt to turn our increasingly self-evident dealing with education in terms of performance and feedback into a matter of concern again and to gather people as a public around this issue. For that reason, this study does not at once attempt to set new rules, standards or to organise different feedback. But that is not because of an ill-placed intellectual modesty or a so-called relativist postmodern stance. It is because the attempt to combine a critical analysis with (new) modes of subjection – similar to a panopticon, synopticon or 360° feedback – creates a power circle. Critique as a public gesture instead aims at making things public, that is, breaking the power circles and turning the state of affairs in governing education into a matter of public concern again.

Notes

1 This chapter is a revised and elaborated version of an article published in *Journal of Educational Policy* (Simons 2007).
2 The quotes from Flemish policy documents and reports are translations of the author.
3 The important discussion on the distinction between disciplinary and sovereign power (and between Foucault and Agamben) cannot be elaborated in this chapter, but see for instance Agamben (1997), and also Simons and Masschelein (2008).
4 For detailed information: http://www.schoolfeedback.be/

References

Agamben, G. (1997) *Homo Sacer. Le pouvouir souverain et la vie nue*, Paris: Seuil.
Arrowsmith, J., Sisson, K. and Marginson, P. (2004) 'What can 'benchmarking' offer the open method of co-ordination?', *Journal of European Public Policy, 11*(2): 311–328.
Barry, A. (1994) 'Harmonization and the art of European government', in C. Rootes and H. Davis (eds) *Social Change and Political Transformation*, London: UCL Press.
Beck, U. (1992) *Risk Society. Towards a New Modernity*, London: Sage.
Brandenburger, A.M. and Nalebuff, B.J. (1996) *Co-opetition*, New York: Doubleday.
Bröckling, U. (2006) 'Und … wie war ich? Über feedback', *Mittelweg, 36*(2): 26–43.

Callon, M. (1986) 'Some elements of a sociology of translation: Domestication of the scallops and the fishermen of St Brieuc Bay', in J. Law (ed.) *Power, Action and Belief: A New Sociology of Knowledge*, London: Routledge and Kegan Paul.

Commission of the European Communities (2006) *Progress Towards Lisbon Objectives in Education and Training (Report Based on Indicators and Benchmarks, Report 2006)*, Commission Staff Working Document, Brussels, 15 May (SEC (2006) 639).

Council of the European Union (2001) *Report from the Education Council to the European Council: On the Concrete Future Objectives of Education and Training Systems*, Brussels, 14 February. http://ec.europa.eu/education/policies/2010/doc/rep_fut_obj_en.pdf

Council of the European Union (2003) *Council Conclusions on Reference Levels of European Average Performance in Education and Training (Benchmarks)*, Brussels, 7 May 2003. http://ec.europa.eu/education/doc/official/keydoc/2003/benchmark.pdf

Council of the European Union (2005) Council conclusion of 23 May 2005 on new indicators in education and training, *Official Journal of the European Union*, C141, 7–8. http://europa.eu.int/eur-lex/lex/LexUriServ/site/en/oj/2005/c_141/c_14120050610en00070008.pdf

Court of Audit (2011) Abstract of the report 'Toezicht op de kwaliteit van het onderwijs door de inspectie' [Monitoring of the quality of education by the inspectorate]. Retrieved from: https://www.rekenhof.be/NL/Publicaties/Fiche.html?id=34994792-c9c2-4a08-b03f-52190aedd19f

Desjardins, R., Garrouste-Norelins, C. and Mendes, S. (2004) *Benchmarking Education and Training Systems in Europe: An International Comparative Study*, Stockholm: Institute of International Education, Stockholm University.

Desrosières, A. (1998) *The Politics of Large Numbers: A History of Statistical Reasoning*, Cambridge: Harvard University Press.

European Commission (2012) *Education and Training Monitor 2012*, Luxembourg: Publications Office of the EU.

Foucault, M. (1977/1989) *Discipline and Punish. The Birth of the Prison*, New York: Pantheon Books.

Foucault, M. (1982) 'Le sujet et le pouvoir', in D. Defert, F. Ewald and J. Lagrange (eds) *Dits et écrits IV 1980–1988*, Paris: Gallimard.

Foucault, M. (1984) *Histoire de la sexualité 2. L'usage des plaisirs*, Paris: Gallimard.

Foucault, M. (2004) *Naissance de la biopolitique. Cours au Collège de France (1978–1979)*, Paris: Gallimard/Le seuil.

Grek, S. (2009) 'Governing by numbers: the PISA 'effect' in Europe', *Journal of Education Policy*, 24(1): 23–37.

Grek, S., Lawn, M., Lingard, B. and Varjo, J. (2009) 'North by Northwest: Quality assurance and evaluation processes in European education', *Journal of Education Policy*, 24(2): 121–133.

Haahr, J. (2004) 'Open co-ordination as advanced liberal government', *Journal of European Public Policy*, 11(2): 209–230.

Larner, W. and Le Heron, R. (2004) 'Global benchmarking: Participating 'at a distance' in the globalizing economy', in W. Larner and W. Walters (eds) *Global Governmentality: Governing International Spaces*, London: Routledge.

Latour, B. (1987) *Science in Action. How to Follow Scientists and Engineers Through Society*, Cambridge: Harvard University Press.

Latour, B. (2005) 'From Realpolitik to Dingpolitik or how to make things public', in B. Latour and P. Wiebel (eds) *Making Things Public. Atmospheres of Democracy*, Karlsruhe and Cambridge: ZKM and MIT Press.

Leterme, Y. (2006) *Toespraak van Minister-President Yves Leterme at Reception of VOKA-Chambers of Commerce and Industry*, 24 January. http://www.voka.be/files/bestanden/2006-01-24_YL_nieuwjaar.pdf

Lisbon European Council (2000) *Presidency Conclusions*, Lisbon, 23–24 March. http://consilium.europa.eu/ueDocs/cms_Data/docs/pressData/en/ec/00100-r1.en0.htm

Lyotard, J.-F. (1979) *La condition postmoderne,* Paris: Les Éditions de Minuit.

Maastricht Treaty (1992) 'Education, vocational training, youth and sport', *The Treaty on the Functioning of the European Union,* Title xii, article 165, para. 1.

Masschelein, J. and Simons, M. (2003) *Globale immuniteit. Een kleine cartografie van de Europese ruimte voor onderwijs* [Global Immunity: A Small Cartography of the European Space for Education], Leuven: Acco.

Mathiessen, T. (1997) 'The viewer society: Michel Foucault's 'Panopticon' revisited', *Theoretical Criminology,* 1(2): 215–234.

McKenzie, J. (2001) *Perform or Else: From Discipline to Performance,* London: Routledge.

Nóvoa, A. and Yariv-Marshal, T. (2003) 'Comparative research in education: A mode of governance or a historical journey?', *Comparative Education,* 39(4): 423–438.

Ozga, J. (2009) 'Governing education through data in England: From regulation to self-evaluation', *Journal of Education Policy,* 24(2): 149–162.

Rose, N. (1991) 'Governing by numbers: Figuring out democracy', *Accounting, Organizations and Society,* 16(7): 673–692.

Rose, N. (1999) *Powers of Freedom. Reframing Political Thought*, Cambridge: Cambridge University Press.

Simon, B. (2005) The return of panopticism: Supervision, subjection and the new surveillance, *Surveillance and Society,* 3(1): 1–20.

Simons, M. (2007) '"To be informed": Understanding the role of feedback information for Flemish/European policy', *Journal of Education Policy,* 22(5): 531–548.

Simons, M. and Masschelein, J. (2008) 'From schools to learning environments: The dark side of being exceptional', *Journal of Philosophy of Education,* 42(3–4): 687–704.

Vandenbroucke, F. (2004) *Beleidsnota 2004–2009: Onderwijs en vorming : vandaag kampioen in wiskunde, morgen ook in gelijke kansen* [Policy 2004–2009: Education and Training: Today Champion in Mathematics, Tomorrow Also in Equal Opportunities], Brussels: Ministerie van de Vlaamse Gemeenschap.

Vandenbroucke, F. (2005) *Toespraak : Studiedag PISA2003 en TIMMS2003, grade 8, 13 mei 2005, aud. Hadewych,* www.ond.vlaanderen.be/beleid/toespraak/050513-studiedag.htm

Vandenbroucke, F. (2006) 'Demand, parental choice and school autonomy. The Flemish case and beyond', paper presented at International OECD seminar, 16 May.

Vinson, K. and Ross, E. (2001, April) 'Education and the new disciplinarity: Surveillance, spectacle, and the case of SBER', paper presented at a roundtable discussion during the annual meeting of the American Educational Research Association, Foucault and Education SIG, Seattle, WA.

Wiener, N. (1950/89) *The Human Use of Human Beings,* London: Free Association Books.

Yeatman, A. (1993) 'Corporate management and the shift from the welfare to the competition state', *Discourse,* 13(2): 3–9.

12 National Qualifications Frameworks Governing Knowledge

Insights from South Africa

Shirley Walters and Samuel Isaacs

Introduction

From the early years of the twentieth century, the relations between education, training and work have become increasingly complex and contested. One example of such contestation is apparent in discourses around Competency Based Training (CBT) and the relationship between this form of training and more classical forms of education that have dominated schooling and higher education. These are found, for example, in the Trivium and Quadrivium that dominated the curriculum of schooling in Europe for hundreds of years and traces of which still remain (Bernstein 1996: 82-90). During the last 30 years, competency based National Qualification Frameworks (NQFs) have emerged as an attempt to manage the relations between education, training and work and, unsurprisingly, have been highly contested. They are highly significant knowledge-based technologies which are intimately linked to policy development and processes of governing knowledge.

The number of NQFs which emerged in the late 1980s in some Anglophone developed countries has grown rapidly with more than 60 countries and at least three regions at various stages of qualifications framework development by 2007, and around 142 by 2013. Their initial emergence was informed by perceptions of fundamental changes in the global economy, which had implications for the traditional divide between education and training and for the formal recognition of workplace and life experience (Illeris 2003: 167). These views complemented the views of business and government, which saw qualification frameworks as a means to make education more relevant to the workplace and as a steering mechanism by which the state could achieve social objectives such as educational reform and equity. South Africa provides an intriguing example of how a confluence of global influences were indigenized and adapted to meet national objectives. While in South Africa the idea of the NQF was 'borrowed' from international processes concerned with global knowledge governance, our argument will show that spaces for negotiation and reappropriation of global knowledge-based technologies are possible within a local context.

South Africa's NQF, which was conceived and established in the transition to a post-apartheid democracy, embodied many of the aspirations of the time, above all, transformation of the apartheid education and training system through an

NQF that addressed access, redress, portability and progression which would enable people to become lifelong learners (Allais 2007: 225). Given the idealism of the times, hindsight understands the impracticalities of the model and of the qualifications and standards setting processes, which emerged as policy was implemented.

This chapter provides background to the development of NQFs internationally. We analyse a critical early period of development of the South African case, in the 1990s, in order to illustrate varying, contested understandings of, for example, legitimacy, governance, accountability, and leadership, guiding educational reform through the creation of an NQF. This was managed by the South African Qualifications Authority (SAQA) in concert with government, Sector Education and Training Authorities (SETAs) and other stakeholders.

We argue for a view of NQFs as work-in-progress and as contestable artefacts of modern society, which can provide spaces for negotiation and reappropriation of global knowledge-based technologies. They have the potential to contribute to the way in which a society manages complex relations between education, training and work by finding 'common ground' between distinct forms of learning.

NQFs in a Nutshell

NQFs are global phenomena which are concerned with global knowledge governance. They are diversely located in industrialized and economically developed countries in the European Union, fast-developing economies in Asia and developing countries in Africa. As Chakroun (2010) describes, NQFs are classifiers that specify the relationship and the horizontal and vertical continuum between different forms of qualifications. The main distinguishing features of NQFs compared with other qualification systems can be summarized as follows: a common definition of qualifications in terms of learning outcomes in most cases covering knowledge, skills and wider competences ranked in terms of levels and an inclusive set of occupational and/or knowledge fields.

In most cases NQFs go beyond the role of classifiers and provide visions that aim to redefine the way qualifications relate to one another and how they are applied and valued in societies. In many cases they are seen as drivers of reform, most often in vocational education and training (VET). As Chakroun (2010) explains, most government documents introducing NQFs refer to the need to: (a) improve the labour market responsiveness of VET; (b) establish pathways between VET and general and higher education; (c) improve the quality and flexibility of VET and other parts of the education and training system; and (d) shift from input to outcome-based systems. While the 'early starter' countries like Australia, Scotland, and New Zealand emphasized VET, increasingly NQFs are aiming to bring all provision, i.e. basic, further and higher education, plus VET, into one system. South Africa was one of the first to do this.

Chakroun (2010) summarizes NQFs' increasingly normative distinctive features. These are: (a) qualifications are independent of the institutions; (b) complex quality assurance systems are foreseen to validate qualifications, accredit institutions and ensure quality assurance in assessment leading to the award of qualifications; and (c) they are seen to make it easier to validate prior learning and to put value on learning programmes that allow for credit accumulation and transfer to assist with the achievement of lifelong learning.

Increasing numbers of articles are being published which both elaborate the benefits of NQFs, and which critique them. Chakroun states that there are two broad policy arguments and rationales put forward in favour of an NQF, namely, internal systemic policy reform and external international recognition of qualifications in a globalized labour market. It is claimed that NQFs facilitate system-wide reforms and increase involvement of stakeholders in the development of qualifications with the result that VET, and other qualifications, are more responsive to labour market needs. NQFs also relate directly to the need for cross-border recognition of qualifications. Governments that are keen to attract foreign capital, to facilitate the mobility of their citizens and, more broadly, to ensure a stake in the global labour market, are increasingly concerned about the transparency and comparability of their national qualifications in relation to those that are produced, awarded and used elsewhere. However, several authors have argued that irrespective of their increasing appeal, NQFs are not necessarily good policy practice, especially in a developing-country context (Young 2005; Allais 2003, 2007). The key argument is that NQFs may achieve little if they are not fit for purpose and if they are not part of a wider strategy. NQFs and their value are, rightly, contested.

We will return to aspects of these debates later in the chapter. First, we provide an historical slice of the development of the South African NQF in order to illustrate how the performance of knowledge wars (Fenwick 2010) appear integral to NQFs and their development. This is not peculiar to South Africa, as Castells (2009: 14) argues:

> [S]ocieties are not communities, sharing values and interests. They are contradictory social structures enacted in conflicts and negotiations among diverse and often opposing social actors. Conflicts never end: they simply pause through temporary agreements and unstable contracts that are transformed into institutions of domination by those social actors who achieve an advantageous position in the power struggle, albeit at the cost of allowing some degree of institutional representation for the plurality of interests and values that remain subordinated. So, the institutions of the state and, beyond the state, the institutions, organizations, and discourses that frame and regulate social life are never the expressions of 'society'.... They are crystallized power relationships; that is the 'generalized means' that enable actors to exercise power over other social actors in order to have the power to accomplish their goals.

If we accept this analysis, then we cannot assume that the debates and discussions within NQFs are politically neutral. The NQF comprises many different types of networks and communities which are part of society and are actively promoting particular interests and values within society. It would be true to say that the NQF, like society, is itself constituted of 'contradictory social structures enacted in conflicts and negotiations among diverse and often opposing social actors'. We argue below that the South African experience bears this out.

Illustrative Insights from South Africa

When the South African NQF (SANQF) was legislated in October 1995, it was the first piece of education and training legislation promulgated by the first democratically elected government. It was significant in that it was *enabling* as opposed to *prescriptive* legislation. The South African Qualifications Authority (SAQA) was established as a statutory body in terms of the SAQA Act of 1995. The SANQF was to be one of the 'first generation' qualifications frameworks. The two international bodies that South Africans could learn from at that time were the New Zealand Qualifications Authority and the Scottish Qualifications Authority. Other important systems' learning came from Canada, Germany, Ireland and England. The concepts underpinning the NQF had to be developed and communicated. Policy and regulations had to be developed in democratic and legitimate ways. Given the transformation imperative of the South African context, this proved no easy task. Organization and systems building at SAQA were difficult. The historical trajectories that pushed South Africa towards transformation also pulled it back.

There were many NQF sceptics. There were also conflicting knowledge perspectives – for example, many argued from globalized western perspectives, others from anti-globalization standpoints, or in favour of indigenous knowledge systems. Given the racialized nature of apartheid education, there was a strong push by trade unionists and social movement activists for the massification of qualifications and the importance of recognition of prior learning. South Africa is a peripheral economy and had been isolated from the world, so there were contradictory pressures to articulate with globalized discursive practices, on the one hand, and to build an equitable education and training system to confront rampant poverty and inequality on the other.

A constant refrain at consultative meetings were variations of the following questions:

- Where in the world are NQFs working?
- Where are the international comparators?
- How much do NQFs cost and is it worth it?

The first SAQA Board, which was a stakeholder, representative body, was appointed by the National Minister of Education in May 1996. The first staff member was appointed in March 1997 as the chief executive; this was Samuel Isaacs, who led the organization for 15 years. At the initial stage of developing and implementing the SANQF in 1997, Samuel describes how they had to find an acceptable and accountable way to proceed with building both SAQA and the SANQF. To do this he, as chief executive, borrowed from the title of Paulo Freire and Myles Horton's (1990) book, and asserted that, 'We will make the NQF Road by walking reflectively, accountably and boldly'. This metaphor recognized that NQFs are social constructions; they require intellectual scrutiny, democratic participation, accountability and bold leadership. They also require funding (Isaacs 2012).

The first SAQA Board stated that the three necessary conditions for success were democratic participation, intellectual scrutiny and resourcing, especially the aligning of financial, organizational and extra-institutional resources. To date, SAQA has put a high premium on its role as 'honest broker' in working with SANQF stakeholders and has striven to take very seriously intellectual scrutiny in its various forms such as academic scrutiny, international comparators and 'world-class best practice'. This is evidenced in its prioritization of impact studies from an early stage (Bolton and Keevy 2012). This approach has stood SAQA in good stead as it faced the many challenges in developing and implementing the SANQF. Meeting the test of rigorous engagement with intellectual scrutiny very often enabled SAQA to establish legitimacy in fulfilling its 'honest broker' role.

From an operational point of view, the following three inter-related sub-systems were required: Standards Setting System; Quality Assurance System; Electronic Management Information System. Each of these systems is complex and demands contextually relevant policy choices. Two sets of regulations were promulgated: The National Standards Bodies' (NSB) Regulations (March 1998) and the Education and Training Quality Assurance Bodies' (ETQA) Regulations (September 1998). The National Learners' Records Database (NLRD) was covered by these regulations, which defined the processes and structures that would be used to develop and implement the core deliverables of these three sub-systems of the SANQF.

Key, complex themes that emanated from these three sub-systems included:

- the democratic participation of stakeholders;
- the integration of education and training;
- separation of standards setting and quality assurance;
- exit-level outcomes and assessment criteria;
- academic freedom and autonomy;
- power shifts and contestations among various stakeholders and role-players;
- sustainable organizational capacity and resources to lead and manage the processes.

From the SAQA Chief Executive's vantage point, it was the power shifts, contestations and the strategies to recognize and manage these that proved the most demanding. As evidence of the contestations, the SANQF was barely operational at the end of 1998 and already the call for its review was being mooted in some sectors, for different reasons. SAQA's ability to lead and manage processes in this climate was severely constrained by funding and other resourcing difficulties. To illustrate this point, SAQA was receiving at that time approximately 20 per cent of its budget from the State and 80 per cent from international donors. The European Union was a significant funder and a disproportionate amount of senior management's time was spent on fundraising and ensuring its proper stewardship for SAQA's sustainability.

The Ministers of Education and Labour did call for a review of the SANQF in 2001. The review report was tabled for public comment by 30 October 2002. A response document was tabled by the Departments of Education and Labour in July 2003 for public comment by October of the same year. The review process remained inconclusive until a Joint Policy Statement was issued by Ministers of Education and Labour in November 2007 and new legislation, the NQF Act (2008), was signed into law in February 2009 and became effective 1 June 2009. The review of the SANQF had taken an official period of seven years but the effect on the SANQF's development and implementation extended from 2000 to 2011 as SAQA staff and Board worked through the uncertainty created by the review process and the transition from the provisions of the SAQA Act to the NQF Act.

After the fourth national democratic elections in 2009 the Department of Education was split into the Department of Higher Education and Training, which includes the Skills Development section of the Department of Labour, and the Department of Basic Education, which deals with schools. This new environment brought significant opportunities to better manage and, in some instances, to placate some key tensions affecting the SANQF. The new architecture of the SANQF and its structures under the NQF Act has SAQA as the oversight body, with three Quality Councils, i.e. Council for Higher Education (CHE), Quality Council for Trades and Occupations (QCTO) and the Council for General and Further Education and Training (called Umalusi) which is concerned, primarily, with schools. This structural move signalled recognition of the deep differences, both organizational and epistemological, between parts of the education and training system.

One of the successes of SAQA has been the establishment and development of an SANQF discourse in South Africa, for example 'NQF levels', 'credits', 'notional learning hours', 'articulation' and 'equivalence'. There are indications that the SANQF is alive, debated, contested and used. It is increasingly being understood, particularly by those most centrally involved in the governance of SAQA and the three Quality Councils, as a framework for communication, co-ordination and collaboration across education, training, development and work (SAQA 2011). It continues to be seen as a key strategy for advancing lifelong learning which requires navigational tools, like guidance advice services, to help individual learners and institutions find their way. SAQA's role as the apex SANQF body in the further development and implementation of the SANQF is pivotal to enabling both access by ordinary citizens to information to study and career opportunities, and to keeping the aspirational goals of the NQF alive through advocacy, research and development. An example of this is the energy it has invested in recognition of prior learning (RPL) through collaborative research partnerships and through participating actively on the 2012 Ministerial Task Team on RPL, in addition to the establishment of its own SAQA RPL Reference Group and new national RPL policy.

A significant change in the global environment has been the development of 'second and third generation' qualifications frameworks (Deij 2009). The global phenomenon of formal national, regional and transnational qualifications frameworks effectively means that no country or region can ignore them for a variety of reasons from 'lifelong learning' through to 'good governance' and 'international trade'. NQFs are an attempt at finding a mechanism to describe and compare complex education and training systems transnationally, perhaps in a similar way to which macro-economic indicators are used to compare national economies.

Important Themes

Contestations

Unsurprisingly, power shifts and contestations remain dominant themes throughout the development and implementation of SANQF. An illustrative example was the deeming of the Council of Higher Education and the General and Further Education and Training Council (Umalusi) as accredited Education and Training Quality Assurance bodies (ETQAs). Initially these bodies had to be accredited by SAQA. The contestation revolved around the argument that SAQA could technically de-accredit these bodies and that this would create an untenable situation for the Minister of Education. In reality, SAQA would have had to undertake a lengthy process of engagement with the parties and the Minister before it would have been able to take such drastic action and then only if the situation warranted it.

A further contestation was the Study Team's Report (2002) that clearly highlighted that 'all was not well between the Department of Education and the Department of Labour'. SAQA was required to report to both these Ministers. The lengthy NQF review process and the later establishment of the Department of Higher Education and Training (DHET), which includes the Skills Development section of the Department of Labour, are illustrative of the contestations. The creation of the new DHET is an attempt to recognize structurally the deep fissures within and between the Departments of Education and Labour. SAQA now only has to report to one Minister of Higher Education and Training. Ironically, Umalusi now reports to both the Minister of Higher Education and Training and the Minister of Basic Education.

The contestations experienced within the SANQF are complex and wide ranging, as Rosemary Lugg's (2009) study elaborates. She very usefully shows how the fractures built into the SANQF point to complex and contradictory challenges that States 'at the margins' face when simultaneously articulating with globalized discursive practices and also seeking to establish equitable national education systems. She suggests that the future of the SANQF cannot be separated from ongoing struggles over the nature of the post-apartheid State, and the forms that ethical leadership might take in the face of demands for a globalized economy on the one hand and rampant local poverty and inequality on the other.

She explains the development of the SANQF and its failure to bring the worlds of education and training closer together through an examination of its discursive construction. By engaging Laclau and Mouffe's (1985) discourse theory, struggles over education policy in the post-apartheid era in South Africa can be located within the broader, complex power struggles between State and institutions of civil society, including struggles over the nature of the State. She describes how discourses join objects within relational systems of meaning, but in excluding possibilities give rise to 'frontiers' or 'antagonisms'. At 'frontiers', meanings are contested and power enacted through two political logics: equivalence and difference. Through a 'logic of equivalence', differences within a discourse are weakened by a shared opposition to an external, excluded force and simultaneously equivalences between internal differences are strengthened. In contrast, practices involving a 'logic of difference' attempt to weaken antagonism by breaking down chains that structure opposing discourse and assimilating elements of it into its own order. She explores how antagonisms were constructed through varying forms of equivalence and difference, shaping education and training policy discourses across the changing political conditions. In addition, she argues that a second set of discursive practices were intertwined with the first, and this she refers to as a 'single system' of education and training. Her study shows how these two discourses constructed the frontier with the Apartheid State differently during the transition; were articulated with globalized discursive practices and were associated with differing forms of the post-apartheid State.

Making a related argument, in 'Whither progressive education and training?', Soudien (2012) argues that much of the South African debate has been about 'quantity'; 'substance' has not come under the same public scrutiny. This reflects acquiescence to the dominance of experts and academics. Whereas he argues that experts have their place, they cannot determine the answers to public interest questions by themselves. He argues that the residual questions of quantity have side-lined the majority of people from substantive democratic engagement. This reflects in the narrow representative democratic polity which has not built on the mass mobilization of the citizenry in opposition to apartheid. It has entrenched an elitist, neo-liberal post-apartheid State. Within the SANQF, the contestation over the legitimacy of broad-based democratic participation of 'stakeholders' in development of qualifications could be seen as illustrative of these struggles over the governing of knowledge.

These struggles have at times reached a crescendo as academics have performed particular knowledge 'wars' (Fenwick 2010). While the purpose here is not to venture too deeply into these, it is important to allude to them (Young 2009; Muller 2009). For example, Joe Muller (2009: 205) uses a socio-epistemic lens or 'knowledge-based' approach to curriculum and qualifications. He traces the historical trajectories of the 'knowledge wars' over several hundred years. He argues that the social, disciplinary and qualification organization are aligned 'in the specialization consciousnesses'. He argues that, when designing a qualification, the most important issue is the 'purpose of a qualification'. He is scathing of the trade unions' struggle slogan of the early 1990s 'from sweeper to engineer'. Similarly he dismisses the ambitions of the SANQF which strives for 'equivalence' and 'articulation' which he says 'of course did neither'. He argues that there can be no moral rule to determine a qualifications pathway. From a knowledge perspective the questions are: what specialization is required, and what are the conceptual demands of the knowledge to be acquired? He and some other influential scholars are either sceptical or hostile to the SANQF. In a debate with Muller, Soudien (2013) referred to his argument as not scientific but 'scientism', which has elitist political consequences.

Other scholars are also engaging actively with knowledge debates that the SANQF embodies (these include, for example, Lotz-Sisitka 2009; Cooper 2005; Parker and Harley 2007; Olvitt 2012). One significant group is deeply involved in studying the praxis of recognition of prior learning (Cooper and Ralphs 2012). They are mapping differentiation of knowledge and learning constructs in RPL practice across different sites to understand more deeply the relationships between knowledge gained through experience and knowledge codified in qualifications. They are asking what knowledge is valued or excluded in the practice and how does it shape the nature of the practice? The RPL research feeds directly into the SANQF as it is funded by SAQA, as are several other partnership research projects between SAQA and South African universities.

The support for potentially 'troubling or transgressive research', has surprised some of the SANQF's critics. But SAQA's approach to contestations has been to try to understand and engage them. There is deep conviction that credibility and effectiveness of an NQF depends on robust intellectual engagement, if the ambitious goals have any chance of success. With the benefit of hindsight there is recognition that mistakes were made in the early years where new systems were too complicated, bureaucratic and technical. The important contribution of critical research studies like those of Allais (2007) who demonstrated this, are acknowledged. The SANQF is seen by SAQA as partly 'an intellectual project' and the important insight is that contestation over 'what knowledge counts', and 'whose voices should be heard', is part of the fabric of an NQF.

The SANQF is about systems change. It has a role in the 'governance of knowledge'. It has a role in 'managing' relationships across education, training, and work. Rather than engaging 'war' over differences, the very real and complex matters require serious intellectual and political engagement. During 2007, SAQA took inspiration from sculptor Orlando de Almeida's work 'Moving into dance'. The work is described as a 'sculpture of seven dancing figures, representing harmony, fluidity and change – symbolic of the transition that has taken place in the country'. Thus the metaphor of 'moving into the NQF dance' was conceived, and has been used, to characterize ways of engaging, shifting, changing, within knowledge flows and boundary negotiations.

Communicative Models

As Parker and Walters (2008) elaborate, building opportunities for lifelong learning requires a clear understanding of 'comparability' and 'transferability' and reiterates the importance of initiatives such as credit accumulation and transfer and recognition of prior learning, which are understood to have the potential to improve access, progression, mobility and portability – nationally and internationally. What instruments, tools and practices can be used for comparability? Moving away from outcomes implies moving towards different approaches to recognizing and evaluating different 'units of comparability'. By themselves, specifications of curriculum content and of assessments do not avoid the conundra of interpretation.

If we can no longer pre-specify the 'unit of comparability', how do we begin to establish a framework for developing communicative models that articulate different forms of learning? We believe that the best way to address these challenges is through research-driven policy, which informs the political and organizational shape of the NQF. In the South African case, there is already a considerable body of research on learning and on the NQF that can provide a foundation for future research. Two theoretical approaches that have become prominent within this research draw on Bernstein's (1996: 169–180) account of different knowledge fields and the power and control relations between and within these fields; and on Lave and Wenger's (1991: 53) notion of communities of practice as learning communities which emerge in workplaces.

For Bernstein, pedagogic discourse is constructed by a re-contextualizing principle, which selectively appropriates, relocates, refocuses and relates other discourses to constitute its own order (Bernstein 1996: 47). This re-contextualization dislocates discourses from their substantive practice and context and relocates them in an arbitrary space according to principles of selective reordering and refocusing that remove the discourses from the social basis of their practice (Bernstein 1990: 184). Understanding the inside of a pedagogic practice, recognizing its intrinsic worth and purpose, is inextricably interwoven with recognizing what is outside of the practice – the social order within which the practice is embedded.

The concept of communities of practice is primarily a means of categorizing a particular set or web of relations between people as having a particular identity, value orientation and purpose (Lave and Wenger 1991: 98). Within a strong community of practice there is a strong sense of shared values and beliefs; a consciousness of, and commitment to, an overall holistic purpose that shapes the activities of the community; and, agreement on the set of practices that constitute 'competent practice' (Wenger 1998: 95). At some level, learning is always induction into a community whose boundaries are marked by commitment to a set of beliefs about what counts as knowledge and skills and what are 'good' values and attitudes to underpin and infuse learning as a process of enlightenment, enhancement and attunement. This approach emphasizes the social and constructive nature of learning. Learning is simultaneously a path to knowledge, initiation into a community of practitioners and a shaping of one's identity. These reflections suggest that when talking about qualifications frameworks it is useful to distinguish between distinct knowledge fields and the ways in which they are cognitively structured and socially organized.

Although we are not advocating the use of these particular theorists, we are suggesting that their productive use in South African research indicates possibilities to explore the development of quality management systems and the role of qualification frameworks within these systems. Recognizing differences between the fields, understanding the nature of their boundaries and hence the possibility of boundary negotiations and crossings will inform how we develop an integrated approach to a national qualifications framework; one that enables comparability between different forms of learning and the different knowledge fields within which learning takes place and between these fields and the world of work.

There have been some suggestions, within South African debates, that the boundaries between the academic field and the 'everyday' field, between school and street knowledge, are very strong and that institutions, curriculum and assessment should be the primary foci of qualifications design and quality assurance. There is a particular emphasis on the importance of institutions as bedrock of quality education and training. This may be correct when applied to schooling and higher education. However, many occupational qualifications are delivered by non-institutional providers or in the workplace, thus raising questions about approaches to quality assurance and development in non-institutional settings. Although the knowledge field of occupationally oriented education is far more context-specific and delivery is less institutionalized, this does not mean that this non-academic knowledge field is content-less, nor that curriculum, pedagogy and assessment are less important. Rather than dichotomizing and demonizing the everyday knowledge field, research is needed into curriculum, pedagogic and assessment practices in these fields to better understand how to improve quality.

In summary, we argue that for an NQF to work optimally, what is required is recognition of the complexity of the knowledge questions involved and a deep commitment of all 'role players' and 'stakeholders' to engage in an 'ideal speech situation' (Habermas 1973:258) on NQF matters. An 'ideal speech situation' requires that all parties communicate openly with one another to educate and inform about their different positions, which can then inform rational debate and discussion, encouraging deep democratic engagement. Amongst SAQA's debates, this aspiration is held while simultaneously recognizing that an NQF is constituted of 'contradictory social structures enacted in conflicts and negotiations among diverse and often opposing social actors' (Castells 2009). Although, the existence of different knowledge fields and communities of practice does make agreement and articulation difficult to achieve, it does perhaps make it all the more worthwhile if the intent is to deepen democratic practices.

Relational Agency

Active stakeholder and role-player participation is essential for building the relationships that facilitate collaborative networks that make shared understandings, shared meanings and shared strategies possible, both nationally and trans-nationally. In South Africa this has led directly to current understanding of the SANQF as a framework for communication, co-ordination and collaboration across education, training, development and work. To this end SAQA, as custodian of the SANQF, has had to work hard and carefully at relationship building in partnership with a wide range of others. One of the results of this careful work was the establishment of an NQF Forum in 2010 that regularly brings together all the CEOs of SAQA, the Quality Councils and the DHET to share concerns and resolve systemic issues.

McMillan (2009) highlights the complexity of human relationships in collaboration, in particular the 'boundary work' that engagement with different communities require. This echoes Edwards' (2007) conception of 'relational agency' and the need for expertise and capacities from 'boundary spanners' (Williams 2010). These are people who demonstrate strong communication skills with ongoing tolerance and willingness to understand the cross-cultural dynamics of interactions and willingness to 'co-create hybrid cultural spaces' (Fryer 2010) where people can collaborate to develop shared visions (Preece *et al.* 2012). There are the beginnings of acknowledgement of the capabilities, skills and attitudes required to effectively negotiate and mediate the complex relationships of diverse, cross-cultural, cross-sectoral spaces and places, as with for example qualifications frameworks. There is need for further research to assist understanding of what these capabilities are and how they are taught and learnt.

Conclusion

NQFs are highly significant knowledge-based technologies that are intimately linked to policy development and processes of governing. The SANQF experience illuminates the contradictory pressures to articulate with globalized discursive practices, on the one hand, and to build an equitable education and training system to confront rampant poverty and inequality on the other. It also shows the importance of coherent and systemic implementation and the slow nature of educational transformation. Qualifications frameworks can play an important role in the transformation of an education and training system, provided that they are seen as important vehicles for knowledge flows and boundary negotiations through communication, coordination and cooperation across national and regional systems, for the public good.

The SANQF introduced new language, procedures and processes, which some found opaque and complex. Systems have continued to be simplified and streamlined in response to this and the NQF is now 'coming of age' with citizens more familiar with its workings. After 15 years of development the South African NQF is seen as an important reference point for new national and regional qualifications frameworks that are developing in many parts of the world. South African experience indicates that qualifications frameworks should be built cautiously, modestly and incrementally. They need to be fit for purpose and not imported inappropriately. Development should have a strong experimental scientific approach in which failures or falsifications are seen as evidence.

South Africa's initial move to privilege CBT or outcome-based education as the template for the whole education and training system through the use of outcomes statements as an up-front, prescriptive and design-down approach, which was intended to create a 'communication's platform' for portability of learning between different knowledge and occupational fields, has not succeeded. The schooling and higher education systems did not 'buy-in' to the approach, nor has South Africa's skills development system prospered. South Africa's deepening skills crisis, which is blamed by many politicians and business leaders on disjunctures between schooling and higher education on one side and the economy and labour market on the other, has been exacerbated by the massive decline in apprenticeships and other types of work-based learning. South Africa's NQF (and here we include all its role-players and stakeholders) has not met the expectations of business with respect to improving the supply of appropriately trained skilled labour or intellectual capital, nor the expectations of labour with respect to increasing access to educational and occupational opportunities. Far from contributing to the development of a lifelong learning system, some argue that the NQF may have at times impeded South Africa's progress.

The reasons for this failure lie in factors internal and external to an outcomes-based NQF. Key amongst external factors was an underestimation of the weaknesses of institutions and the lack of competent educators and trainers inherited from Apartheid. Key amongst the internal factors was conceptual confusions and contestations over what was meant by competences and outcomes (and forms of learning underpinning their achievement) and how they might best be described in qualification statements and used for quality assurance. Central to both sets of factors was a lack of clarity about the purposes of the NQF with stakeholders having very different perspectives and objectives. They ranged from the State's perspective of an administratively driven quality management system that could steer the education and training system towards its economic and political objectives to organized labour's view of the NQF as a portal to lifelong learning with strong emancipatory and empowering objectives.

With hindsight, the SANQF has provided a space for negotiation and re-appropriation of global knowledge-based technologies within the local context. We therefore argue that NQFs are best understood as a work-in-progress. They are contestable artefacts of modern society, which can contribute in a modest way to how a society manages the relations between education, training and work by finding common ground between distinct forms of learning and their articulation with workplace practices in the interests of the public good. This can best be done through a strong research-driven collaborative approach to NQF development that seeks 'means of portability', ways of enabling boundary crossings through building relational agency, of improving quality and relevance and of understanding better different forms and sites of learning.

NQFs aim to bring multi-faceted, diverse pedagogical, political and organizational interests into a relationship with one another in order to build coherence in a complex system. They are a significant development in the governing of education across the globe. They are articulated with contradictory national and globalized discursive practices and inevitably reflect these. They are strategic mechanisms for the governing of knowledge. However, they also can be re-appropriated to address, in a modest but important manner, aspects of lifelong learning in ways which contribute to greater equity and social justice.

References

Allais, S. (2003) 'The National Qualifications Framework in South Africa: a democratic project trapped in a neo-liberal paradigm', *Journal of Education and Work*, 16(3): 305–324.

Allais, S. (2007) 'The rise and fall of the NQF: A critical analysis of the South African National Qualifications Framework', unpublished doctoral dissertation, Johannesburg: University of the Witwatersrand.

Bernstein, B. (1990) *The Structuring of Pedagogic Discourse: Volume IV, Class Codes and Control*, London: Routledge.

Bernstein, B. (1996) *Pedagogy, Symbolic Control and Identity: Theory, Research, Critique,* London: Taylor and Francis.

Bolton, H. and Keevy, J. (2012) 'How are we doing in relation to NQF objectives? Measuring the impact of the South African NQF', *SAQA Bulletin,* 12(2): 273–292.

Castells, M. (2009) *Communication Power,* Oxford: Oxford University Press.

Chakroun, B. (2010) 'National qualification frameworks: from policy borrowing to policy learning', *European Journal of Education,* 45(2): 199–216.

Cooper, L. (2005) 'Towards a theory of pedagogy, learning and knowledge in an "everyday" context: A case study of a South African trade union', PhD thesis, University of Cape Town, South Africa.

Cooper, L. and Ralphs, A. (2012) 'Towards a conceptual framework: RPL as a specialized form of boundary pedagogy', paper presented to SAQA Seminar, October, Pretoria.

Deij, A. (2009) 'Towards a common understanding of the development stages of national qualification frameworks', European Training Foundation (ETF) Working Paper on NQF developments (unpublished).

Edwards, A. (2007) 'Relational agency – professional practice: a CHAT analysis', *An International Journal of Human Activity Theory,* 1: 1–17.

Fenwick, T. (2010) 'Let the river run: Education futures and globalization', Keynote address to the Vice Chancellor's Annual Julius Nyerere Lecture on Lifelong Learning, University of Western Cape, South Africa, October.

Freire, P. and Horton, M. (1990) *We Make the Road by Walking: Conversations on Education and Social Change,* Philadelphia: Temple University Press.

Fryer, M. (2010) 'How to strengthen the third mission of the university: The case of the University of British Columbia learning exchange', in P. Inman and H.G. Schuetze (eds) *The Community Engagement and Service Mission of Universities,* Leicester: NIACE.

Habermas, J. (1973) 'Wahrheitstheorien', in H. Fahrenbach, ed., *Wirklichkeit und Reflexion, Zum Sechzigsten Geburtstag fur Walter Schutz,* Pfullingen: Neske.

Illeris, K. (2003) 'Workplace learning and learning theory', *Journal of Workplace Learning,* 15(4): 167–178.

Isaacs, S. (2012) 'Making the NQF road by walking reflectively, accountably and boldly', *SAQA Bulletin,* 12(2): 75–99.

Laclau, E. and Mouffe, C. (1985) *Hegemony and Socialist Strategy: Towards a Radical Democratic Politics,* London: Verso.

Lave, J. and Wenger, E. (1991) *Situated Learning: Legitimate Peripheral Participation,* New York: Cambridge University Press.

Lotz-Sisitka, H. (2009) 'Insights from an environmental education research programme in South Africa', in L. Cooper and S. Walters (eds) *Learning/Work: Turning Work and Lifelong Learning Inside Out,* Cape Town: HSRC Press.

Lugg, R. (2009) 'Making different equal? Rifts and rupture in state and policy: The National Qualifications Framework in South Africa', in L. Cooper and S. Walters (eds) *Learning/Work: Turning Work and Lifelong Learning Inside Out.* Cape Town: HSRC Press.

McMillan, J. (2009) 'What happens when the university meets the community? Service-learning, activity theory and 'boundary work' in higher education', Seminar Paper, Division for Lifelong Learning, University of the Western Cape.

Muller, J. (2009) 'Forms of knowledge and curriculum coherence', *Journal of Education and Work,* 22(3): 205–226.

Olvitt, L. (2012) 'Ethics oriented reflexive deliberations of novice environmental educators', unpublished doctoral dissertation, Rhodes University, Grahamstown, South Africa.

Parker, B. and Harley, K. (2007) 'The NQF as a socially inclusive and cohesive system: communities of practice and trust', *SAQA Bulletin,* 10(2): 27–37.

Parker, B. and Walters, S. (2008) 'Competency based training and national qualifications frameworks: insights from South Africa', *Asian Pacific Education Review,* 9(1): 70–79.

Preece, J., Ntseane, P. G., Modise, O. M. and Osborne, M. (2012) 'The African university and community engagement in context', in: J. Preece, P. G. Ntseane, O. M. Modise and M. Osborne (eds) *Community Engagement in African Universities: Perspectives, Prospects and Challenges.* London: NIACE.

SAQA (South Africa Qualifications Authority) (2011) *Annual Report 2011,* Pretoria.

Soudien, C. (2012) 'Whither progressive education and training in South Africa?', The 3rd Ben Parker Memorial Lecture, 6 March, SAQA, Pretoria.

Soudien, C. (2013) 'Debating educational futures', panel discussion at the close of the South African Education Association (SAERA) 30 January, Klein Kariba Resort, Limpopo Province, South Africa.

Study Team Report (2002) *Report of the Study Team on the Implementation of the National Qualifications Framework Department of Education and Department of Labour,* Pretoria.

Young, M. (2005) 'National Qualifications Frameworks: Their feasibility for effective implementation in developing countries', in *Focus Programme on Skills, Knowledge and Employability, Skills Working Paper No. 22.* Geneva: International Labour Office.

Young, M. (2009) 'Education, globalization and the "voice of knowledge"', *Journal of Education and Work,* 22(3): 193–204.

Wenger, E. (1998) *Communities of Practice: Learning, Meaning, and Identity,* New York: Cambridge University Press.

Williams, P. (2010) 'Special agents: The nature and role of boundary spanners', paper presented to the ESRC Research Seminar Series – 'Collaborative Futures: New Insights from Intra and Inter-Sectoral Collaborations', University of Birmingham. www.changetropics.org.

13 Standardization of Professional Knowledge and Practice

The Regulatory Role of Professional Associations in Norway

Monika Nerland and Berit Karseth

Introduction

With its emphasis on creating uniformity across space and time, standardization is a key means to governing knowledge and practice in the professions. Standards are necessary to secure common knowledge and educational requirements as the basis for work. However, they also set boundaries for what is possible, and when addressing work performance they provide means for comparison that often are used for accountability purposes (Ozga *et al.* 2011). Hence, they serve the dual purpose of securing quality and control.

While professional associations historically have played an important role in these processes, their roles are transformed with the rise of global knowledge circuits and increased international regulation. Moreover, while their role historically has been linked to educational standards, their engagement in the era of lifelong learning may be considerably extended to other arenas (Watkins 1999).

This chapter discusses how professional associations in three different fields engage in developing, regulating and securing collective knowledge in their respective areas of expertise, with special emphasis given to standardization. Efforts to regulate collective knowledge and modes of enactment are basically about constructing consistency in practice across sites, that is, creating and distributing standards (Timmermans and Epstein 2010). Such efforts may, however, be generated to address different concerns and with different forms of justification. The questions we raise are: What characterizes approaches to standardization in different associations as means to regulate knowledge and secure knowledge-based practice? And how are the approaches taken related to wider governing spaces at the national and European levels?

The discussion draws on a study of three key organizations in Norway (Karseth and Nerland 2007; Nerland and Karseth 2013) that all assume responsibilities and functions as professional associations: the Norwegian Nurses Organization, the Union of Education Norway and the Norwegian Institute of Public Accountants. We discuss how different types of standards have different implications for practice, and propose the need for a more nuanced discussion about standardization in the professions as well as its implications for professional education and work. We commence, however, by introducing professional associations as regulatory agencies and by situating their work in a wider regulatory context.

188 Monika Nerland and Berit Karseth

Professional Associations as Regulatory Agencies

Professional associations are key regulatory agencies in their respective fields (Freidson 2001; Greenwood *et al.* 2002). They constitute a site for formal organization in which different voices and viewpoints meet, norms are negotiated and agreements achieved. They also decide on formal rules and procedures to be followed by members in different organizations.

Professional associations are often regarded as conservative and protective agencies that strive to maintain jurisdiction over their given domain of work by resisting changes. In recent times, however, researchers have shown how professional associations also act as change agents that contribute to legitimizing and enhancing change introduced by external forces (see, e.g. Greenwood *et al.* 2002; Noordegraaf 2011). Moreover, during the last few decades, researchers have pointed to a shift in the foci of professional associations towards an increased emphasis on collective knowledge and on securing their members' opportunities for continuous learning (Watkins 1999). This concerns, among other things, the circulation of knowledge and the opportunities for practitioners to stay updated on advancements within their areas of expertise. At the same time, conceptions of professional development are quite ambiguous (Cervero 2001; Friedman and Phillips 2004), and different stakeholders may have different expectations as to the kinds of regulations and support structures needed (Morgan *et al.* 2008).

The wider environment in which professional associations are embedded is also in transition. Among the changes facing professions and professional associations today is the increase in transnational regulations (Ozga *et al.* 2011). Evetts (2011, 2012) discusses in this regard how the emergence of professional federations at the European level constitutes new mechanisms of regulation, e.g. related to the need for aligning educational requirements and standards for good practice in a European market for professional services. International relations form an important context for the regulatory work of professional associations at the national level as well. Such relations may be especially important for their knowledge-regulatory efforts, as science-generated knowledge and standards for practice typically are seen as universal. Moreover, as pointed out by Faulconbridge and Muzio (2011), efforts to standardize knowledge in the professions typically have multi-scalar influences.

In sum, these studies reflect a renewed orientation towards knowledge development and knowledge regulation in the professions, in which professional associations play a key role. In spite of this, research that focuses specifically on professional associations' work directed towards their collective knowledge base (rather than their professionalization efforts more broadly) is limited, especially from a comparative perspective. However, some examples do exist, indicating that there are interesting differences among professions as to whether regulatory efforts are directed towards profession-external or profession-internal relationships (Karseth and Nerland 2007), i.e. the balance between what Zietsma and Lawrence (2010) describes as 'boundary work' and 'practice work.'

The present chapter discusses the different approaches professional associations take in their regulatory efforts by employing concepts and perspectives from what has been called the 'sociology of standards' (Timmermanns and Epstein

2010). Standardization is commonly defined as a process of constructing uniformity across space and time, through the generation of agreed-upon rules (Bowker and Star 1999; Timmermans and Epstein 2010). In this sense, it is not a new phenomenon to the professions. Standards have always been critical for professional work performance, as they form the basis for collective actions and shared conventions of good practice.¯

What is more characteristic of our times is that standards become more explicit and linked with formal regulations (Timmermans and Epstein 2010; Fenwick 2010). This is partly due to the emergence of a 'culture of performativity' and new accountability regimes, which bring attention to organizational control and generate expectations to make visible which actions are taken and what knowledge they rely on. Standards are often used for the dual purpose of securing the quality of professional work and to make the principles and decisions taken more transparent for user groups and other stakeholders (Evetts 2011). At the same time, the increased formalization is related to the need for coordinating actions and services across wider geographical contexts. In this regard, we have seen a growth of standard-setting agencies, whose regulatory efforts may have global aspirations. They form agencies at the macro level that also play a key role in the regulation and distribution of knowledge, e.g. like the Cochrane Collaboration does in the medical domains.

Standards can have different origins, take different forms, vary in the degree of flexibility, and be directed towards different aspects of work. In the context of health care, Timmermans and Berg (2003) distinguish among four types of standards: *design standards, performance standards, terminological standards* and *procedural standards*. The first type refers to specifications of technologies or instruments that are used in work, while the second refers to specifications of outcome. The third deals with professional knowledge in terms of concepts/vocabulary for identifying problems and envisioning solutions, while the fourth is directed towards procedures for good practice (Timmermans and Berg 2003; Timmermans and Epstein 2010; Nes and Moen 2010). The different types of standards will thus be directed towards different aspects and phases in work; they engender different allocations of responsibilities and they may take different forms relative to their underlying domain of expertise and principles for validation.

A core issue in current debates about professionalism is the relationship between standardization and discretionary decision-making, that is, the degree and space for flexibility when standards meet professional work with specific clients (Forrester 2000). Standardization is often regarded as a threat to professionalism, as it may undermine the space for judgement in work towards specific clients (Strathern 2000; Styhre 2011). As discussed above, however, it is not given that standardization implies a detailed prescription of professional actions. An interesting question is thus how standardization is approached and carried out in different professional contexts.

A Study of Three Professional Associations

We use the term 'associations' as a label for professional organizations that engage in efforts to regulate knowledge and competencies in their respective fields. A

distinguishing feature of the professional sector in Norway is that such organizations are established at the national level and that there is no strong organizational
division between unions and associations. The reasons for this are that traditionally the state has always been a strong partner and constitutive force, and that
labour markets as well as professional services have been regulated in collaborative
efforts between the state, the professions, employers and educational institutions
(Østerud and Selle 2006). This strong role of the state has contributed to position
Norway as a relatively slow adopter of neoliberal market strategies (Falcounbridge
and Muzio 2011). Yet, Norway participates in the European arenas that aim to
harmonize educational systems and standards for knowledge production, and the
knowledge base for professional work is becoming increasingly internationalized.
Hence, an interesting question is what approaches the professional associations
take in this new and extended context.

The organizations attended to are the Norwegian Nurses Organization, the
Union of Education Norway and the Norwegian Institute of Public Accountants.
The Norwegian Nurses Organization (NNO) was established in 1912. The association speaks on behalf of all registered nurses, nurse specialists, midwives and
public health nurses in Norway, and has about 96,000 members. The Union of
Education Norway (UoE) was founded in 2002 as a merger between two previous
teachers' unions and is the largest trade union for teaching personnel, comprising
about 150,000 members. The Norwegian Institute of Public Accountants (DnR)[1]
is the professional body for registered public accountants and state-authorized
public accountants in Norway, and has about 5,000 members. The association was
established as an institute for state-authorized public accountants in 1930, but
merged with its sister organization for registered public accountants in 1998.
More than 90 per cent of the state-authorized public accountants in public practice in Norway are members of the Institute.

These selected professional bodies operate in the same national context;
however, their professional fields are structured and regulated in different
ways. Among other things, they differ as to their number of members, their
role in collective bargaining and their market relations. As to similarities, all
associations organize professionals who hold at least a bachelor's degree in a
professional programme provided by a university college or university in
Norway, which is regulated through national curricula. Furthermore, all are
entrusted with a position from which they contribute to the provision of critical services in society, and they are all challenged to explicate and secure their
collective knowledge as a basis for these services. We may also argue that all of
them represent continuity, as the services they are concerned with have existed
for more than 50 years. Although the organizations may also be involved in
traditional union activities, our focus is on their role as regulatory agencies for
knowledge in their respective fields.

The study we draw upon comprises analyses of documents produced from 2005
to 2011, as well as interviews with key informants in the respective organizations who
were responsible for issues concerning knowledge regulation and professional development. Due to differences in organizational structure and modes of operation, the
types of documents differ somewhat among the organizations. However, the main

documents selected for analysis include formal documents, such as statutes, ethical codes and legal regulations; approved policy documents, such as strategic plans, annual reports, and congress and board decisions; policy statement documents, such as letters to the government and comments; documents describing requirements and guidelines for practice; and finally, historical descriptions of the profession provided by or approved by the association in question. For more information about the study, see Karseth and Nerland (2007) and Nerland and Karseth (2013).

Approaches to Standardization in the Three Associations

Our study revealed that all associations were concerned with standardization of knowledge and practice, and that this issue was one of increasing concern, but also that they engaged themselves in quite different ways. We will discuss the approaches taken and the challenges that seemed to arise under three thematic headings: types of standards and their interplay, their efforts to secure spaces for professional discretion and the wider international context for their approaches to standardization.

Types of Standards and Their Interplay

All the types of standards categorized by Timmermanns and Berg (2003) were present in the associations' regulatory efforts, but their relative emphasis and interrelationship varied. Starting with the NNO, this association was heavily involved in developing and distributing procedural standards for nurses' work. Important in this regard was the NNO's ownership (until 2012) of a publishing house that has developed the Practical Procedures for the Nursing Service (PPS), a commercial ICT-based repository containing a set of basic, standardized nursing procedures that adhere to legal regulations, national standards, professional guidelines and research-based knowledge (see Nes and Moen 2010 for further descriptions). Procedural standards are also supported by various documents comprising guidelines for the performance and documentation of nurses' clinical work. The emphasis on procedural standards in this association is combined with a strong attention towards terminological standards. The NNO has, for instance, established a council (*terminologiråd*) to assess the terminology used in the electronic patient record (EPR) system in Norway and recommended the International Classification of Nursing Practice (ICNP) as the terminology system for documentation of nursing care (Rotegaard and Ruland 2010). Through these efforts, the NNO is an active initiator and mediator of standards in the nursing profession. Moreover, its work is characterized by standardizing knowledge and practice from 'within' the knowledge domain rather than emphasizing external benchmarks or outcome measures. Procedural and terminological standards play a core role; however, these may increasingly be seen as interlinked with design standards as new and more advanced technological systems are introduced, such as the EPR.

The approaches taken in the Union of Education are quite different from those of the NNO. Securing a space for differentiation in teachers' work to allow for personalized teaching has been and still is a central concern for the UoE. Hence, the UoE engages itself in resisting attempts from national and local authorities to standardize teachers' work and to regulate the teacher profession more strongly. In recent years, there has been a shift in the discourse towards emphasizng teaching as a research-based activity. This was reflected in the agenda and documents produced for the national congress in 2009. As stated by the president in her opening speech to the congress:

> A stronger approach towards research is the way to go. We have to use research as a basis for the development of our profession. But we have to be able to be critical of research of lower quality. We know that all results have to be seen in a pedagogical context. There are no recipes that will work always and everywhere.
>
> (Hjetland 2009: 8)

Rather than encouraging procedural standards, the UoE advocates terminological standards as the way to develop a collective knowledge base beyond everyday language and to ground practice in research. Its efforts are ambiguous, however, and it is not clear how this terminology should be developed. While expressing a need for a professional language that standardizes terminology and ensures stability in meaning across different sites, there is a concern that languages reflecting other fields, such as the language of management, will take over as the main vocabulary defining professional work and contribute to undermining education as a public good and teaching as an ethically responsible activity. In addition, the UoE engages itself in securing equal standards for teachers' working conditions, such as regulations concerning the teacher-to-student ratio and available resources in schools. Hence, more than regulating professional knowledge per se, this association is concerned with securing conditions for professional knowledge to develop and spread from below.

The DnR speaks explicitly about the importance of standardization and regards it as a prime responsibility to ensure that Norwegian audit practices are at all times in line with international standards. The DnR's engagement in this respect is oriented towards the implementation and use of formal terminological and procedural standards. Moreover, this is primarily related to translating standards proposed by international agencies into different contexts of auditing work. As the representative for DnR explained in the interview:

> Very few standards are created in Norway. For the most part, we act as translators. [...] If Norwegian legislation, for instance the Limited Liability Companies Act, states that something else needs to be done, we will adjust it. If not, the standard is directly translated.

The Institute also engages in clarifying the use of these standards by offering a consultancy service for members. Moreover, by developing and distributing a Web-based audit support system called *Descartes*, the DnR develops and promotes procedural and terminological standards. The system links audit standards to the work-flow of the audit process and the standards themselves rest heavily on specialized terminology (Mathisen and Nerland 2012).

In sum, we find an interesting continuum of regulation here; the stronger the emphasis is on procedural standards, the stronger is the regulation of professional practice as a series of justified actions. The regulation of professional knowledge is related both to terminological and procedural standards. While the NNO and the DnR engage actively in developing and circulating procedural standards in their respective professions, the UoE is more reluctant on this matter. All associations emphasize terminological standards, however for somewhat different purposes. This is seen by the UoE and the NNO as a way to strengthen the research–practice relationship and by the DnR as a matter of securing consistency in the interpretation of (inter)national legislation.

An interesting finding is also that the different types of standards seem to support each other as much as representing different approaches. Emphasis on output measures put forward by external audit agencies generates a stronger emphasis on procedural standards, which again often has terminological standards as a prerequisite. Efforts to promote and develop one type of standards in professional associations are therefore likely to generate an emphasis on other types of standards, hence creating a self-reinforcing attention towards standardization.

The implications of the approaches taken for the professional project are, however, not clear-cut. On the one hand, standards are important in the jurisdictional work of the profession, as they help to define the competencies needed for professional work and thereby allocate responsibilities to practitioners in protected work spaces. On the other hand, standards may regulate practice in ways that limit the space of action for the professionals in their daily work. We will thus continue by discussing two types of challenges that seem significant for the professional associations in their engagement with standardization: the need to combine standardization with a concern for securing spaces for professional discretion, and the challenges emerging from increased regulation of professional education and work on the transnational level.

Securing Spaces for Professional Discretion

The approaches to standardization described above are shaped by the history and normative basis of the different professions and their associations. While standardization of professional work is seen as appropriate and necessary by the DnR, its normative basis is questioned by the UoE. For the NNO, standardization of professional knowledge and work is seen as legitimate; however, the documents from NNO also underline that this must be reconciled with the history of the profession and nursing as an independent field of knowledge.

One issue in this respect concerns how the standards may incorporate and mobilize different forms of knowledge. Both the NNO and the UoE argue that professional discretion must be based on a broad repertoire of knowledge sources. This was brought forward as an attention towards the complexity of the professional field and an expressed need to protect the values of practice-based and personal knowledge when research-based knowledge is gaining a strong footing. For instance, the NNO states the need to combine different approaches and argues that the different sources of knowledge lay the groundwork for knowledge-based practice:

> The use of knowledge-based practice implies that nurses use various sources of knowledge in clinical practice, among others research-based knowledge. At the same time, research-based knowledge is insufficient. Professional judgment based on clinical experience and ethical assessment, together with the patient's wishes must be the basis for nursing actions. In addition, the framework that nurses work under influences how clinical practice is performed.
>
> (NNO 2008: 6)

A similar concern emerged in the data from the UoE, which stated that evidence-based practice in the field of education should be defined broadly and needs to include a variety of perspectives and methods of inquiry (Utdanningsforbundet 2008: 35). A main concern for this association is to protect the autonomy of the individual teacher and to secure equal conditions for teachers' professional practice across schools and districts.

In the DnR's efforts, the main threat towards professional discretion is not as much about balancing forms of knowledge as it is about the degree of detailed regulations in the terminological and procedural standards. While the Institute promotes standardization in active ways, the association is concerned with securing a space for judgement in auditing work, and strives to avoid a too-detailed system of standards (DnR 2008, 2009). As explained in the interview, international standards are significantly more detailed than Norwegian ones: 'If the international standards comprise 2,000 pages, the Norwegian ones constitute about 300 pages. And if you turn to the American ones, they are 20,000 pages . . .'. Thus, the DnR engages itself in simplifying international standards to facilitate their use in Norwegian contexts and to avoid overregulation. Moreover, the Institute is concerned with taking an active role in the development and distribution of new standards in Norway and to take a lead in this work in relation to the state authorities (Bredal 2005; Karseth and Nerland 2007).

Another question with regard to professional discretion is what the different types of standards potentially do. Given that professional work is characterized by collective ways of performing tasks and solving problems, as much as by the knowledge base, procedural standards are especially important. As regards the professions targeted in this chapter, and from the perspective of professionalism, we would argue that it is crucial that the development of procedural standards is in the hands of the profession itself. This is because procedural standards are directly related to the performance of work; they represent ways of operationalizing the collective knowledge base and – provided that they are not too detailed – are important for safeguarding discretion, as well as trust, in professional services. Our analysis shows that the NNO and the DnR pay extensive attention to this work and see it as their responsibility. The UoE seems reluctant, however, and by and large leaves this work to external stakeholders. This approach seems more vulnerable in the long run, as the standards promoted in this profession may be generated from various audit agencies rather than from 'within' the expert domain. While the argument for not engaging itself in standardizing the processes of work is presented as a concern for protecting professional jurisdiction, the opposite may in fact be the result.

The Extended Professional Project: Relations to Knowledge Regulation at the European and International Levels

The institutionalization and regulation of professional expertise and services in Norway can be characterized by the active involvement of a strong and interventionist state (cf. Faulconbridge and Muzio 2011). Furthermore, as noted earlier, Norway has been a slow adopter of neoliberal market strategies by supporting a strong role of the state in the provision of public services. In other words, the state's regulatory role is important in understanding the process of professionalization. Yet it is crucial to capture how certain professions also reflect a local orientation and a local interdependency.

As mentioned above, one of the significant changes facing professions and professional associations today is the increase in transnational regulations. One aspect in this respect is the regulation of higher education in order to establish a more convergent and unified area of European higher education. Another aspect is the regulation of trade and labour markets through organizations such as the WTO and the EU. The development towards a more global labour market implies also an increased number of supra-national professional associations that coexist with national associations (Faulconbridge and Muzio 2011; Evetts 2011).

Our analysis shows that all three associations participated in international collaboration through membership in different organizations at European and international levels. Additionally, the importance of Nordic cooperation was highlighted in the interviews. This was seen as an increasingly important arena to develop shared initiatives and be capable of informing standards launched at the European level. What the associations sought to influence was, however, varying.

One issue at stake concerns the level of qualifications needed in order to practice the profession. This issue is particularly highlighted by the NNO, as education in nursing in Europe is offered on different levels by different institutions in the educational sector. An important matter in the NNO's educational policy is to defend a unified science-based professional programme, which leads to master's programmes. The NNO's work on procedural standards implies a need to stay in touch with the latest advances in medical treatment and to bring these insights to Norwegian health services. The notion of universalism at play in this association is related to scientific evidence, and the knowledge work enacted to manage the local–global relationship takes the form of promoting science-based procedures and guidelines for nursing practice. The importance of procedural standards and evidence-based practice is in line with the policy of the International Council of Nurses (ICN 2012).

In the case of the UoE, the emphasis on formalizing standards for teachers' work in terms of teacher-to-student ratios and educational requirements, combined with the reluctance to define collective knowledge and best practices in the profession, generates a positioning of the Union as a watchdog for government initiatives and regulations. This again brings organizational issues to the forefront. These concerns related to conditions and educational equity are also issues that are at the core for Education International (EI) – the world's largest federation of unions – which represents about 400 organizations across the globe.

In the field of education, national policy makes increasing reference to an international reform agenda. However, while the teaching profession is increasingly influenced by international benchmarking and performance standards (e.g. PISA and TIMSS), the UoE does not seem to engage itself extensively on the international scene. Our interpretation of this matter is that the transnational trends in the teaching profession are filtered through the bureaucracy in which the state is a prime actor. Hence, much of the work related to adjusting and aligning national regulations to international standards is enacted by the state and its agencies.

The engagement of the DnR on the international scene is motivated by a general interest for securing consistency in legislation and standards for accountancy work across national boundaries. Moreover, as an important part of its professional project, the Institute is concerned with taking a lead in promoting new standards in Norway. Throughout its history, the Institute has strived to initiate changes in regulations before such changes are sought by the national authorities as a way of maintaining a sense of professional jurisdiction (Bredal 2005; Karseth and Nerland 2007). This work is increasingly related to its extended engagement on the Nordic and European scene, as national regulations often are derived from international regulations.

To sum up, our analysis of the international work of the associations with regard to knowledge regulation and standardization shows that the way associations act reflects the distinctiveness of their respective professional fields. The NNO defines its knowledge base as universal, and international collaboration is embedded in an international conceptual knowledge base. This association performs its knowledge-regulative effort in close relation to science and engages in producing, distributing and warranting profession-specific knowledge for different purposes. The knowledge regulation of the UoE reflects weak ties to a conceptual knowledge base. It seems that the international work mainly is concentrated towards ensuring good educational conditions. By focusing on societal responsibility and equality, however, the approaches taken in the teacher profession imply a risk that it will be exposed to external regulation, as there may be a lack of procedural standards that are generated from 'within' their expert domain.

Conclusion

Efforts to regulate and secure knowledge in and for professional work – and the engagement of professional associations in this respect – take place within contested terrain in which different concerns need to be negotiated on a continuous basis. At the same time, we have shown that standardization in the professions can take very different forms and that the effects on standards of professional knowledge and practice are not clear-cut. While too-detailed standards for practice may be seen as a threat to professional discretion, common standards are also a prerequisite for discretionary decision-making. Moreover, in the context of increased internationalization and transnational regulations of professional work, profession-specific standards may take on new functions. Such standards can be seen as intermediaries providing connection points between local work and wider circuits of knowledge (Timmermanns and Epstein 2010; Nes and Moen 2010; Jensen *et al.* 2012).

At the same time, the development of such standards needs to be understood in a wider context that stretches beyond the nation state. The interplay between transnational, national and local agencies is an interesting issue in this respect, and is in need of more research that can reveal governing mechanisms within specific professions and how these are influenced by global knowledge cultures (Knorr Cetina 2007). As noted by Faulconbridge and Muzio (2011: 142), the rise of supra-national professional bodies means that access to practising the profession and professional standards are now controlled at multiple levels. As argued by these authors, the professional project has become transnational (ibid.). For associations at the national level, this implies requests for extended engagement in space and time, in which the epistemic and political dimensions of their work may be difficult to separate.

The professional associations will become increasingly important knowledge agents in a society where knowledge, as well as the market for professional services, becomes internationalized. Their identity as national member associations is likely to continue; however, by participating in different networks on the international scene their activities and priorities may change. We therefore suggest that a future research agenda should pay more attention to their efforts to regulate knowledge and practice, and that more comparative analyses across professions – as well as profession-specific analysis across nations – should be conducted in this respect. Additionally, looking into how policies for knowledge regulation travel from one professional sector to another is also essential in order to understand the knowledge-regulative efforts of professional associations and processes of standardization.

Acknowledgement

The two authors have contributed equally to this work, which has been conducted as part of the *Learning Trajectories in Knowledge Economies* (LiKE) project funded by the Research Council of Norway. Results from the study we draw upon were previously published as an article in the *Journal of Education and Work* (Nerland and Karseth 2013). Hence parts of the text, in particular the description of types of standards and the presentation of the Norwegian associations, have appeared in this publication.

Note

1   DnR is the official abbreviation for the Institute's name in Norwegian ('Den norske Revisorforening'). We have chosen to use this throughout the text as the Institute does not have an English acronym.

References

Bowker, G.C. and Star, S.L. (1999) *Sorting things out. Classification and its consequences,* Cambridge, Ma: MIT Press.

Bredal, D. (2005) 'Revisor og revisjon gjennom 75 år: Historie, forening og fag' [Auditor and accountancy in 75 years: History, association and discipline], *Revisjon og regnskap,* 7: 8–19.

Cervero, R.M. (2001) 'Continuing professional education in transition, 1981–2000', *International Journal of Lifelong Education* 20(1): 16 –30.

DnR (2008) *Årsberetning 2008* [Annual report 2007], Oslo: Den norske Revisorforening.

DnR (2009) *Årsberetning 2009* [Annual report 2009], Oslo: Den norske Revisorforening.

Evetts, J. (2011) 'Sociological analysis of professionalism: past, present and future', *Comparative Sociology* 10: 1–37.

Evetts, J. (2012) 'Similarities in contexts and theorizing: Professionalism and inequality', *Professions & Professionalism* 2(2). http://dx.doi.org/10.7577/pp.322

Faulconbridge, J.R. and Muzio, D. (2011) 'Professions in a globalizing world: Toward a transnational sociology of the professions', *International Sociology* 27(1): 136–152.

Fenwick, T. (2010) '(un)Doing standards in education with actor-network theory', *Journal of Education Policy,* 25(2): 117–133.

Freidson, E. (2001) *Professionalism: The Third Logic,* London: Polity Press.

Friedman, A. and Phillips, M. (2004) 'Continuing professional development: developing a vision', *Journal of Education and Work* 17(3): 361–376.

Forrester, G. (2000) 'Professional autonomy versus managerial control: the experience of teachers in an English primary school', *International Studies in Sociology of Education,* 10(2):133–151.

Greenwood, R., Suddaby, R. and Hinings, C.R. (2002) 'Theorizing change: The role of professional associations in the transformation of institutionalized fields', *Academy of Management Journal,* 45(1): 58–80.

Hjetland, H. (2009) Opening speech at the Congress of Union of Education Norway, 2 November.

ICN (2012) *Closing the Gap: From Evidence to Action,* Geneva: International Council of Nurses.

Jensen, K., Lahn, L.C. and Nerland, M. (2012) 'Professional learning in new knowledge landscapes: A cultural perspective', in K. Jensen, L.C. Lahn and M. Nerland (eds) *Professional Learning in the Knowledge Society* (pp. 1–24), Rotterdam: Sense Publishers.

Karseth, B. and Nerland, M. (2007) 'Building professionalism in a knowledge society: Examining discourses of knowledge in four professional associations', *Journal of Education and Work,* 20(4): 335–355.

Knorr Cetina, K. (2007) 'Culture in global knowledge societies: Knowledge cultures and epistemic cultures', *Interdisciplinary Science Reviews,* 32(4): 361–375.

Mathisen, A. and Nerland, M. (2012) 'The pedagogy of complex work support systems: Infrastructuring practices and the production of critical awareness in risk auditing', *Pedagogy, Culture & Society,* 20(1): 71–91.

Morgan, A., Cullinane, J. and Pye, M. (2008) 'Continuing professional development: Rhetoric and practice in the NHS', *Journal of Education and Work,* 21(3): 233–248.

Nerland, M. and Karseth, B. (2013) 'The knowledge work of professional associations: Approaches to standardization and forms of legitimization', *Journal of Education and Work.*

Nes, S. and Moen, S. (2010) 'Constructing standards: a study of nurses negotiating with multiple modes of knowledge', *Journal of Workplace Learning,* 22(6): 376–393.

Noordegraaf, M. (2011) 'Remaking professionals? How associations and professional education connect professionalism and organizations', *Current Sociology,* 59(4): 465–488.

NNO (2008) *Sykepleie: Et selvstendig fag* [About Nursing as an Independent and Professional Field], Oslo: Norsk Sykepleierforbund.

Østerud, Ø. and Selle, P. (2006) 'Power and democracy in Norway: The transformation of Norwegian politics', *Scandinavian Political Studies,* 29(1): 25–46.

Ozga, J., Segerholm, C. and Simola, H. (2011) 'The governance turn', in J. Ozga, P. Dahler-Larsen, C. Segerholm and H. Simola (eds) *Fabricating Quality in Education: Data and Governance in Europe*, London: Routledge.

Rotegaard, A.K. and Ruland, C.M. (2010) 'Patient centeredness in terminologies: Coverage of health assets concepts in the International Classification of Nursing Practice', *Journal of Biomedical Informatics,* 43: 805–811.

Strathern, M. (2000) 'The tyranny of transparency', *British Educational Research Journal,* 26(3): 309–321.

Styhre, A. (2011) *Knowledge Sharing in Professions: Roles and Identity in Expert Communities,* London: Gower.

Timmermans, S. and Berg, M. (2003) *The Gold Standard: The Challenge of Evidence-Based Medicine and Standardization in Health Care*, Philadelphia: Temple University Press.

Timmermans, S. and Epstein, S. (2010) 'A world of standards but not a standard world: Towards a sociology of standards and standardization', *Annual Review of Sociology,* 36: 69–89.

Utdanningsforbundet (2008) 'Evidens og evidensdebattens betydning for utdanningssystemet', temanotat 6 [About evidence and its impact on the educational system], Oslo: Utdanningsforbundet.

Watkins, J. (1999) 'Educating professionals: The changing role of UK professional associations', *Journal of Education and Work,* 12(1): 37–56.

Zietsma, C. and Lawrence, T.B. (2010) 'Institutional work in the transformation of an organizational field: The interplay of boundary work and practice work', *Administrative Science Quarterly,* 55: 189–221.

14 Governing Education in China

PISA, Comparison and Educational Regions

Philip Wing Keung Chan and Terri Seddon

Introduction

The 2009 results for the Organisation for Economic Co-operation and Development's (OECD) Programme for International Student Assessment (PISA) ranked China highest of the 65 participating countries. While scholars outside China celebrate the 'stunning success' of Shanghai in all three areas assessed, the ranking has attracted comment about Shanghai not being representative of all of China. This chapter reports the results of the 11 other participating Chinese regions and considers the implications of the OECD allowing the PISA results of one Chinese city to be used as a basis for comparison of other nation states' results.

The chapter is organised in four sections. The first section outlines the history of educational governance in China and comments on the role of PISA in governing. The concept of 'network governance' is introduced to focus the analysis on the transaction of knowledge resources as a means of governing. The use of this theoretical framework in relation to Chinese education is addressed and the methodology is outlined. The main body of the chapter documents the multiple agencies and administrative processes behind PISA in Shanghai and then considers PISA in the rest of China. PISA results from 11 other regions of China are reported and related to the overall 2009 PISA results worldwide. The repercussions of the Shanghai PISA result in China and abroad indicate that there was Shanghai 'PISA fever'. The implications of these results and the consequent PISA fever raises questions about the effects of the OECD shifting from nation states to city states as the unit of analysis. It also raises questions about educational governance in China and Chinese-styled network governance.

PISA as a Means of Governing

Prior to the Open Door Policy in 1978, Chinese society was often described as 'closed, conservative, authoritarian and hierarchical' (Qi and Tang, 2004, p. 466). Education in that period was centralised and monopolised by the state (Mok, 1997; Yang, 2004). Under such a governance model, the Ministry of Education (MOE) took responsibility for the design of curricula, syllabuses and textbooks, student admission and graduate job assignment and also exerted control over budgets, salary scales and personnel issues (Mok, 2003). Provincial and local education commissions and bureaus were simply mediators of national policy (Mok, 2005).

After Deng Xiaoping introduced the notion of a 'socialist market economy' in 1992, China remained a socialist state but was increasingly shaped by market forces (Bray and Qin, 2001). The transition period from a planned economy to a market economy transformed all aspects of Chinese policy-making, from isolationist, politics-oriented policies to economics-oriented policies (Sun, 2010; Yang *et al.*, 2007). The flourishing market economy and the policy of decentralisation deeply influenced China's educational development. Changes in the State's role in regulating and financing educational services showed that China's educational development was undergoing marketisation (Kwong, 1996), with decentralisation occurring at all levels of government and all sectors of the education system (Cheng, 1994b).

In a global economy, the success of an education system is no longer simply benchmarked against national standards (Schleicher, 2012). Governance of education is also shaped by internationally benchmarked tests of student achievement. It is an approach that has gained increasing popularity with governments around the world. They monitor and measure the performance of their country's education system to guide their education reform. China is not immune from this trend: international benchmarking via tests, such as PISA, provide information that meets central governments' 'demands for data about operation and resources' (Ozga, 2009, p. 150).

The OECD launched PISA in 1997 as an international assessment and worldwide evaluation of 15-year-old students' academic performance in three key subjects: Reading, Mathematics and Science literacy. The PISA survey was first conducted in 2000 and was repeated every three years. To date, over 70 countries and economies have participated and PISA results have become an important reference point from which to evaluate education systems and judge educational outcomes worldwide (Schleicher, 2012). A PISA report is treated as a comprehensive world education ranking that identifies which country's students perform best in Reading, Mathematics and Science (Lee and Lee, 2012).

PISA results provide a new global standard that affects national education reform and policy-making in participating countries. The use of statistics is a powerful tool, used by both media and government (Stack, 2006). PISA's statistical results have come to represent the success or failure of education systems. They are a status indicator. PISA results prompt media coverage that drives policy reform. Such 'PISA fever' goes viral across nation states as education ministers, policy-makers, researchers, administrators and educators obsessively pursue the status of Top Performing Education Systems that equip their students with twenty-first-century skills (Lee and Lee, 2012).

China first participated in PISA in 2009. Twelve regions in China were tested but only the Shanghai region result was released. So Shanghai appeared to represent China as a whole. Yet China is a big country, comprising 22 provinces (Taiwan is disputed territory), four municipalities, five autonomous regions, and two special administrative regions: all are at different stages of economic development. The eastern coastal regions of China are relatively well-developed and richer than western inland regions.

China's decentralisation shifted financial responsibility from central government to local government. This move from a centralised system with a narrow revenue base to a decentralised system with a diversified revenue base produced provincial and regional disparities (Cheng, 1994a). It increased disadvantage in economically undeveloped regions. For example, in 2001, provincial governments in the central and western regions did not have sufficient funds to support compulsory education (primary school Year 1 to secondary school Year 3). The central government responded by putting more money into these regions but they remain relatively poorer than eastern coastal regions (Zhao, 2008).

These educational disparities across China raise questions about the OECD's decision to allow the results of Shanghai, one of the richest cities in the eastern coastal region of China, to be used as a basis for comparison with other nation states.

Network Governance – a Theoretical Framework

China's economic and social transition since the 1978 Open Door Policy is linked to changes from centralised to decentralised practices of governing. In Western social science, this transition is described as a shift from 'government' to 'governance' (Jessop, 1998). The concept of 'network governance' provides an analytical framework for understanding how decision-making processes are embedded in and realised through networks.

Political Science Perspectives

The idea of governance is as old as human civilisation (Malik, 2002). Etymologically, the notion can be traced to the Greek verb *kubernan* (to pilot or steer) and was used by Plato to describe how to rule people effectively (Kjær, 2004). However, the concept of 'governance' has been elaborated as governments reoriented policy-making processes by drawing on economic theories, particularly agency theory and transaction cost theory that make particular assumptions about individual motivations, relationships between principal and agent, and the efficient use of contracts (Giguere, 2006). These economic policy frames offered strategies to address complex economic and social problems but also presented problems of coordination.

The move away from centralised government was accompanied by changing modes of coordination through states, markets and networks. Where 'government' refers to decision-making through a privileged or sovereign authority, 'governance' refers to practices of governing through multiple entities. Markets offer one means of coordination. Networks become significant when complex problems are not amenable to simple solutions and cannot be realised either through single agencies or the operation of markets. In these circumstances networks become significant because coordination occurs through smaller-scale localised interest groups that operate as different political systems and create many decision-making centres with considerable cultural diversity (Rhodes 1996).

Theories of network governance developed through studies of policy communities in political science. Heclo and Wildasvsky (1974) analysed the British Treasury Department and the private government of public money. They defined a 'policy community' as a cluster of personal relationships between major political and administrative actors in a policy area. In America, studies of elite policy-making documented policy communities consisting of small, exclusive sets of actors: congress, administrative agencies and lobbying groups interact and exchange resources (Heclo, 1978). Such research focused attention on horizontal coordination in policy-making, involving individual actors in concrete policy processes (Hanf and Scharpf, 1978).

The idea that the policy community operated as a 'network' built on pluralist theory. Bentley (1967) and Truman (1971) pointed to the existence of horizontal relations between government, administration and organised interests. Government was revealed as a 'network of activities' (Bentley, 1967, p. 261) in which actors were self-organising in policy processes. They were able to 'resist government steering, develop their own policies and mould their environments' (Rhodes, 2000, p. 61). These policy processes operated through exchange of resources and negotiations, and the game-like interactions were 'rooted in trust and regulated by rules of the game negotiated and agreed by network participants' (Rhodes, 2000, p. 61). Knowledge is a key resource in these transactions: in its own right and as a means towards better negotiation and engagement within relations of resource exchange (Kersbergen and Waarden, 2004).

By the 1980s, 'network governance' became an accepted descriptor for policy making arrangements distinguished by modes of coordination: hierarchical control (state-centralist or government-focused) and horizontal coordination (centreless or polycentred society) (Hanf and Scharpf, 1978). British network analysis suggested that this new governance mode hollowed-out the state (Rhodes, 1994), becoming 'a collection of inter-organisational networks made up of governmental and societal actors with no sovereign actor able to steer or regulate' (Rhodes, 1997, p. 57). By contrast, Dutch network research focused on ways of managing networks, by examining the practical consequences of multi-actor approaches to governance (Kickert *et al.*, 1997). Contrasting hierarchical relations where power operates through demands, they highlighted how multiple local actors interacted in ways that enabled and coordinated exchanges of information resources and goals (Koppenjan and Klijn, 2004; Klijn, 2008).

Policy Sociology of Education

Policy sociology of education builds on and elaborates these political science traditions by emphasising cultural understandings of knowledge and practice. The seminal work of McPherson and Raab (1988) was significant because their study of educational governing centred on political cultures of education. They approached the workings of government anthropologically to reveal the values and practices of actors, and how governing occurred through regulation of knowledge via curriculum, qualifications and employment practices. The idea of 'policy community' was also extended beyond the state to recognise the 'set of persons and groups which stretches across the divide between government and outside interests, and which is directly involved in the making and implementation of policy' (McPherson and Raab, 1988: 472).

Expanding political sociology in this way framed up persistent debates about knowledge as a means of control (Young, 1971). Education was a social institution and a means of social and economic reproduction and transformation. This political sociology of education was reconfigured as 'policy sociology' with market reform of education in the 1980s (Dale, 1989). Studies of political cultures of education interrogated changes in education policy processes, cultural dimensions of market governance and its effects in civil society. This research revealed struggles over cultures of educating that were initially conceptualised as hegemonic cultural politics (Gramsci, 1971) and then re-read through theories of discourse (Foucault, 1982). Practices of governing occurred through macro-level policy processes and through the governmental effects of micro-practices of power (Ball, 1990; Marginson, 1997). Both were mediated by power-knowledge relations that became evident in ways of using words to drive the 'conduct of conduct' in and through relationships (Dean, 1999).

This 'governance turn' in education policy sociology (Ozga, 2009, p. 158) connected political sociology of education and studies of governmentality. The state is understood to be a network of relations that locates governing in networks of actors and discursive strategies to regulate and discipline citizens (Popkewitz, 1996). Contemporary educational reforms shift the work of governing from government through a bureaucratic state to market mechanisms that endorse the proliferation of agencies that operate as localised centres of power and influence in policy processes. The state still dominates and, therefore, does not 'hollow-out' but the work of governing opens selectively to allow other actors to influence government policies. These heterarchical modalities of governance represent 'a new modality of state power, agency and social action and indeed a new form of state' (Ball, 2008, p. 748).

Knowledge and Policy

With this transition towards a 'post-bureaucratic' state, governments seek new forms of intervention and action in societies. Network governance demands the continuous generation of new skills and knowledge to legitimate state actions (Rhodes, 2007). Coordination no longer relies just on conformity to rules and standardisation of bureaucratic procedures or professional qualifications. Instead it operates through new regulatory devices that operationalise quasi-markets and evaluative states in ways that affect individual's attitudes and behaviours:

> [I]n the quasi-market models, it is above all competitive pressure through the intervention of an 'informed' user parent that encourages the school to improve its educational services. In the evaluative state model, regulation occurs more through evaluation of processes and results and through incentives or sanctions meted out to schools according to their 'progress' and results.
>
> (Maroy, 2012, p. 69)

Knowledge/information is central to these emerging regulatory devices. Market mechanisms depend on users making choices based on good information; evaluation-based knowledge supplies the demand for information. These knowledge-information flows are linked through the design of assessment technologies and reporting processes that underpin regulatory instruments, such as funding formulae, key performance indicators and performance assessment processes, such as PISA. These 'knowledge-based regulatory tools' organise and also legitimise policy decisions: evaluative knowledge-for-policy feeds into market mechanisms that, in turn, govern knowledge of practice. Their 'objective measures' are selectively screened through knowledge networks that comprise particular knowledge workers (e.g. professionals, experts, think tanks, professional organisations, and educational researchers) and ordered as valued inputs to evidence-based policy action (Pons and van Zanten, 2007).

Governing through networks encourages innovation but regulates practice through the standardisation of norms, justifications and institutional referents (Maroy, 2012). The vocabulary of public education reform is disciplined by discourses of 'efficiency', 'accountability' and 'quality' that provide a normative frame within which shared goals are constructed. For example, public education reform in the United States affirms 'participatory collaboration between citizens and the agencies of government' to improve the quality of public provision (Liebman and Sabel, 2003, p. 271). Yet as the words become embedded in knowledge-based regulatory tools they also reorient practice, justifications and judgements, endorsing 'open cultures' that align with free-market social logics, and romance private firms as 'goods', while relegating established bureaucratic and professional standardisation in education as 'closed cultures' and 'bads'.

This normative logic of comparison underpins international benchmarking using knowledge-based regulatory tools, such as PISA. PISA reorients the reference point for making judgements about education away from established national debates about education, social justice, and the significance of system-based practices and cultures in reproducing or transforming societies. Instead, PISA assessments centre debate on 'quality' measures and the comparative ordering of results along a normative 'good'–'bad' continuum. National education systems are represented by tests results based on indicators that are treated as objective measures of performance and then ranked.

Yet PISA is premised on particular methodologies of comparative education. PISA's 'facts' are 'objects of knowledge brought into view and highlighted in a conceptual system in which specific processes are seen as problems' (Nóvoa and Yariv-Mashal, 2003, p. 426). Indicators are treated as having universal validity and these indicators are assumed to be a sufficient basis for comparison. These methodological choices produce 'thin' knowledge that can be generalised. It is contradicted by the 'thick' knowledge that develops in particular places, as countries and their educators engage in everyday processes of defining and solving problems, framed by their established histories and traditions.

This contradiction between 'thin' and 'thick' knowledge is central to contemporary politics of network governance. PISA is a knowledge-based regulatory tool that has constructed a world ordering of national education systems. However, it is vulnerable to questions about the legitimacy of its 'facts' that rest on particular processes of problematisation, conceptual frameworks and methodological strategies used to build knowledge for policy. PISA 'facts' become legitimate when they are accepted as appropriate generalisable measures of performance and as comparisons between countries. Building this kind of agreement across multi-agency networks depends upon a knowledge politics that also denigrates those knowledges that are generated in particular places through historically embedded knowledge processes. These politics of partnership require network actors to prioritise and endorse the network prior to the networked entities (Seddon *et al.*, 2004).

In this light, the inclusion of Shanghai in the 2009 PISA results seems curious. When methodological choices are central to the alignment of knowledge and policy that legitimises network governance, questions about the validity of comparison and its unit of analysis become critical.

Methodology

In this exploratory study we investigate PISA as an instrument of governing in networks by examining the knowledge base that informs the PISA 2009 results. We focus on the unit of analysis in PISA 2009 comparison where the OECD published Shanghai results but China conducted PISA tests in 11 regions as well as Shanghai. We ask two questions. First, is it legitimate to compare educational results from Shanghai and from the national education systems of other countries? Second, what does the PISA survey reveal about network governance in China, testing was?

Network governance has been described in various Chinese public policy processes, using the Chinese terms *zhengce wangluo* (policy network) or *wangluo guanzhi* (network governance). These processes have been studied in relation to reform of taxation in rural areas (Tang, 2004), politics in provincial legislatures (Xia, 2008), housing and estate policy (Zhu, 2008) and public health insurance reform (Zheng, Jong *et al.*, 2010). In education, Mok (2001) examined the shift from 'state control' to a 'state supervision model' in Chinese higher education, where power was decentralised from education bureaucracies to create, in their place, devolved systems of schooling that restructure state-education relationships and shifts state control. Law and Pan (2009) examined private education legislation in China using game theory. They found educational legislation in China to be a dynamic game involving repeated negotiation, cooperation and/or competition among interested actors, each with their own goals, authorities, information sources and strategies.

The concept of 'network governance' was used to investigate changing state-education relations under China's Modern Enterprise System (Chan and Seddon, 2012). This policy shift occurred in 1993 when economic pressures in state-owned enterprises (SOEs) prompted central government to disconnect SOEs from SOE schools. SOEs are the foundation of China's industrial base and dominate strategic areas of heavy industry, such as iron and steel, coal, metallurgy, chemicals, energy production, and petroleum exploration (Steinfeld, 1998). They contribute significant resources to education by providing a diversified range of SOE schools, from childcare centres to higher-education institutions, throughout China. In this respect, they operate like a mini-welfare state. In 1994, there were SOE schools, including 314 higher-education institutions. The study 21,323 focused on SOE schools in the Ministry of Railways in Harbin and Shenzhen. Harbin in Heilongjiang province has the biggest numbers of SOE schools. Shenzhen in Guangdong Province has much smaller numbers. It is not typical of the rest of China but it is the most economically prosperous city in southern China in terms of per capita income (Chan, forthcoming).

This comparative research found evidence of network governance in China but also noted different practices of governing in the two cities. For example, the Modern Enterprise System shifted educational governance arrangements in ways that threatened retirement benefits of retired SOE schoolteachers. In Shenzhen, these retired teachers formed networks to connect other retired teachers in different cities to exchange information, and mobilised the support of public media and councillors to increase their bargaining power with government officials. By contrast, the Harbin retired teachers trusted their school principals and the officers in railway education departments to act in their best interests. These different strategies to influence government policy making indicate that the these governance reforms shifted education in SOE schools away from a highly centralised system of government and, instead, coordinated actors decision-making processes through resource exchanges and stakeholder motivations to contribute to collective decisions.

The analysis draws on secondary data, official documents, and media reports and our prior empirical research into regional disparities and Chinese network governance. First, we traced the reactions and responses to media reports about the Shanghai result in PISA 2009 that were collected on the website of the Shanghai Academy of Educational Sciences. Second, we searched for reports on the other 11 regions participating in PISA 2009 in Chinese journal articles, public media and institutional websites. We found the names of participating regions in public media and government reports. The regional results were available through a Chinese journal article in which the author referred to the regions as A to K, rather than fully identifying them. We can only reliably match Zhejiang province to region E, so the names of participating regions in our analysis will be Shanghai, Zhejiang and regions A to K (except E). Ranking the regions' results revealed regional variations across China. Third, we calculated China's average to find the aggregate picture of China's PISA results. We mapped this average against the OECD average and also entered the Chinese regions into the list of top 15 PISA 2009 to see how many regions in China fitted into the list. This procedure revealed China's average and 12 regional results in the PISA 2009 ranking.

PISA in Shanghai

The scores of Shanghai in PISA 2009 far surpass those of students from the top nations in the previous triennial PISA assessments since 2000. Former leaders in Reading, Mathematics and Science are shown in Table 14.1. Shanghai students' scores of 556 in Reading, 600 in Mathematics and 575 in Science gave them a 17-point margin over South Korea in Reading, a 38-point margin over Singapore in Mathematics and a 21-point margin over Finland in Science (OECD, 2009). Moreover:

> The Shanghai students not only outperformed the rest of the world but also had the largest percentage of test takers performing at the highest level. In Mathematics, for example, 27% of them reached level 6 defined as capable of advanced mathematical thinking and reasoning, versus 3% of the students from OECD countries and 2% of U.S. students.
>
> (Mervis, 2010, p. 1461)

Table 14.1   Global education ranking in PISA

Year	Global Education Ranking in PISA (Reading, Mathematics, Sciences)
2000	Finland, Japan, South Korea
2003	Finland, Hong Kong, Finland
2006	South Korea, Taipei, Finland
2009	Shanghai, Shanghai, Shanghai

Source: OECD (2000, 2003, 2006, 2010a).

These results were the outcome of a PISA project that was lead and coordinated operationally by the Shanghai Municipal Education Commission (SMEC) (Lu, 2009). The Shanghai PISA (SHPISA) Secretariat and Research Centre at the Shanghai Academy of Educational Sciences (SAES) administered the test, under the leadership of Professor Minxuan Zhang. Zhang was the previous president of SEAS (2005–2009), the deputy director-general of the SMEC (2009–2011) and is now president of the Shanghai Normal University. He is also an observer representing China-Shanghai on the PISA Governing Board and programme manager for Shanghai PISA (OECD, 2012).

The Shanghai PISA project involved a number of actors organised in a clear division of labour. The SHPISA Secretariat was responsible for implementing the decisions made by the project operations team, which undertook planning, organisation and coordination of works. The SHPISA Research Centre was responsible for test papers, questionnaires, examination manuals, examination standards, the translation and revision of score management manuals, training for test supervisors and school examiners, student sampling and data management, as well as carrying out PISA research tasks. The Shanghai Education Examination Institute managed the test affairs, which include printing of papers, promotional materials and candidate's test documents, students' commemorative pen production, management of marked papers and results data entry. The Assessment and Research Office in the SMEC was responsible for the recruitment of assessment experts, training for the test markers, proposed and revised test topics and contents (Lu, 2009). PISA 2009 in Shanghai also involved five department units and four direct-controlled institutions under SMEC, admissions offices of 19 district education bureaus, assessment experts, quality monitoring experts, 375 supervisors and management staff on the test day, 152 schools and 5,115 students (Zhang, 2009).

On 17 April 2009, SHPISA conducted the first formal test in accordance with PISA requirements and technical standards. SHPISA selected 5,115 students from a test sample of 152 schools in Shanghai using statistical methods (Westate – PPS) and KeyQuest software (Lu, 2009; Shanghai PISA, 2010). The data met minimum OECD requirements of at least 150 schools and 4,500 students (OECD, 2008). Within this student cohort in Shanghai, 89.9 per cent were from public schools and 10.1 per cent from Minban (private) schools. They included 39.5 per cent of students from urban schools and 60.5 per cent from rural schools; 49.4 per cent male students and 50.6 per cent female students (Lu, 2009).

PISA in Other Regions of China

Apart from Shanghai, the National Education Examination Authority (NEEA) of the Ministry of Education in China selected 11 regions to participate in PISA 2009. They included eight provinces (Hainan, Hebei, Hubei, Jiangsu, Jilin, Sichuan, Yunnan, Zhejiang), one autonomous region (Ningxia), one municipality (Tianjin) and one district (Beijing – Fangshan) (Examination Bureau of Hainan Province, 2012). Shanghai was not included under the NEEA, but was administered by Shanghai PISA. These regions, together, contain more than 6.5 million students and 20,000 schools. The NEEA finally selected 19,256 students from 613 schools (Examination Bureau of Hainan Province, 2012).

Table 14.2 shows the PISA 2009 result for Reading, Mathematics and Science in all 12 regions of China. Apart from Shanghai, Zhejiang province, Region D and Region B are ranked the top three regions in China, while Region H, Region I and Region G are ranked the bottom. For Reading, while China's average is 486, seven marks less than the OECD average (493); five regions (Shanghai, Zhejiang, Regions D, B and A) are above the OECD average and seven regions below the OECD average. In Mathematics, China averages 542, 46 marks more than the OECD average (496), with ten Chinese regions above the OECD average and two regions below. In Science, China has an average of 517, 16 marks ahead of the OECD average (501). Eight Chinese regions are above the OECD average for Science and four regions are below. The data show that there is good performance in Mathematics and Science in China when viewed against the OECD and a slight under-performance in Reading relative to the OECD average. It also shows a large regional variation in education across China.

Table 14.2 PISA 2009 result in Chinese regions

No.	Region	Reading	Mathematics	Science	Total
1	Shanghai	556	600	575	1731
2	Zhejiang	525	598	567	1690
3	Region D	522	585	558	1665
4	Region B	509	564	531	1604
5	Region A	498	568	535	1601
6	Region F	481	549	523	1553
7	Region K	497	536	503	1536
8	Region C	483	533	512	1528
9	Region J	469	519	500	1488
10	Region H	450	520	497	1467
11	Region I	435	482	468	1385
12	Region G	407	453	437	1297
	China average	486	542	517	1545
	OECD average	493	496	501	1490

Source: OECD (2010b); Xue (2012).

Table 14.3 shows an updated world ranking of PISA 2009 by adding the results of the Chinese regions. In Reading, four Chinese regions are ranked amongst the top 15 in the world. They are Shanghai, Zhejiang, Region D and Region B. In Mathematics, eight Chinese regions are ranked with the top 15 in the world and five of them are in the top five – Shanghai, Zhejiang, Region D, Region A and Region B. In Science, six Chinese regions are ranked among the top 15 in the world; Shanghai, Zhejiang and Region D are in the top three. Some regions in China (such as Zhejiang or Region D) performed almost as well as Shanghai in Mathematics and Science.

Table 14.3 PISA 2009 result (including Chinese regions)

Rank	Reading		Mathematics		Science	
	Country (Region)	Mark	Country (Region)	Mark	Country (Region)	Mark
1	China (Shanghai)	556	China (Shanghai)	600	China (Shanghai)	575
2	South Korea	539	China (Zhejiang)	598	China (Zhejiang)	567
3	Finland	536	China (Region D)	585	China (Region D)	558
4	Hong Kong SAR	533	China (Region A)	568	Finland	554
5	Singapore	526	China (Region B)	564	Hong Kong SAR	549
6	China (Zhejiang)	525	Singapore	562	Singapore	542
7	Canada	524	Hong Kong SAR	555	Japan	539
8	China (Region D)	522	China (Region F)	549	South Korea	538
9	New Zealand	521	South Korea	546	China (Region A)	535
10	Japan	520	Chinese Taipei	543	New Zealand	532
11	Australia	515	China (Region C)	543	China (Region B)	531
12	China (Region B)	509	Finland	541	Canada	529
13	Netherlands	508	Liechtenstein	536	Estonia	528
14	Belgium	506	China (Region K)	536	Australia	527
15	Norway	503	Switzerland	534	China (Region F)	523
	China average	486	China average	542	China average	517

Source: OECD (2010b); Xue (2012).

Table 14.4 PISA 2009 result (including China average)

Rank	Reading		Mathematics		Science	
	Country	Mark	Country	Mark	Country	Mark
1	South Korea	539	Singapore	562	Finland	554
2	Finland	536	Hong Kong SAR	555	Hong Kong SAR	549
3	Hong Kong SAR	533	South Korea	546	Singapore	542
4	Singapore	526	Chinese Taipei	543	Japan	539
5	Canada	524	*China*	*542*	South Korea	538
6	New Zealand	521	Finland	541	New Zealand	532
7	Japan	520	Liechtenstein	536	Canada	529
8	Australia	515	Switzerland	534	Estonia	528
9	Netherlands	508	Japan	529	Australia	527
10	Belgium	506	Canada	527	Netherlands	522
14	Poland/Iceland	500	Belgium	515	*China*/Switzerland	*517*
28	*China*/Italy	*486*	Hungary	490	Iceland	496

Source: OECD (2010b); Xue (2012).

Table 14.4 provides a challenging view of China's global position, by incorporating the 12 Chinese regions as a China average, then comparing the result with other countries and regions. China ranked 28th, 5th and 14th in Reading, Mathematics and Science respectively, in 2009.

Shanghai and PISA Fever

It is no surprise that the 2009 PISA result generated massive attention in China and abroad. It was the first time China had participated in PISA and yet the great achievements were based on Shanghai results. The common reaction of the foreign media was shock. SHPISA summarised the reactions into four categories (Lu and Zhu, 2011) – praise, reflection, questioning and scarification:

1 *Praise* – the ability of Shanghai students is high. The *New York Times* ran an article, 'Top Test Scores From Shanghai Stun Educators', saying that 'With China's debut in international standardised testing, students in Shanghai have surprised experts by outscoring their counterparts in dozens of other countries, in Reading as well as in Math and Science' (Dillon, 2010, para. 1).
2 *Reflection* – students' abilities in their home countries or regions are backward when compared with Shanghai: they must strive to catch up.
3 *Questioning* – Chinese students achieved good results, but they still lack creativity.
4 *Scarification* – Chinese students spend most of their time studying subject knowledge rather than extracurricular activities like sports, art and other aspects. They pay the price for getting a good grade in academia.

The general reaction of Chinese media, domestic and overseas, was not one of shock about the PISA result and the examination ability of Chinese students. In contrast to the foreign media, it revealed six perspectives:

1   *Pride* – People in Shanghai celebrated their students' achievement and education.
2   *Questioning* – Some people doubted the sample reliability.
3   *Not an unexpected outcome* – Some people believed the PISA test primarily reflected the result of knowledge-based education. Shanghai students have these achievements because of their strong ability in testing.
4   *Heavy academic burden* – Shanghai students carry a tremendous cost to achieve these good results.
5   *Result of elite education* in Shanghai.
6   *One-off nature of the exam* had limited applicability.

Despite the mix of affirmation and questioning among both international and Chinese commentaries, Shanghai was identified as a competitor. For example, a new book, *Surpassing Shanghai* (Tucker, 2011), treats Shanghai as a model for American education to surpass. The release of the PISA 2009 results prompted the Danish Prime Minister to set the new goal of putting Denmark in the top five in PISA. Canada also expressed a need to improve the PISA scores and PISA ranking (Breakspear, 2012). These are examples of 'PISA fever' based on sensationalisation of PISA results but, in the case of Shanghai, the results are based on errors of comparison.

First, Shanghai is not a country and is also not representative of China. The Chinese PISA results vary across Chinese educational regions and Shanghai is one of the biggest commercial centres and industry powerhouses in China. It is better resourced than other regions (Baird *et al.*, 2011), drawing the elite to the Yangtze delta, it is a magnet for the best students in the country. Consequently, Shanghai has been a forerunner in educational reform in China in areas such as curriculum change, reducing teacher and student workloads, and small class teaching (Baird *et al.*, 2011). A recent OECD video (OECD, 2013) documents how Shanghai has put tremendous effort into strengthening weaker schools with positive effects in these schools.

Second, using the PISA result of a single Chinese city as if it was a country-to-country comparison is invalid. This error of comparison previously occurred in Canada. Media coverage in Canada regionalised the PISA results and affirmed 'good' Alberta, the 'so-so' Ontario, and 'bad' Atlantic Canada. This error produced a normative ordering of Canadian provincial education systems and also prompted the Alberta Ministry of Education of Learning to over-claim that 'the [PISA 2000] test showed that Alberta has one of the best education systems in the world because of the high quality of teaching and curriculum' (Stack, 2006, p. 56). Yet Canada did not use the Alberta data to represent the whole country. It reported national PISA results, not a particular sub-set of the national data.

These comparison errors reveal the normative impact of PISA on education policy and policy-making of participating countries and economies (Breakspear, 2012). Governments cite PISA results to legitimise particular education policies and justify education reforms. There was a perceived 'crisis' of education in

Japan when the 2003 PISA result showed a decline from being the top performer in 2000. The PISA 2000 result ranked Germany 20th among 32 participating countries, creating a 'PISA-shock' that had tremendous impact on the German education system, leading to a new concept of school management, new quality control measures and a balance of centralisation and decentralisation of education (Lawn and Grek, 2012).

First, is it legitimate to compare educational results from Shanghai and from the national education systems of other countries? Second, what does the PISA survey reveal about network governance in China?

Conclusion

The OECD's publication of Shanghai results in PISA 2009 raises many questions. However, it appears to undercut the legitimacy of the PISA world ranking of national education systems on two grounds. First, it focuses attention on the unit of analysis. At the national scale, PISA provides a benchmarking device for evaluating the quality, equity and efficiency of school systems in some 70 countries that comprise nine-tenths of the world economy (OECD, 2010a). Presenting Shanghai, a city, as one of the OECD partner economies compares apples and oranges. It has implications for the ranking of OECD countries and policy decisions based on these countries' positions. Conversely, treating Shanghai as a proxy for China over-claims China's educational standing because the PISA evidence does not acknowledge the educational advantage of Shanghai relative to other regions of China that were also tested.

Second, the use of Shanghai results in PISA 2009 problematises the politics of knowledge associated with PISA indicators. The OECD claims PISA indicators and 'thin' knowledge are a generalisable measure of national educational performance. This claim is set against the 'thick' knowledge claims of educational researchers and professionals embedded within national education systems. Yet Shanghai's government officials and educational researchers worked together using the PISA tests and close to minimum sample size ($N = 5,115$) to create particular knowledge about Shanghai's educational performance. This knowledge building process appeared to be separated from a parallel China PISA project ($N = 19,256$) that surveyed 11 regions other than Shanghai but with results not released to the world. The implication is that particular knowledge about educational performance was represented in the 2009 PISA comparison, not the more generalised results based on PISA tests across China.

This case study of PISA 2009 results provides evidence of network governance at a global scale that produced the OECD's inclusion of Shanghai results in PISA 2009. However, the two Chinese PISA projects provide evidence that China's is also governing through networks, rather than operating as a centralised state. At a global scale the inclusion of Shanghai in PISA 2009 indicates a negotiated agreement between the OECD and China. At a national scale, the development of two separate PISA projects and the inclusion of Shanghai data rather than Chinese data also suggest that agreements are being negotiated in ways that recognise a multiagency arrangement.

References

Baird, J.-A., Isaacs, T., Johnson, S., Stobart, G., Yu, G., Sprague, T. and Daugherty, R. (2011) *Policy Effects of PISA*. Oxford University Centre for Educational Assessment.

Ball, S. J. (1990) *Politics and Policy Making in Education: Explorations in Policy Sociology*. London: Routledge.

Ball, S. J. (2008) 'New philanthropy, new networks and new governance in education', *Political Studies*, 56(4), 747–765.

Bentley, A. F. (1967) *The Process of Government*. Cambridge, MA: Belknap Press of Harvard University Press.

Bray, M. and Qin, G. (2001) 'Comparative education in greater China: Contexts, characteristics, contrasts and contributions', *Comparative Education*, 37(4), 451–473.

Breakspear, S. (2012) 'The policy impact of PISA: An exploration of the normative effects of international benchmarking in school system performance', OECD Education Working Paper, OECD Publishing.

Chan, P. W. K. and Seddon, T. (2012) 'Network governance in education: The case of Chinese state-owned enterprise school', *The International Journal of Continuing Education and Lifelong Learning*, 4(2), 117–136.

Cheng, K. M. (1994a) 'The changing legitimacy in a decentralizing system: The state and education development in China', *International Journal of Educational Development*, 14(3), 265–269.

Cheng, K. M. (1994b) 'Issues in decentralizing education: What the reform in China tells', *International Journal of Educational Research*, 21(8), 799–808.

Dale, R. (1989) *The State and Education Policy*. Milton Keynes: Open University Press.

Dean, M. (1999) *Governmentality: Power and Rule in Modern Society*. London: Sage.

Dillon, S. (2010) 'Top test scores from Shanghai stun educators', *The New York Times*. Retrieved 13 January 2012, from http://www.nytimes.com/2010/12/07/education/07education.html?pagewanted=all&_r=0

Examination Bureau of Hainan Province (2012) 'Introduction of PISA in China', Retrieved 11 January 2013, from http://218.77.181.27/phtml/2012/10/24/2732.html

Foucault, M. (1982) 'The subject and power', *Critical Inquiry*, 8(4), 777–795.

Giguere, S. (2006) 'Local governance for economic development: Practice ahead of theory', Governments and Communities in Partnership conference, Centre for Public Policy, University of Melbourne, Australia.

Gramsci, A. (1971) *Selections from the Prison Notebooks*. London: Lawrence and Wishart.

Hanf, K. and Scharpf, F. W. (1978) *Interorganizational Policy Making: Limits to Coordination and Central Control*. London; Beverly Hills: Sage Publications.

Heclo, H. (1978) 'Issue networks and the executive establishment', in S. H. Beer and A. S. King (eds) *The New American Political System* (pp. 87–124). Washington, DC: American Enterprise Institute for Public Policy Research.

Heclo, H. and Wildavsky, A. (1974) *The Private Government of Public Money: Community and Policy Inside British Politics*. London: Macmillan.

Jessop, B. (1998) 'The rise of governance and the risks of failure: The case of economic development', *International Social Science Journal*, 50(155), 28–43.

Kersbergen, K. V. and Waarden, F. V. (2004) '"Governance" as a bridge between disciplines: Cross-disciplinary inspiration regarding shifts in governance and problems of governability, accountability and legitimacy', *European Journal of Political Research*, 43(2), 143–171.

Kickert, W. J. M., Klijn, E.-H. and Koppenjan, J. F. M. (1997) *Managing Complex Networks: Strategies for the Public Sector*. London: Sage Publications.

Kjær, A. M. (2004) *Governance*. Malden, MA: Polity/Blackwell.

Klijn, E.-H. (2008) 'Networks as perspective on policy and implementation', in S. Cropper (ed.) *The Oxford Handbook of Inter-organizational Relations* (pp. 118–146). Oxford; New York: Oxford University Press.

Koppenjan, J. and Klijn, E.-H. (2004) *Managing Uncertainties in Networks: A Network Approach to Problem Solving and Decision Making.* London; New York: Routledge.

Kwong, J. (1996) 'The new educational mandate in China: Running schools running businesses', *International Journal of Educational Development, 16*(2), 185–194.

Law, W.-W. and Pan, S.-Y. (2009) 'Game theory and educational policy: Private education legislation in China', *International Journal of Educational Development, 29*(3), 227–240.

Lawn, M. and Grek, S. (2012) *Europeanizing Education: Governing a New Policy Space.* Oxford: Symposium Books.

Lee, W. O. and Lee, S. K. (2012) 'Learning from success', in E. L. Low (ed.) *PISA: Lessons For and From Singapore* (pp. 6–7). Singapore: National Institute of Education.

Liebman, J. S. and Sabel, C. F. (2003) 'A public laboratory Dewey barely imagined: The emerging model of school governance and legal reform', *Review of Law and Social Change, 28*(2), 183–304.

Lu, J. (2009) 'PISA 2009 Shanghai Implementation Report', *Research in Educational Development*(24), 72–75.

Lu, J. and Zhu, X. (2011) 'How to treat the PISA 2009 Shanghai result – Commentary on the secondary students from China Shanghai, first to participate in the International Benchmark Test', *Shanghai Research on Education, 1*, 17–19.

Malik, A. (2002) 'State of the art in governance indicators', *Human Development Report 2002* (pp. 1–31). United Nations Development Program.

Marginson, S. (1997) *Markets in Education.* St. Leonards, NSW: Allen and Unwin.

Maroy, C. (2012) 'Towards post-bureaucratic modes of governance: a European perspective', in G. Steiner-Khamsi and F. Waldow (eds) *Policy Borrowing and Lending in Education.* London: Routledge.

McPherson, A. and Raab, C. D. (1988) *Governing Education: A Sociology of Policy since 1945.* Edinburgh: Edinburgh University Press.

Mervis, J. (2010) 'Shanghai students lead global results on PISA', *Science, 330*(6010), 1461.

Mok, K. H. (1997) 'Retreat of the state: Marketization of education in the Pearl River Delta', *Comparative Education Review, 41*(3), 260–276.

Mok, K. H. (2001) 'From state control to governance: Decentralization and higher education in Guangdong, China', *International Review of Education, 47*(1/2), 123–149.

Mok, K. H. (2003) 'Globalisation and higher education restructuring in Hong Kong, Taiwan and Mainland China', *Higher Education Research and Development, 22*(2), 117–129.

Mok, K. H. (2005) 'Globalization and educational restructuring: University merging and changing governance in China', *Higher Education, 50*(1), 57–88.

Nóvoa, A. and Yariv-Mashal, T. (2003) 'Comparative research in education: A mode of governance or a historical journey? ', *Comparative Education, 39*(4), 423–438.

OECD. (2000) *Knowledge and Skills for Life: First Results from PISA 2000* (p. 322), OECD Publishing .

OECD. (2003) *Learning for Tomorrow's World: First Results from PISA 2003* (p. 323), OECD Publishing.

OECD. (2006) *PISA 2006: Science Competencies for Tomorrow's World* (p. 390), OECD Publishing .

OECD. (2008) *School Sampling Preparation Manual – PISA 2009 Main Study* (p. 98), OECD Publishing.

OECD. (2010a) *PISA 2009 at a Glance.* OECD Publishing.

OECD. (2010b) *PISA 2009 Results: What Students Know and Can Do – Student Performance in Reading, Mathematics and Science,* Vol. I. Retrieved 13 March 2013, from http://dx.doi.org/10.1787/9789264091450-en

OECD. (2012) 'PISA Governing Board', Retrieved 2 January 2013, from http://www.oecd.org/pisa/contacts/pisagoverningboard.htm#Shanghai

OECD. (2013) 'Strong performers and successful reformers in education: Shanghai, China', Retrieved 15 March, 2013, from http://www.pearsonfoundation.org/oecd/china.html

Ozga, J. (2009) 'Governing education through data in England: From regulation to self-evaluation', *Journal of Education Policy, 24*(2), 149–162.

Pons, X. and van Zanten, A. (2007) 'Knowledge circulation, regulation and governance', *KnowandPol Literature Review,* 10–38.

Popkewitz, T. S. (1996) 'Rethinking decentralization and state / civil society sistinctions: The state as a problematic of governing', *Journal of Education Policy, 11*(1), 27–51.

Qi, W. and Tang, H. (2004) 'The social and cultural background of contemporary moral education in China', *Journal of Moral Education, 33*(4), 465–480.

Rhodes, R. A. W. (1994) 'The hollowing out of the state: The changing nature of the public service in Britain', *The Political Quarterly, 65*(2), 138–151.

Rhodes, R.A.W. (1996) 'The new governance: Governing without government', *Political Studies,* 44(4), 652–67.

Rhodes, R. A. W. (1997) *Understanding Governance: Policy Networks, Governance, Reflexivity and Accountability.* Bristol, PA: Open University Press.

Rhodes, R. A. W. (2000) 'Goverannce and public administration', in J. Pierre (ed.) *Debating Governance: Authority, Steering, and Democracy* (pp. 55–90). Oxford: Oxford University Press.

Rhodes, R. A. W. (2007) 'Understanding governance: Ten years on', *Organization Studies, 28*(8), 1243–1264.

Schleicher, A. (2012) 'Lesson from PISA – About some of the world's best-performing education systems', in E. L. Low (ed.) *PISA: Lessons for and from Singapore* (pp. 9–13). Singapore: National Institute of Education.

Seddon, T., Billett, S. and Clemans, A. (2004) 'Politics of social partnerships: A framework for theorisingv *Journal of Education Policy,* 19(2), 123–142.

Shanghai PISA. (2010) *Quality and Equity: A Brief Report of the Programme for International Student Assessment 2009 in Shanghai, China.* Shanghai: Shanghai Educational Publishing House.

Stack, M. (2006) 'Testing, testing, read all about it: Canadian press coverage of the PISA results', *Canadian Journal of Education, 29*(1), 49–69.

Steinfeld, E. S. (1998) *Forging Reform in China: The Fate of State-Owned Industry.* Cambridge; New York: Cambridge University Press.

Sun, M. (2010) 'Education system reform in China after 1978: Some practical implications', *The International Journal of Educational Management, 24*(4), 314.

Tang, H. F. (2004) 'Policy network and policy consequence: The analysis of the changing allocation pattern in the rural taxation', *The Journal of CPC Zhejiang Provincial Party School,* 1, 31–36.

Truman, D. B. (1971) *The Governmental Process: Political Interests and Public Opinion.* New York: Knopf.

Tucker, M. S. (2011) *Surpassing Shanghai: An Agenda for American Education Built on the World's Leading Systems.* Cambridge, MA: Harvard Education Press.

Xia, M. (2008) *People's Congresses and Governance in China: Toward a Network Mode of Governance.* New York: Routledge.

Xue, P. (2012) 'The comparative research between the abilities of urban and rural students in Zhejiang: Based on PISA test results', *Zhejiang Social Sciences,* 6, 95–100, 128.

Yang, R. (2004) 'Toward massification: Higher education development in the People's Repulic of China since 1949', in J. C. Smart (ed.) *Higher-Education - Handbook of Theory and Research* (Vol. XIX, pp. 311–374). The Netherlands: Kluwer Academic Publishers.

Yang, R., Vidovich, L. and Currie, J. (2007) 'Dancing in a cage': Changing autonomy in Chinese higher education', *Higher Education, 54*(4), 575–592.

Young, M. (1971) *Knowledge and Control: New Directions for the Sociology of Education.* London: Collier-Macmillan.

Zhang, M. (2009) 'What do we learn from PISA assessment', *Research in Educational Development, 24*, 75–76.

Zhao, L. (2008) 'Between local community and central state: Financing basic education in China', *International Journal of Educational Development, 29*(4), 366–373.

Zheng, H., Jong, M. D. and Koppenjan, J. (2010) 'Apply policy network theory to policy-making in China: The case of urban health insurance reform', *Public Administration, 88*(2), 398–417.

Zhu, Y. (2008) 'Housing problem and solution in China', *Wuhan Univeristy Journal (Philosophy and Social Sciences), 61*(3), 345–350.

15 New Governing Experts in Education

Self-Learning Software, Policy Labs and Transactional Pedagogies

Ben Williamson

Governing Experts

The governance of education is increasingly intertwined with database technologies. This chapter examines the emergence of the 'public policy lab' as a new actor in educational governance with governing expertise in data technologies and techniques. Public policy labs are a hybrid organizational form combining elements of the political think tank, the social enterprise and the R&D lab from the computer technology industry. Such labs operate as cross-sectoral mediators who translate ideas and processes from the domain of database-driven computing into educational policy proposals. They are becoming increasingly significant policy actors with the governing expertise and capacity to contribute to national positioning and the 'fabrication' of comparability in the wider global policy competition (Ozga *et al.* 2011).

Drawing on a study of the think tank Demos, the social enterprise the Innovation Unit, and Nesta (the National Endowment for Science, Technology and the Arts) in England, the chapter shows how these organizations promote themselves as intermediary governing experts. They exercise the capacity to diagnose the problems of contemporary schooling, and activate the competencies of learners as governing resources to solve those problems. My emphasis is on their aspirations, ambitions and objectives for the future of education: on their attitudes towards the present and the models of invention they adopt. Focusing specifically on analysis of reports and web materials produced by Demos, the Innovation Unit and Nesta, I argue that these texts act as relays for ideas that are intended to change ways of thinking about education. Methodologically, I view these texts as material and virtual forms which assemble, circulate and implant potentially agenda-changing ideas, and as intermediary devices or 'intellectual techniques' for 'producing conviction in others' (Rose 1999: 37). These material and virtual techniques transform education by making it problematic, thinkable, intelligible, and hence practicable in new ways.

By mobilizing such techniques, these policy intermediaries act cross-sectorally through relationships with government agencies, commercial organizations and the third sector to promote reformatory ideas in education. They contribute to 'policy networks' of new governing experts in the UK (Ball and Junemann 2012), as well as in European education policy (Lawn and Grek 2012) and globalizing policy processes (Rizvi and Lingard 2010), who are carving out an interstitial governing space in-between the think tank, the social enterprise and the digital R&D lab. Within this emerging space of governance, new policy discourses, ideas, practices, knowledge and data are constantly being mediated between the public, private and third sectors, and between the political, academic and commercial fields. They are linked to wider transnational 'governing discourses' of the knowledge economy, lifelong learning, data collection and comparison (Lawn 2003). The discourse of 'soft' is a key element of these governing discourses, found in soft governance, soft power, soft paternalism, soft systems thinking, soft behavioural competencies and soft skills, as well as in software and soft computing (Williamson 2013).

Significantly, these cross-sectoral organizations take particular technological forms as 'diagrams' (Barry 2001) for reinventing public education. These diagrams, drawn from the discourses and imagery of computational forms and experimental R&D processes in the ICT industry, include soft computing, data analytics, adaptive technologies, big data and other Web 2.0 technologies based on database-driven processes. These technologies are today significant since 'the sociotechnical instantiation of many aspects of the contemporary world depend on database architectures and database management techniques' and the technical processes of 'ordering, sorting, counting, and calculating' that they mediate (Mackenzie 2012: 335, 338).

Through the entwining of such database-driven technologies with public services in England, many services are now being reconfigured to meet specific individual needs; a process which requires knowledge and information about service users to be 'collated, monitored and interpreted by service providers, and even used as the basis for forecasting future needs' (Grek and Ozga 2010: 285). Person-responsive public services require the collection and analysis of individuals' 'digital traces', or 'data that is generated routinely as a by-product of our everyday experiences', and the 'pervasive mobilization of transactional data to know and evaluate the performance of populations' (Ruppert and Savage 2012: 74). For Thrift (2005) the mobilization of powerful technologies to know, calculate, act upon and ultimately 'make up' individuals as new kinds of citizens, workers or learners, is a key technique in 'knowing capitalism'.

Consequently, within the field of public services, the collection and storage of digitized datasets and the availability of analytics software is generating and making available new ways of managing and mediating the relationship between service provider and service user. The focal public policy labs in this chapter are seeking to usher in new forms of learning in which transactional data generated as a product of their use of data-based computational applications may be used to know and act upon learners. In particular, they are promoting new data-based computational forms such as adaptive technologies, learning analytics, and self-learning software that can (or have the potential to) automatically collect, collate and calculate learner data.

The mobilization of database technologies in education is intensifying an emerging form of 'governing knowledge', or 'governing through data', which uses knowledge about learners as a 'governing resource' (Ozga 2008). It augments existing disciplinary regimes of monitoring and surveillance of learners for 'these technological devices do not merely mobilize already existing actors but are active in making them up' (Ruppert and Savage 2012: 87). Through the governing expertise of self-learning software, individual learners are to be reassembled and reactivated according to measurable performance criteria that can be collected, collated and calculated in databases. Individualized performance data may then be utilized as evidence of 'what works' best in education reform, thus signalling the legitimacy of the governing strategies used to construct, promote, disseminate and implement them. This produces a feedback loop within which individual learners' data may be used to inform policy on which pedagogies and practices work best. In the process, learners are to undergo a series of transformations or 'translations' (Ozga *et al.* 2011): school pupils are to be translated into learners, learners into performances, performances into data, and data into locally, nationally and globally comparable databases, tables and visualizations. Learning is to be made knowable, measurable and calculable, and learners made up as transactional data resources to be collected, collated and calculated into comparable governing knowledge. In these ways, education is to become a self-regulating system which uses database-driven processes both to generate new pedagogies and as comparable evidence in a wider global policy competition.

In outline, the chapter examines the emergence of the idea of the public policy lab as a new kind of intermediary policy actor that is operating to mediate and translate key governing discourses into policy and practice. These constitute an emerging form of cross-sectoral governing expertise. The chapter proceeds to focus specifically on how such public policy labs are seeking to promote and mobilize their expert knowledge on particular computational forms, especially database-driven soft computation, data analytics and self-learning software. This is generating new kinds of transactional pedagogies facilitated by the capacity of databases to identify and know learners through their mediated transactions. Through such database-driven systems, learners are to be activated as 'calculable' governing resources whose individual competence and performance is to be collected, collated and calculated as data for comparison in globally competitive educational policy programmes.

Governing Softly

The governance of education is increasingly understood as taking place through cross-sectoral networks of public, private and third sector interdependencies that criss-cross national and transnational borderlines. 'Networked governance', as this style of governing is termed, is decentralized and characterized by fluidity, looseness, complexity and instability (Ozga *et al.* 2011; Williamson 2012). As opposed to the hard bureaucratic power of centralized government authority and control, 'post-bureaucratic' networked governance is conceived as 'soft power' which works through techniques of attraction, seduction, persuasion and the cultivation of support and shared interest across networks of loosely associated actors. Soft forms of governance include self-regulation, self-evaluation, self-governance and governing through the capacities of the governed, rather than the hard government of centralized targets and external regulation.

Educational 'policy networks' are a specific form of post-bureaucratic governance. Policy networks consist of individual intermediaries, interlockers and 'policy entrepreneurs whose 'good ideas' straddle sectoral problems (Ball and Exley 2010). Made up primarily of experts from think tanks, policy institutes, multilateral agencies, media consultancies and experts in public relations, they 'perform the role of conveying ideas between different areas of the production, distribution, or circulation of ideas' in order to 'influence the decision-making process' (Lawn and Grek 2012: 75). Their participation in 'reinventing public education' involves 'moving from a bureaucratic/professional knowledge about education, a part of the public sector, to individualized, personalized and integrated knowledge about a society' (Grek and Ozga 2010: 272). The shift to individualization and personalization is bringing about the emergence of new forms of governing expertise, and a new kind of governing expert whose claim to authority rests on the capacity to know, assess and act upon the individual – through the collection, collation and calculation of data – rather than to seek to reform the more cumbersome bureaucratic systems of the public sector.

These claims depend on innovative new database-driven technologies that can perform complex processes of data collection, aggregation and analysis on the performance of individuals and populations. The use of powerful databases and analytics software to collect and generate performance data on education, or 'learning' as it has been reconceived, has been integral to the formation of new techniques of governance. The soft governing logics of data seek to link the supranational to the individual 'through their collective but individualized investment in their own learning' (Ozga *et al.* 2011: 85). Individualizing technologies of personal performance data are part of how individual actors have come to construe their own 'responsibilized' autonomy, interests, problems and aspirations for the future as intrinsically linked with those of governing authorities (Rose 1999). In the specific education context, soft governance, learning and data are intertwined as data is used 'to govern by activating the capacities of the individual' (Ozga *et al.*2011: 88).

Assembling Public Policy Labs

What are public policy labs and how do they operate as actors in educational governance? In this section I identify some key characteristics of the public policy lab and explore how their objectives and aspirations are contiguous with wider governing discourses.

Network Mediators

The Innovation Unit is a social enterprise first formed within the Department for Education and Skills in 2002 and spun-out as an independent not-for-profit organization in 2006 with a mission to innovate in public services. The Innovation Unit is an important actor in the genealogy of public policy labs, both in terms of its discursive production of ideas about cross-sectoral innovation in education and its role in assembling the concept of the public policy lab itself. In the field of education, its aim is to create an 'innovation ecosystem' for education in which 'schools no longer have a monopoly on 'academic' learning', and learning is supported beyond school by the internet, mobile technologies, and a 'vastly increased number of education providers' (Innovation Unit 2012a: n.p.). In this ecosystem, education is reimagined as a dispersed, boundary-free zone of suppliers that bisect and traverse sectoral borderlines and digitally networked pedagogies that break free of the classroom. The monopoly of the school and its pedagogical, curricular and assessment techniques are challenged by a market of competitors from outside of the bureaucratic organs of the education system. The imagery of the innovation ecosystem for education acts as a template both for reimagining education and for generating new positions of reformatory expertise.

What kinds of experts are being positioned to do this work? An Innovation Unit pamphlet entitled *Honest Brokers: Brokering Innovation in Public Services* (Horne 2008: 3) describes 'innovation intermediaries' that 'have existed in other sectors for years – such as innovation and science parks, incubators, accelerators, exchanges, labs and studios'. The blurb asks, 'Where is the Silicon Valley for public services in Britain?' Horne (2008: 4) focuses on emerging 'brokering organizations that have succeeded in fostering innovation in education'. These organizations ostensibly mediate both knowledge and relationships for their clients, and their work is characterized as being concerned with affecting the culture of the system to make it more conducive to the development and spread of innovation.

Another Innovation Unit pamphlet, *A D&R System for Education* (Bentley and Gillinson 2007), similarly translates models from other sectors into education. Both authors were formerly associated with Demos, the 'radical centre' think-tank responsible for making cross-sectoral thinking possible in public services reform. Drawing on agile methods from 'open source' R&D, the authors propose 'an education R&D system and strategy which is more open and flexible', involves 'open communities of collaboration', 'opportunities for innovation that is both multi-disciplinary and inter-disciplinary' and 'makes the most of user-driven innovation and demand to shape new methods and create knowledge' (Bentley and Gillinson 2007: 19). Their version of 'D&R' puts the emphasis first on experimental development, rather than traditional R&D with its 'pipeline' model of basic research followed by application. They use examples of networked 'hubs and clusters' of cross-sectoral relationships between commercial ICT, university research labs, independent research institutes and think-tanks, and policymakers; and advocate the creation of a 'National Evidence Centre' which would 'synthesize, test and validate evidence of effectiveness for new research findings and methods, and develop and diffuse this knowledge base in direct collaboration with users of that knowledge' (Bentley and Gillinson 2007: 32).

Honest Brokers also announces the formation of a 'Public Services Innovation Laboratory', to be 'run by Nesta, in partnership with many existing innovation intermediaries':

> The Laboratory will trial new methods of supporting innovation, search for innovation in public services around the world, disseminate lessons to delivery organizations, develop training, tools and services for practitioners and influence policy. ... The Laboratory could become a service provider to other innovation intermediaries, helping them build capacity, educate demand . . . and create an evidence base for what works in social innovation. . . . The Laboratory could become a 'system influencer' campaigning for changes in policy. . . .
>
> (Horne 2008: 33–34)

The Public Services Innovation Lab is now a permanent department within Nesta. Formerly a public body, Nesta became an independent not-for-profit organization in 2012 to promote innovation in public services. Its webpage states that 'Nesta's Innovation Lab supports innovators in public services, society and business to develop radical new responses to the most pressing social and economic challenges'.

Its key themes include 'Digital Education', and some of its cross-cutting topics include 'data and technology', 'open innovation', 'digital disruption', 'civic engagement', 'creative economy', 'social good', 'video games' and 'Web 2.0', and 'transformation'. It assumes an intermediary role to iterate between the big picture and individual innovations. It has been closely involved in establishing the national network of 'What Works Centres', including a major report, *Making Evidence Useful: The Case for New Institutions* (Mulgan and Puttick 2013). These centres are being tasked with collecting evidence on 'what works' in innovation across sectors, primarily by carrying out randomized control trials. The centre for education, managed by the Educational Endowment Fund (EEF) shares its evidence through a 'Teaching and Learning Toolkit' which summarizes educational research for teachers and schools. Relatedly, Nesta has established the 'Alliance for Useful Evidence' and a 'Standards of Evidence Framework' – a common language for talking about data and evaluation – and is involved in the creation of a free online 'app' called 'Randomise Me' which permits anyone to set up and carry out their own randomized control trial (Mulgan and Puttick 2013). Demos and the Innovation Unit are interorganizationally networked with the lab through a variety of relationships, partnerships and co-authored publications.

Nesta documentation describes the lab as a prototype for 'social science parks' and 'public policy labs'. The public policy lab is defined as 'not so much a think tank but an experimental workshop that prototypes new forms of public service delivery' by working across 'the public, private and social enterprise sectors to create socially useful and usable ideas' (Nesta 2013a). Based on the Nesta prototype, the public policy lab is imagined and promoted as a new kind of cross-sectoral actor in public services reform which works by actively trialling and evaluating new services. The public policy lab extends the role of the think tank into the domain of R&D, with a particular emphasis on innovative experimental development and the production of evidence and data of what works in public service reform.

Discursively, the lab acts to position education as a public service which is to be made governable as a networked, interconnected system rather than a centrally controlled bureaucracy. In the Nesta report *Systems Innovation*, Mulgan and Leadbeater (2013: 7) – both formerly of Demos and associates of the Innovation Unit – argue that public services could be improved through an 'interconnected set of innovations, where each influences the other, with innovation both in the parts of the system and in the ways in which they interconnect'. The report represents systems innovation as a networked and interconnected phenomenon, a form of soft systems thinking. It is illustrated with a series of 'systems maps' and 'diagrams' of the 'dynamics of the system' which detail the 'feedback or feed-forward loops', points of 'influence or leverage', and their 'critical causal links' (Mulgan and Leadbeater 2013: 10). Again, the 'intermediaries' such as networks, research institutes, consultancies and think tanks are positioned to 'link big ideas to individual innovations', 'orchestrate advocacy and campaigns', promote policy, develop coalitions and networks, and 'change minds', 'attitudes and cultures' (Mulgan and Leadbeater 2013: 20–21). Internet companies Google, Apple and Amazon are identified as visible recent examples of systems innovations, and the form of the network is specified as a reformatory diagram:

We have embraced vast new systems for creating, sharing, processing and analysing information from the Internet and the world wide web, through to new
generations of mobile phones, and social media to the possibilities of cloud
computing, the semantic web, and the Internet of Things. These digital platforms could allow us to create more distributed, networked, systems to achieve
feats of coordination previously associated with large hierarchical organizations.

(Mulgan and Leadbeater 2013: 30)

In the report the potential of networked systems to develop and deliver digital and
open online learning is counterposed with the overt problematization of schooling as an outdated relic of industrialization.

How can the public policy lab be understood? Demos, Nesta, and the Innovation
Unit are cohabitees of an emerging interstitial space in educational governance, an
experimental space in which new ideas may be combined from across sectors and
fields. They work by gathering, balancing and assembling various institutionalized
resources from across the academic, political, and commercial domains, and assembling those resources into unique packages, and their power 'lies in their ability to
claim for themselves a kind of mediating role' between 'resources captured from
other fields' (Medvetz 2012: 178). The liminal, cross-sectoral hybridity of these
organizations creates the new expert position of the 'mediator', who is able to seize or
appropriate big abstract ideas generated in one place and move them on through new
combinations and interactions in order to make them practical, usable, 'buzzy' and
marketable (Osborne 2004: 441). Mediators must be able to produce, brand and
market their ideas as unique new policy packages in order to appear innovative and to
mobilize political, public and media support simultaneously. Understood as a governing expert in the education policy context, the mediator is a participant in policy
networks whose effect is 'to create a think tapestry of communication, organizational and network relations, stable and unstable linkages' which combine traditional
actors in the field of education with 'those conventionally considered peripheral to
education governance', such as 'commercial interests and technological innovators'
(Lawn and Grek 2012: 82). The notion of the networked mediator captures the expert
governing style of the public policy lab organizationally and discursively established
by Nesta, Demos and the Innovation Unit.

Material Techniques

A central element in how public policy labs operate as networked mediators is
their capacity for communication. These organizations all deploy a variety of
printed materials and online, virtual materials which are, to paraphrase Demos
co-founder Mulgan (2006), intended to 'change the way people think' about education. All publish reports and pamphlets as free internet downloads on a Creative
Commons license for widespread access and redistribution. Their websites are
promoted as accessible, useful and evidence-based sources of expert knowledge.
The Nesta website features extensive blogging facilities which enable its teams to
communicate their projects on an ad hoc basis. Many of the virtual and printed
materials generated by Nesta, the Innovation Unit and Demos contain illustrative

diagrams, visualizations and images that act to transform complex abstract problems into seemingly practicable courses of action.

The Innovation Unit's school reform programme Learning Futures, for example, has produced a guidebook, *Learning Futures: A Vision for Engaging Schools*, from an ensemble of text, imagery, infographic and diagrammatic forms. It features a diagrammatic visualization of an imagined educational system in which the individual learner is to be linked up to a network of other relationships, institutions, spaces and practices. The visualization freezes into one single position a set of 'extended learning relationships' with teachers, tutors, experts, mentors, coaches, peers, employers and families; an image of the 'school as basecamp' which is connected to industry, local businesses, cultural institutions, community organizations, and the internet; and a commitment to a 'learning commons' of project-based learning, co-construction, democratic community, and collaborative enquiry pedagogies (Innovation Unit 2012b: 11). In the accompanying text, the document refers to 'the 4 Ps of engaging activities' that include a 'place-based curriculum, purposeful projects, passion-led teaching and pervasive opportunities for research and constructive challenge' (Innovation Unit 2012b: 8). These '4 Ps' juxtapose physical and virtual settings, the idea of authentic and practical activities that 'foster agency', the importance of personal emotions, and ideas about 'learning outside the classroom' through online research, into a set of 'criteria' and 'design features' for 'every aspect of the way the school is organized: its structure, culture, and the use of space, place and time' (Innovation Unit 2012b: 8). Throughout, the publication is punctuated with break-out boxes, testimonials, bulletpoints, buzz-phrases, and other visual imagery and photographs. Together, these discursive and bibliographic elements capture and stabilize a complex assemblage of concepts, ideals, possibilities and proposals for the future of schools.

A critical perspective would suggest that materials such as these put a highly mediatized gloss on educational problems. This would be an analytical simplification of the mediating techniques mobilized by the Innovation Unit, Demos and Nesta. Another analytical approach is to view their reports, pamphlets and websites as material techniques that mediate policy ideas from amongst political, social scientific, and digital R&D resources and embed them in material form within educational policy discourses. They perform what Latour (1986: 3) would describe as the transformation of ideas and concepts into 'inscriptions' such as 'signs, prints and diagrams' that can affect how we argue, think and believe; they are material techniques of thought. For Latour (1986: 7) the power of an inscription device such as a graphic, image, diagram, and so on, is to stabilize ideas, problems, concepts, explanations and arguments in one place; make those ideas legible and intelligible; amenable to being moved around and copied and reproduced in other places; and reshuffled, recombined and superimposed with others. Ultimately, through such processes, inscriptions can be used to measure and modify what is 'out there'. As Latour (1986: 27–28) puts it, 'realms of reality that seem far apart' are just 'inches apart, once flattened on to the same surface'. This makes it possible to see and make connections previously unthinkable.

Public policy labs act by producing material and virtual inscription devices that are innovative and make use of cutting-edge techniques to be mobilized, reproduced and made amenable to combination and juxtaposition. Fenwick and Edwards (2010: 11) argue that educational texts, pedagogic guides, curricular documents, web resources and other materials themselves act as 'mediators' which translate and fix a complex network of relationships in one place. As virtual forms which are circulated through informational networks, the material and virtual forms generated by public policy labs are themselves mediating techniques which combine ideas from across the academic, political and commercial ICT arenas, stabilize them in new forms such as pamphlets, diagrams and infographics, and then mobilize them as unique policy packages. These material and virtual techniques of thought translate problems, ideas, practices and concepts from different sectors and arenas into shared vocabularies, interests and agendas for intervention, and they superimpose the seemingly distant governing discourses of the knowledge society and lifelong learning with the commercial ICT arena and the mundane practices of pedagogy. Through such juxtapositions, combinations and superimpositions these intermediary devices generate a shared representation of a governable educational domain.

Based on an initial genealogical exploration of the public policy lab in education governance, then, we can summarize that Demos, Nesta and the Innovation Unit act as cohabitees of a new kind of interstitial governing space that is in-between the think tank, the social enterprise and the digital R&D lab. They operate as mediators of ideas from the political, social scientific and digital arenas, reassembling them into unique material and virtual packages that can be branded, marketed, promoted and reinserted anew into educational policy debate. These organizations are commensurate with wider educational governing discourses and new forms of governing expertise amongst cross-sectoral policy networks.

Data-Processing Pedagogies

What do public policy labs want to happen? This section explores some of the particular policy packages that have been assembled by the public policy labs now operating in England. These intermediary policy packages seek to make particular computational forms legible, intelligible and thinkable as potential solutions to the contemporary problem of schooling. In particular I focus on how schooling is being reimagined in terms of big data and data analytics.

Big Data

The role of big data in education needs to be put in the wider context of the reimagining of public services by Demos, Innovation Unit and Nesta. In a Demos pamphlet entitled *The Civic Long Tail: Big Data and the Wisdom of the Crowd,* Leadbeater (2011) suggests making big data a template for governance. In the report's reformatory vision, technological diagrams of data mining, algorithms, cloud computing, the social web, intelligent systems and the 'hopeful web' are interwoven with the political imaginary of a smarter, more open and more intelligent form of 'Government 2.0':

> Government 2.0 is about improving people's relationships with government, either as citizens through the political process, as funders through taxation or as service users. Community 2.0 is about enlarging and empowering citizens' relationships with one another ... about communities looking after

themselves more effectively and the web providing a platform for unfolding communitarian creativity.

(Leadbeater 2011: 18)

Demos researchers Wind-Cowie and Lekhi (2012: 63) likewise argue that big data 'should be viewed as a transformative agent that has the potential to revitalize, reinvigorate and renew public services'. Moreover, Demos researcher Bartlett (2012: 20) claims that the benefit of collecting and analysing users' personal information and behavioural data is the production of 'services and applications that are more tailored to users' needs'. The discourse here is both of technological innovation and the 'democratization of public services' in parallel, as Wind-Cowie and Lekhi (2012: 10) articulate:

> The dynamics of service improvement through data use draw equally from technological and democratic sources. From the technological perspective, identifying problems in service delivery can be seen as a similar process to debugging software.

Such approaches presuppose that analytics software and data, and its networked and interactive forms, now offer diagrams for more democratic and participatory forms of public service, particularly for education.

Commensurately, the learner at the centre of Demos's vision of education is imagined as a self-managing and autonomous individual able to use the web to facilitate more personalized and self-directed educational services, while teachers are reimagined as 'brokers' guiding learners to mobilize their own resources and knowledge in order to 'make better choices for themselves' (Leadbeater *et al.* 2008: 11). Big data is positioned as a resource for personalized learning which would operate by mobilizing 'democratic intelligence: the ideas, know-how and energy of thousands of people' in a 'liberal, open society' where 'public institutions and professionals' are repositioned to 'educate us towards self-help and self-reliance as much as possible' (Leadbeater *et al.* 2008: 79–80).

Data Analytics

As part of its Digital Education programme, Nesta is promoting discourses that legitimate, justify and work to persuade people to act in relation to the database-driven processes that increasingly 'make up the material-social life of people and things' in 'contemporary information societies, network cultures and so on' (Mackenzie 2012: 335, 337). Mobilizing the powers of such thinking as a 'diagram on the basis of which reality might be refashioned and reimagined' (Barry 2001: 87), Nesta has sought to reconstitute the future of learning through database-driven practices.

Consequently, Nesta has advocated 'adaptive learning technologies' which use student data, algorithmic 'learning analytics' and feedback mechanisms to adapt and personalize learning:

> Adaptive learning technologies use student data to adapt the way information is delivered to a student on an individual level. This data can range from online test scores to session time (how long users spend on a single exercise) to records

of where a user has clicked or touched while figuring out a problem. Based on this feedback, the programme will understand which content to point the user at next – planning a personalized learning journey.

(Nesta 2013a)

According to Nesta (2013b) statements, these adaptive technologies have potential to provide 'digital tutors' that are responsive to learners; and intelligent online platforms that can use data gathered from learners to become smart enough to predict, and then appropriately assist and assess, their progression. Importantly, these adaptive technologies depend on constructing datasets of vast populations of learners, so that any individual's profile in the system can be compared with the entire population of learner profiles, in order to generate real-time predictions and automatically change pedagogy. The database-driven logic of comparison between the individual and population in adaptive learning software runs parallel to the governing discourses of data and comparison in education policy.

Similarly, in Innovation Unit documents proposing new ideas for the future of schools, the role of data-based analytics technologies is represented in the ideal of personalized learning driven by automated digital performance assessment technologies which can generate 'playlists' of lessons for students based on prior assessments (Hampson *et al.* 2012). These automated performance assessment technologies are programmed with the capacity to learn through interaction with other devices and users. Self-learning software which depends on human–computer interaction, calculative technologies and feedback loop mechanisms, has the potential to 'second-guess the user, becoming a part of how they decide to decide' – a key technique of 'knowing capitalism' (Thrift 2005: 184). As Demos researchers have argued (Wind-Cowie and Lekhi 2012), public services platforms including those in education should be equipped with the most up-to-date analytics software in order to generate the kind of everyday personal, behavioural and transactional data about citizens that commercial ICT companies such as Amazon, Google and Facebook utilize to generate targeted search results, recommendations and tailored online services. Translated into education in the form of learning analytics, digital tutors and intelligent adaptive technologies, the result is the automatic production of personalized pedagogies through database-driven calculating technologies.

After the notion of 'transactional politics', which describes the political power of identifying and knowing people on the basis of their transactional data (Ruppert and Savage 2012), learning analytics and adaptive educational technologies may be seen as *transactional pedagogies*. Through transactional pedagogies learners are to be known, calculated and acted upon on the basis of their mediated transactions, human–computer interactions, and the collation and analysis of their personal, informational and behavioural data through database-driven and automated self-learning software. In putting transactional data and automated analytics software at the centre of the personalization of pedagogy, Demos, Nesta and Innovation Unit are acting as gatekeepers with the mediating power to make such database technologies into significant pedagogic actors. This is a transactional politics which 'knows' learners, sorts and aggregates them on the basis of personal and behavioural data, responds with an algorithmically generated personalized pedagogy, and then generates measurable metrics of data which can feed back into the policy process.

A key issue emerging from these developments concerns the assumptions about the learner that are programmed into learning analytics and its subjectifying effects. Learning analytics does not merely measure, evaluate and produce data for the judgement of teachers. Instead, these increasingly automated systems can come to their own pedagogic judgements, autonomously forecast learners' future development, and calculate the most appropriate courses of pedagogic intervention. These database technologies close the loop in the relationship between the objectives of governance, and the aspirations of individuals whose learning is now to be translated and expressed in the dominant governing discourses of data, evidence and comparison in an increasingly globalized educational policy arena. They make up learners as 'calculable persons' with 'calculating mentalities' who are enmeshed in 'networks of calculation' both as active and self-calculating participants and as the objects of others' calculations (Rose 1999). Learners are made up by such subjectifying techniques both as calculable resources and as self-calculating individuals whose competencies are to be activated to generate data for comparison in a global competition between policy programmes. Indeed, beyond this, the transactional pedagogies of analytics and adaptive software are disassembling individual learners into 'transactional actors' defined by their specific transactions through data switches, impulses, profiles, and circuits (Ruppert and Savage 2012). Education is increasingly to be governed through transactional learning data, and through the measurement and comparison of nonhuman transactional learners.

Calculative technologies of individualized performance data and feedback have made data into the dominant governing resource in education, and data analysis and processing into one of the central components in the forecasting, controlling and shaping of the knowledge economy (Lawn and Grek 2012). In the future visions of intermediary public policy labs such as Nesta, Demos and the Innovation Unit, education is not to be governed through its national education systems, but through activating the self-calculating competences of individuals. The new database-driven transactional pedagogies govern by knowing, evaluating, and then acting upon the capacities and subjectivities of learners. In this way, as they are promoted and inserted into learning practices through the interventions of public policy labs such as Nesta, these calculative technologies have the potential to become part of the flow of data that now constitutes a dominant source of educational governance in England as well as transnationally. Through public policy labs, learning is being reconstituted as continual calculative process and learners are being transformed through automated pedagogies both into self-calculating individuals and into calculable data resources for collation and comparison in the databases of global educational policy.

Conclusion

Public policy labs are an emerging, prototypical form of cross-sectoral governance in public services generally and education specifically. The public policy labs of Demos, Nesta and the Innovation Unit act as policy intermediaries to broker alignments between commercial R&D in the ICT industry and the policies and pedagogies of public education. They deploy reports and other virtual and material forms, which are intended to inject new ideas into education policy. These texts act as material techniques of thought and their objective is to make particular policy problems and solutions thinkable and their solutions practicable. The ideas they contain are created from a constant juxtaposition and recombination of ideas from the public, private and third sectors and from the fields of politics, social science and digital R&D. These public policy labs act as new kinds of 'governing experts' that are contributing to new forms of educational governance through interstitial, cross-sectoral policy networks whose interest is in marketable ideas and techniques that could change the ways that people think about education.

Discursively, these policy intermediaries have begun to interweave ideas about smart self-learning software, big data, analytics and other database-driven processes with ideas about personalized and lifelong learning. Self-learning software can collect, collate and calculate learner data, and automatically generate prescriptions for subsequent pedagogy. The juxtaposition of self-learning software with schooling is leading to the possibility of the automatic production of pedagogy facilitated by calculative techniques and algorithmic processes. The new policy package of 'learning analytics' and adaptive self-learning software being promoted and supported by Nesta is a current example of how governance by cross-sectoral intermediaries is ushering into the policy space a concern with database-driven computational forms. Learning analytics puts smart self-learning software based on adaptive algorithmic processes into school. This is introducing into education new 'transactional pedagogies' in which the pedagogic act is being socio-technically co-constituted by individual learners in interaction with commercially produced data analysis devices, self-learning software and automated calculative techniques which depend on comparison between big datasets of individual and population data. Transactional pedagogy is the ideal form for schooling in 'knowing capitalism' and is part of the shift towards 'governing knowledge' practices which monitor and assess data on individuals' learning in order to forecast or calculate any necessary interventions. With the emergence of transactional pedagogy, learners are being reconstituted as transactional learners and governing resources to be activated through self-learning software in order to fabricate globally comparable and calculable policy data.

References

Ball, S.J. and Exley, S. (2010) 'Making policy with "good ideas": policy networks and the "intellectuals" of New Labour', *Journal of Education Policy* 25(2): 151–169.

Ball, S.J. and Junemann, C. (2012) *Networks, New Governance and Education*, Bristol: Policy Press.

Barry, A. (2001) *Political Machines: Governing a Technological Society*, London: Athlone Press.

Bartlett, J. (2012) *The Data Dialogue*, London: Demos.

Bentley, T. and Gillinson, S. (2007) *A D&R System for Education*, London: Innovation Unit.

Fenwick, T. and Edwards, R. (2010) *Actor-Network Theory in Education*, Abingdon: Routledge.

Grek, S. and Ozga, J. (2010) 'Re-inventing public education: The new role of knowledge in education policy making', *Public Policy and Administration* 25(3): 271–288.

Hampson, M., Patton, A. and Shanks, L. (2012) *10 Ideas for 21st Century Education*, London: Innovation Unit.

Horne, M. (2008) *Honest Brokers: Brokering Innovation in Public Services*. London: Innovation Unit.

Innovation Unit (2012a) '21st century education', Innovation Unit website. Available online: http://www.innovationunit.org/knowledge/our-ideas/21st-century-education (accessed 28 May 2013)

Innovation Unit (2012b) *Learning Futures: A Vision for Engaging Schools*, London: Paul Hamlyn Foundation/Innovation Unit.

Latour, B. (1986) 'Visualization and cognition: thinking with eyes and hands', *Knowledge and Society* 6: 1–40.

Lawn, M. (2003) 'The 'usefulness' of learning: the struggle over governance, meaning and the European education space', *Discourse: Studies in the Cultural Politics of Education* 24(3): 325–336.

Lawn, M. and Grek, S. (2012) *Europeanizing Education: Governing a New Policy Space*, Oxford: Symposium.

Leadbeater, C. (2011) *The Civic Long Tail: Big Data and the Wisdom of the Crowd*, London: Demos.

Leadbeater, C., Bartlett, J. and Gallagher, N. (2008) *Making It Personal*, London: Demos.

Mackenzie, A. (2012) 'More parts than elements: how databases multiply', *Environment and Planning D: Society and Space* 30: 335–350.

Medvetz, T. (2012) *Think Tanks in America*, London: University of Chicago Press.

Mulgan, G. (2006) 'Thinking in tanks: The changing ecology of political ideas', *The Political Quarterly* 77(2): 147–155.

Mulgan, G. and Leadbeater, C. (2013) *Systems Innovation: Discussion Paper*, London: Nesta.

Mulgan, G. and Puttick, R. (2013) *Making Evidence Useful: The Case for New Institutions*, London: Nesta.

Nesta (2013a) '13 predictions for 2013', Nesta website. Online: http://www.nesta.org.uk/news_and_features/13for2013 (accessed 28 May 2013).

Nesta (2013b) 'Decoding learning', Nesta website. Online: http://www.nesta.org.uk/areas_of_work/public_services_lab/digital_education/assets/features/more_and_better_learning_using_technology (accessed 28 May 2013).

Osborne, T.S.D. (2004) 'On mediators: Intellectuals and the ideas trade in the knowledge society', *Economy and Society* 33(4): 430–47.

Ozga, J. (2008) 'Governing knowledge: research steering and research quality', *European Education Research Journal* 7(3): 261–272.

Ozga, J., Dahler-Larsen, P., Segerholm, C. and Simola, H. (eds) (2011) *Fabricating Quality in Education: Data and Governance in Europe*, London: Routledge.

Ozga, J., Segerholm, C. and Simola, H. (2011) 'The governance turn', in Ozga, J., Dahler-Larsen, P., Segerholm, C. and Simola, H. (eds) *Fabricating Quality in Education: Data and Governance in Europe*, 85–95, London: Routledge.

Rizvi, F. and Lingard, B. (2010) *Globalizing Education Policy*, London: Routledge.

Rose, N. (1999) *Powers of Freedom: Reframing Political Thought*, Cambridge: Cambridge University Press.

Ruppert, E. and Savage, M. (2012) 'Transactional politics', *The Sociological Review*. Special Issue: Sociological Review Monograph Series: *Measure and Value* (edited by L. Adkins and C. Lury), 59, supplement s2: 73–92.

Thrift, N. (2005) *Knowing Capitalism*, London: Sage.

Williamson, B. (2012) 'Centrifugal schooling: Third sector policy networks and the reassembling of education policy in England', *Journal of Education Policy* 27(6): 775–794.

Williamson, B. (2013) 'Soft openings: The psychotechnological expertise of third sector curriculum reform', *Pedagogy, Culture and Society*, 21(2): 217–238.

Wind-Cowie, M. and Lekhi, R. (2012) *The Data Dividend*, London: Demos.

Index